AMERICAN GRASSLANDS

American Grasslands provides a comprehensive review of select laws and policies that have shaped modern western agriculture. Through compelling stories of famous and lesser-known ranches, the book explores the trajectory of law and policy that has consolidated power in certain western ranchers and agricultural enterprises. Drawing lessons from historical events such as the Dust Bowl and the current climate and extinction crises, the book illustrates the harmful externalities of agricultural activity and the need for meaningful reform. The book also addresses recent national calls for social and racial justice in the context of western agriculture and disputes over access to public resources such as water, land, and wildlife. After highlighting the problems created by current laws and policies, the book offers practical recommendations for future legal and policy reform. *American Grasslands* is a must-read for anyone interested in the history and future of western agriculture and the role of law and policy in shaping it.

Hillary M. Hoffmann is an author, legal scholar, and nonprofit leader with expertise in natural resources and Indigenous law and policy. She has been a law professor since 2008, winning the Richard L. Brooks Prize for Distinguished Faculty Scholarship in 2020. She is also the coauthor of *A Third Way: Decolonizing the Laws of Indigenous Cultural Protection* (2020).

American Grasslands

RECKONING WITH THE LAW AND POLICY THAT SHAPED AGRICULTURE IN THE WEST

HILLARY M. HOFFMANN

CAMBRIDGE
UNIVERSITY PRESS

CAMBRIDGE
UNIVERSITY PRESS

Shaftesbury Road, Cambridge CB2 8EA, United Kingdom

One Liberty Plaza, 20th Floor, New York, NY 10006, USA

477 Williamstown Road, Port Melbourne, VIC 3207, Australia

314–321, 3rd Floor, Plot 3, Splendor Forum, Jasola District Centre, New Delhi – 110025, India

103 Penang Road, #05–06/07, Visioncrest Commercial, Singapore 238467

Cambridge University Press is part of Cambridge University Press & Assessment, a department of the University of Cambridge.

We share the University's mission to contribute to society through the pursuit of education, learning and research at the highest international levels of excellence.

www.cambridge.org
Information on this title: www.cambridge.org/9781009573917

DOI: 10.1017/9781009573900

When citing this work, please include a reference to the DOI 10.1017/9781009573900

First published 2025

A catalogue record for this publication is available from the British Library

Library of Congress Cataloging-in-Publication Data
NAMES: Hoffmann, Hillary M., 1975– author.
TITLE: American grasslands : reckoning with the law and policy that shaped agriculture in the West / Hillary M. Hoffmann.
DESCRIPTION: Cambridge, United Kingdom ; New York, NY : Cambridge University Press, 2025. | Includes bibliographical references and index.
IDENTIFIERS: LCCN 2024023552 | ISBN 9781009573917 (hardback) | ISBN 9781009573900 (ebook)
SUBJECTS: LCSH: Agricultural laws and legislation – West (U.S.) | Law reform – West (U.S.)
CLASSIFICATION: LCC KF1682 .H64 2025 | DDC 343.7307/6–dc23/eng/20240528
LC record available at https://lccn.loc.gov/2024023552

ISBN 978-1-009-57391-7 Hardback
ISBN 978-1-009-57394-8 Paperback

To my parents, my sister, and to Pleasant Valley.

Contents

Prologue

The origins of this book lie deep in my past, but the moment that my ideas crystallized into maturity happened only a few years ago. One cold and windy late spring morning in the early 2020s, I was trying to go for a hike on BLM-managed land in southern Utah. I had a narrow window of time before I had to head east and north, back to the airport in Salt Lake City to catch a flight home. To reach the trailhead, I had to drive across a creek that had temporarily flooded the road, which appeared to be knee-deep. This is a common scenario in the southwest – where it is often uneconomical to build a bridge or dig a culvert to account for a few weeks of seasonal flooding each year. Drivers are accustomed to having to gauge whether they can cross, then determine whether to make their way through the flowing water. I could roughly estimate the depth of this water because there were live measuring tapes standing in the middle of the road (that was now a creekbed) in the form of a small herd of cattle. They were distributed across the width of the road in a way that blocked any attempt I might make to cross. As I sat in the car and waited for them to move on, and out of my way, I had nothing to do but think. The longer I sat, and particularly as my precious window of time rapidly dwindled, the more I thought. I thought about the cows, the water, and the land surrounding us, which was all public land managed by the Department of Interior's Bureau of Land Management (BLM). I also wondered where these cows had come from, whether they were supervised, and whether it would be worth it to continue sitting there, given that they might never move. I thought about how, if I were a cow in the middle of the desert, I probably would stand in cool running water all day, too, rather than wandering the parched nearby remnant of a field with no shade in sight.

I ended up waiting for a little more than an hour, but the cattle never moved, so eventually I turned around and left. The hike would have to wait, but the thoughts continued. During those hours it took to drive north to the airport in Salt Lake City, my thoughts ran deeper, into the history of this area, the role of private agriculture in the development of land and water rights in the West, and to so many other topics that were the genesis of the chapters of this book. Of course I knew, from my years of working with natural resources and public land laws, that the reason the cattle were freely roaming on public land, wallowing in a creek that flows directly into a national park, is that their owners held certain privileges on public lands, derived from privileges their predecessors established almost a century earlier. I knew that the water they were wallowing in was likely almost entirely privately controlled, despite crossing federal public lands. The laws that secured this framework date back even further, to the late 1800s, when Congress passed a series of statutes that allowed homesteaders, miners, and other individuals and corporations to secure private rights in what were then, and still are, public resources in the West.

The arc of natural resources and public lands law reveals tensions underlying the situation at the wash, although it usually does not resolve them to the complete satisfaction of anyone. The little scenario that unfolded that day illustrated this well. I was the representative of the public, wanting to use "my" public lands to hike (and relive a cherished childhood memory), and the cows were the representatives of private interests who want to use this area to water their livestock, possibly free of interference from recreationists like me. In my view, the cows got in my way and prevented me from accessing "my" public lands. In their view, maybe, the cows were here first and this was their pasture. I wondered what would happen if I called the local BLM field office and asked them to remove the cattle so I could cross, but I quickly discarded that thought, guessing that they likely would not do much, if they were even near enough to take action before I had to leave. But as I drove north, I began a familiar exercise of extrapolating this scenario across the West, thinking about all of the land and water subject to similar tensions. I also imagined how this scenario could have escalated. It probably would not have gotten close to the armed conflicts described in Chapter 9 of this book, but certainly could have gotten rather heated, relatively fast.

Resource competition breeds fear and uncertainty, and in the West, this fear has at times led to violence, and even full-blown wars. Livestock and human beings have died over resources like land, grass, and water, and well into the 2020s, there is really no end in sight. I knew this not only in my professional experience, but I knew it in my bones. Growing up in one of these states, agriculture and public lands were dominant themes in my life, ebbing and flowing as I roamed the national forest and BLM lands surrounding my childhood home and then moving into the realm of my work once I graduated from law school and began working with the various laws that govern natural resource and public land use in the West. I was born in Steamboat Springs, Colorado, on the ancestral lands of the Yamparika Ute people. The 7-acre property my parents established in a 2,000-acre valley in the heart of the Colorado Rockies could barely be properly labeled a ranch, given its small size. But my childhood years on this little gem of a property near the headwaters of the Colorado River planted a lot of seeds that ran through my mind that day driving away from the wash: seeds of questions involving the interplay between public lands and agriculture, tensions over "rights" to resources and how they worked in such a strange way in the West, and musings on grass, fences, ranches, and the deep sense of belonging to a place that arises from working on and with land and animals every day.

The West of my childhood is the West as I am defining it for the purposes of this book. It does not include the Pacific coast, nor its coastal mountain ranges, but starts in the drier portions of the Pacific coast states and reaches across the Great Basin of Nevada and Idaho to Montana, Wyoming, and south to Utah, Colorado, New Mexico, and Arizona. These areas are home to the western ranches of my childhood, and the ones depicted in so many Hollywood films and television shows, with cowboys on horseback herding livestock across vast open ranges. Like so many ranches in this region, our family's land was surrounded by federal public lands – the Routt National Forest on one side, BLM lands on another, and the Service Creek Wilderness less than five miles to the south. It was also located above public mineral rights managed by the BLM, in an arrangement known as a "split estate," which is another dominant land tenure theme throughout the West.[1] The proximity to public lands had attracted my parents to this property in the 1970s – the nearby open spaces were free to access and use, contained thousands of acres of pristine hiking and backcountry skiing, and offered perquisites like free Christmas trees every December, if we could cut and haul them out.

Our property had a mix of aspen and pine trees, a hay meadow, several barns for the sheep, and two creeks that we were legally obligated to let flow unimpeded and unused down to a neighbor's ranch because that family owned the rights to their waters. Even though it was small, it still qualified as a ranch in my mind because our land produced a crop – hay – and our sheep were wild. We kept them fed, watered, and gave them the basic shelter of their barn, while they in turn produced wool every spring that my mom would knit into sweaters, hats, and mittens. Also, much to my horror, we docked the lambs in the spring (tails and testicles) and then sent them to the butcher in the fall, when they would return in white paper packages that we stored in the freezer and ate throughout the winter.

In this idyllic valley surrounded by mountains and vast undeveloped tracts of federal public lands, I never questioned the role of agriculture. It just seemed to make sense that people would raise livestock here – water was abundant, the temperatures were never high enough to scorch crops or parch herds, and sun was plentiful, although the growing season was incredibly short due to the long winters, which could last half the year. It seemed like there was a lot of land, and certainly enough for the number of people who wanted to use it, whether for raising livestock or for hiking, fishing, hunting, and other things people did in this region, like skiing. Ranchers coexisted with ski racers and miners and aside from the occasional grumblings by the former about the endless stream of "newcomers," life just went along. There were no standoffs, no occupations of Forest Service offices, and definitely no FBI sting operations or deadman roadblocks over grazing disputes.

[1] A split estate results from a legal severance of mineral rights lying under a given parcel of land from the surface rights above. James Rasband, *et al.*, Natural Resources Law and Policy, p. 1163 (Foundation Press, 3rd ed. 2016).

In this part of western Colorado, in the 1980s, no one was yet raising livestock for any purpose other than to supply meat, and no one was raising species of livestock other than sheep, horses, or cattle. That would change in the ensuing decades, but as of then, the biggest agricultural controversies in this area were the same ones that had permeated the community dating back to the early 1900s – tensions between sheep ranchers and cattle ranchers and between all ranchers and wildlife. As far as the former, if you raised sheep, the cattle ranchers looked down on you, and you knew to keep your head down at county commission meetings and local bars, to avoid any dustups. And regarding the latter, if wildlife were bothering your livestock, in any way, you simply had to call the state agency charged with wildlife "management," and they would send rangers out to shoot, poison, or trap the offending beasts and cart them away.[2] Otherwise, the peace was kept and things worked for these ranches much like they might have fifty years before.

Things were a little more tense to the south and west of us, though. Down there, in the desert, I could detect resource tension and scarcity issues even as a child. On the five-hour drive from our home to the public lands in southern Utah where we camped every year (near the location of the aforementioned missed hiking opportunity), we passed a lot of ranches. I could spot them easily by the gate and the arch near the highway, with the telltale brand sign front and center. Sometimes the cows did not appear for a few miles after passing the ranch entrance, was although it could be a much larger distance. On the bigger ranches, I only knew that the cattle belonged to the ranch because my parents would talk about the massive size of these operations as we drove, and we all wondered aloud how it came to be that one family or one person could have so much land. Some of these ranches took hours to cross, even at highway speeds.

As I finished middle school and began high school, I read more about the history and ecology of Colorado and Utah, and these desert ranches raised even more questions. Plant life was so scarce, especially in southern and eastern Utah, and shade was hard to find. There was little grass, and so much sagebrush. I wondered if the cows ate sagebrush (and whether they liked it). Then I wondered what impact their presence had on other species, because it was not hard to calculate the resource scarcity scenario even from the window of a passing car. There were hundreds of cattle in some places, and there was just not very much to eat or drink. On one of our family trips, we went further south in Utah than we had gone before, seeking to escape the crowds that had begun to amass in the region around Moab and the national parks in its immediate vicinity, including Arches National Park and Canyonlands National Park. We were looking for less visited public lands, and we found them to the south, in a never-ending series of canyons and cliffs in San Juan County. We ended up camping for most of the trip, but for a treat on the last night,

2 *See, e.g.*, Mike Koshmrl, *Wyoming Spends Record $4.2 Million to Kill Coyotes, Other Predators*, WyoFile (June 1, 2023), https://wyofile.com/wyoming-spends-record-4-2-million-to-kill-coyotes-other-predators/.

we stayed in a guesthouse, where I found a series of black and white photographs on a wall-mounted pegboard in the lobby. The moment I first saw them, tacked to the wall amid shelves of maps, books, petrified corncobs, bird nests, and other desert tokens people gather when they visit places like this, I stopped and stared for a long time. Normally it would be the book spines that I would gravitate to, in search of the next title by Wallace Stegner or Everett Ruess that might unveil a previously unknown nugget or two about the history of this place. But that day, it was these photos that drew me in. They were photos of tall grasses, seemingly thriving in the desert.

Many years later, I found out this was ricegrass, or Indian ricegrass, as the plants are commonly known. *Achnatherum hymenoides* is an endemic species that is one of the most widely adapted native grasses of Utah's grassland regions.[3] It is hardy, drought tolerant and thrives at elevations between 3,000 and 10,000 feet. It was once hard to miss, with plants regularly growing waist-high and appearing throughout the nooks and valleys nestled at the base of the red rock canyons and cliffs.[4] Ricegrass thrives in the cool climate of these high desert elevations and has adapted to a wide variety of soils found in the rocky, sandy, stony, and shallow soils of the semidesert region of southeastern Utah. It does not survive in wet or poorly drained soils,[5] which also makes the plant perfectly suited to the desert, and it can thrive even in soils high in lime, salt, and alkali. Ricegrass is a foundational grass species in the foothills and semidesert grasslands of Utah, which historically and today, are also the places where people usually want to settle down. As I learned more about this grass species during the research for this book, I learned that it used to grow in the area surrounding the wash where I had my frustrating interaction with the wallowing cattle.

Judging from their appearance in the guesthouse photos alone, these grasses were once healthy and abundant. The old wooden structures in the background of the photo looked like they came from a movie set. Settling down in this little town in the early 1900s, when the photos were taken, would not have been a bad decision, especially for a budding rancher, as ricegrass is well suited for domestic livestock and provides excellent forage for spring and summer grazing seasons.[6] Ricegrass can even sustain livestock through the winter, with plants retaining their taste and appeal well after being harvested and dried. A field of ricegrass would also attract birds, like upland game species such as mourning doves, pheasants, and

3 Horton, Howard, Interagency Forage and Conservation Planting Guide of Utah, Utah State University Extension Service. Publication EC433. Logan, UT, p. 67 (1989); Utah State University, *Range Plants of Utah: Indian Ricegrass* (last accessed Oct. 10, 2023), https://extension.usu.edu/rangeplants/grasses-and-grasslikes/indian-ricegrass.

4 Roger M. Hybner, U.S. Department of Agriculture, Natural Resources Conservation Serv., Plant Materials Technical Note No. MT-74: Indian Ricegrass, p. 1 (Sept. 2011).

5 Horton at 67.

6 *Id.*

others, which found the plant's abundance of plump and nutritious seeds an excellent food source. Some of these birds could be hunted to supplement livestock production, and one could paint a picture of a nice life here as a newly arrived family in the spirit of Laura Ingalls Wilder's experience in *Little House on the Prairie*.

As with any Hollywood story, though, there is more context behind this scenario than one could understand from the photos. Like other desert plants, ricegrass cannot sustain year-round grazing by herds of domestic livestock, or even three-season grazing, because the plants depend on the moisture of the early growing season in the spring to complete their normal growth and food storage cycles.[7] So, if ranchers use ricegrass pastures to sustain their cattle herds, they must remove their stock during the spring to allow the plants to go through their flower and seed formation stages before the moisture they need to complete these processes is drained or evaporates from the soil. Also, even during the seasons when the plants are mature and capable of sustaining grazing, ranchers cannot allow more than 60 percent of the plant growth to be removed, or the plants will die.[8] The ranchers in southern Utah found this out through trial and error, and the results of their experiment can be seen in areas like the one I set out to hike in, where there is no longer any ricegrass to be seen.

Ricegrass also had a relationship with people long before the Euro-American settler colonizers arrived in southeastern Utah in the late 1800s. Indigenous Peoples used this grass to make flour, and it was a preferred source of meal, due to its flavorful taste and protein-laden seeds. This flour was combined with water to create a "mush," with a distinct nutlike flavor. People and animals alike in southern Utah wanted to eat ricegrass and like most plants, there were limits to the harvest levels it could sustain over time. So, a logical assumption explaining the difference between the area in the guesthouse photos and the view I could see from the guesthouse window – devoid of any ricegrass whatsoever – is that the plant was overharvested or overgrazed. And that is, in fact, exactly what happened.

The chapters that follow analyze how this happened, not only with ricegrass but also so many other grass and plant species in the West, but they also explore the cascading effects of laws and policies that facilitated overgrazing and resource depletion. They highlight key laws and policies that created or responded to inflection points in the trajectory of agriculture throughout the West and explore the intersections of natural resources laws, Indigenous law and policy, property law, and water law in the evolution of the West. They relate, in an abbreviated fashion, the relatively rapid transition from Indigenous stewardship to settler colonizer models of resource allocation and explore the consequences of these transitions, including wildfire frequency and intensity, drought, invasive species, and declines in wildlife populations. And no discussion of any of these issues in the West would be complete without exploring the role of climate change in resource allocation.

7 *Id.*
8 *Id.*

While this might sound somewhat foreboding, the following chapters also reveal that these acute threats may spur change that could be good for the West, in so many ways. For example, deconstructing old patterns can allow for an accounting of the racial and social inequities that settler colonialism has wrought throughout the region over the past century and a half, while allowing legal reform that avoids the mistakes of the past. In addition, the percentage of federal land in the West, and the federal government's role in managing and regulating its use, has traditionally been resented by western ranchers, which has led to the conflicts that are described in Chapters 4–9. Viewed from a different perspective, these federal lands are the lands of all Americans and should reflect the collective values and diversity of the entire population. At the lower end of the spectrum, in Montana, the American public owns 30 percent of the state, but at the higher end, the American public owns more than 60 percent of the land in states such as Idaho and Utah (without accounting for unceded Tribal lands that may be restored to Indigenous Nations, or other land tenure adjustments that might occur as a result of the reckoning this book calls for). This reality means that the federal government, as a trustee for the American public, will remain present in these states, but perhaps not in the same way as in the past, as Chapter 10 will explore.

Discovering the extent to which law and policy lay at the root of the challenges that plants like ricegrass have faced was incredibly exciting to me, because the intersection of law, policy, and more recently, racial and social justice, is where I have spent the bulk of my career. What I found during the years I interviewed ranchers and researched the statutes, judicial opinions, and regulations in the pages that follow is that law and policy are inextricably intertwined with power, which is true almost everywhere, but especially in regions such as the Rocky Mountains, the Great Basin, and the Colorado Plateau, where resources are scarce. Controlling access to scarce resources creates power, and powerful people have historically been the ones to create natural resources and property laws, which has resulted in myriad laws that consolidate this power. I also found, not surprisingly, that the issues of resource scarcity in the West intersect with race, socioeconomic class, race and ethnicity. One only needs to google "water" and "the West" to find a series of news articles exploring the water shortages facing this region, which tend to impact Tribal Nations, rural regions, and people of color most acutely.[9]

Yet, many resource challenges of the twenty-first century are not new to the West, and this region has sustained agricultural enterprises on a significant scale for over

[9] Sharon Udasin, *Wester Tribes Face Challenges Capitalizing on Water Rights: Study*, THE HILL (Apr. 19, 2023), https://thehill.com/policy/equilibrium-sustainability/3959010-western-tribes-face-challenges-capitalizing-on-water-rights-study/; Leslie Sanchez, *et al.*, *The Inequitable Exposure of Socially Vulnerable Groups to Water Shortages across the United States*, ENVTL. RES. LETT. 18, p. 7 (2023), www.fs.usda.gov/rm/pubs_journals/2023/rmrs_2023_sanchez_l001.pdf.

4,000 years, if not longer.[10] The history of the West has been inextricably intertwined with resource scarcity and agricultural ingenuity since well before the arrival of Europeans in the 1500s, with Indigenous histories documenting sustained dryland farming operations in locations that receive only inches of precipitation annually, for hundreds of years prior.[11] Once European immigration and colonization began, new agricultural practices and customs were adapted and added to the agricultural landscape, with some of them sustaining populations for centuries. But others did not fare as well. The homesteading era of the 1800s brought more aspiring ranchers and farmers than the land could sustain, and the region collapsed under the pressure. This, of course, was the now famous Dust Bowl that wreaked havoc on the US economy, as well as the ecology of the Midwest and West.

The rule of law – which was used to address the causes of the Dust Bowl and has so often been used throughout history to relieve pressure on finite resources, address resource conflicts, and establish a durable system of land and resource use – sometimes outstays its usefulness, though. And in the case of agriculture and public lands in the West, it is seen by many as having outstayed its usefulness for perhaps a half-century or longer, continually failing western ranchers, conservationists, wildlife, and the public more broadly. The rules of law analyzed in Chapters 1–3 often fail to allocate resources in a way that reflects the values of twenty-first-century America, which has begun to discard the principles of the so-called lords of yesterday, who amassed power and privilege and wielded them against the land and those less powerful and privileged.[12] The pattern readers will note is that those with the power to establish permanent systems of resource allocation and resource exclusion were usually from somewhere else, and their desire to be of this new place, and securely of this new place, caused them to be deeply and personally invested in the rules of law they were crafting for the arguable benefit of "everyone," including the first peoples of this region. The power these lords of yesterday wielded over natural resources has permeated much of the legal system that governs resource allocation and use in the West. And the descendants of yesterday's lords still reign unchallenged, in pockets throughout the region.

But the story cannot be viewed only through the binary lens of colonizers and colonized. Law and policy had profound and permanent consequences for African Americans who wanted to move West after the Civil War, in search of land and the American dream that had been sold to them. Like Indigenous Peoples, they were

10 Craig Childs, House of Rain: Tracking a Vanished Civilization Across the American Southwest, p. 13 (Little, Brown & Company 2006).

11 U. of Ariz. Indigenous Resilience Ctr., "The Man Working to Sustain Hopi Dry Farming in Arizona" (Sept. 2, 2022), available at https://resilience.arizona.edu/news/man-working-sustain-hopi-dry-farming-arizona#:~:text=It%20is%20Hopi%20women%20who%20%E2%80%9Cown%E2%80%9D%20the%20fields%2C,crop%20genetics%20carried%20on%20from%20generation%20to%20generation

12 Charles Wilkinson, Crossing the Next Meridian: Land, Water, and the Future of the West, pp. 20–21 (Island Press 2013).

excluded from the process of law and policymaking that influenced their access to land, water, and ultimately, legal rights that would be necessary to secure their future and the success of their dream. Yet, they were not colonizers in the sense that the white immigrants were, having little to no support for their westward migration and attempts at land acquisition from far-flung politicians and power brokers in the east. African Americans who succeeded in amassing the resources to move West found themselves attempting to farm in foreign landscapes, where the skills they had acquired during the slavery and sharecropping eras in the south were often of little practical value. Their dream also included the mirage of equality and freedom, which had begun to appear in law, but had not been recognized by those who controlled the banks, land offices, legislatures, Governor's offices, and executive branch agencies. As hard as they were willing to work to make their dream a reality, the forces of institutional and structural racism were continually working against them, as they still do today.

The chapters that follow will tell the story of how agriculture evolved in the West, from the precontact era until the present, highlighting some of the most influential laws and policies that shaped the modern tableau of agricultural use in this region. They will explore law and policy through the stories of several agricultural operations to highlight the aspects of these laws that profoundly impacted land, water, wildlife, livestock, and people. Read in sequence, the chapters trace the arc of agricultural stewardship, depicting how so many laws and policies were developed to resolve resource scarcity or crises of one form, but while attempting to fix the problems they were created to solve, they often caused new and unexpected externalities, which have continued through the present day.

This book represents, in several ways, the culmination of much of my prior research in the areas of natural resources law, Indigenous law and policy, environmental governance, and in the subspecialty area of federal grazing law. It grew from the thoughts I ruminated on during my drive away from the wash that day in southern Utah, which took me back to my childhood and the photos I saw in that guesthouse. In the car that day and so many other days before and since, I have imagined a West in which some of the resource tension dissipates and the ricegrass might once again grow and thrive. There is room for agriculture in this vision, but not in the form it has taken to date. Instead, the new agricultural reality of the West must reflect the diversity that permeates the region, allowing it to truly serve all the people who live there. In my imagination, this land could once again contain healthy, regal grasses, representing a visible sign of ecological health, and a rejection of the agricultural colonization that has so damaged it. Whether that is a dream or could one day be reality remains very much an open question – one that will not be entirely resolved by the ensuing pages of this book. However, the exploration that follows might provide a foundation from which to build this new framework – a framework that protects land, water, and plants, and embraces the present diversity of people, customs, and stewardship practices of this beautiful and beloved region.

Introduction

If there is always an individual who can exclude all others from access to any given area, then individuals will endeavor by cultivation or other improvements to maximize the value of the land.[1]

– Richard Posner

In 2018, the Paramount Network premiered "Yellowstone," a television series that quickly became a ratings boon.[2] The show featured Kevin Costner as John Dutton, the descendant of European-American emigrants who homesteaded the largest fictional ranch in Montana history. As the episodes rolled out, viewers were introduced to the fictional Yellowstone Dutton Ranch and the challenges its ownership posed for the Dutton family. They watched, captivated, as constant drama unfolded surrounding the family during its never-ending battle to keep the ranch, which was the only home that generations of Duttons had ever known. Somewhat surprisingly for a cable television show, the writers accurately depicted many modern challenges of operating a large ranch in a state like Montana. Located adjacent to a national park and national forests, the show documents wildfire threats, the burden of state, and federal government regulations protecting endangered species, along with threats like drought, financial hardship, and predatory land developers (mostly from California) seeking to pounce on the Duttons' land. In a twist on the usual Western drama, viewers got a glimpse into Dutton's challenging and complex relationship with the fictional Tribal nation whose lands his ancestors settled under the federal homestead laws.

"Yellowstone" captured the resource challenges and sociopolitical dynamics of Montana and the West in a way that clearly resonated with people across the

1 Richard A. Posner, Economic Analysis of Law, p. 30 (3rd ed. 1986).

2 Nicole Bitette, *The Audiences Behind "Yellowstone's" Success*, Paramount (Aug. 23, 2019) (noting that the series is "the most-watched cable series on TV for a second straight summer," thanks to national audiences tuning in to watch the "compelling" stories that are not "too dystopian or too cerebral."), www.paramount.com/news/content-and-experiences/the-audiences-behind-yellowstone-success.

country and around the world. Even for the viewer steeped in history, law, and policy, including the history of Indigenous land loss and white settlement, Dutton's struggle evokes a certain empathy because of the way that his family's relationship to the land is portrayed. The Duttons seem to belong to the peaks and valleys of the Yellowstone Dutton Ranch, and it seems to belong to them. But on a slightly deeper level, viewers are no doubt captivated because the storylines of this show are the ones that Americans of most generations grew up with, in one form or another. Whether it is John Wayne or John Dutton, Americans have had a national fascination with Western stories involving settler colonialism, exploration, family legacies, human connection with rugged and beautiful land, and of course, with the relationship of cowboys and Indians. People seem particularly captivated by all the strange rituals, norms, and values that authors and screenwriters in this genre have so compellingly told, time and time again, for nearly a century.

Even though viewers are given brief glimpses of the past through flashback segments that illustrate the challenges and successes of previous generations, and of Dutton as a young father, the show tells the story of these descendants of white European immigrants who established their massive ranch from only one perspective – their own. Though it is made clear that these lands were once Tribal lands, the story of Tribal divestiture and Dutton acquisition is vague and largely brushed over. It is unclear to viewers whether the federal government took this land from a Tribe and then sold or gave it to the Duttons, or perhaps negotiated with a Tribe to purchase or otherwise acquire it by treaty. All viewers get are clips depicting Indigenous Peoples camped along the banks of the river that passes through the modern-day ranch, occupying tipis and hunting game species like bison. They are brief glimpses of the past and seem to suggest that, for a time, Tribal members and the Duttons used the same land without conflict. Successive episodes document the modern pressures facing the descendants of the original Duttons and those Tribal members, with the former trying to keep "their" land from being sold and subdivided, and probably developed, and the latter pursuing self-determination on their reservation through ranching and gaming. Almost every episode alludes to the past conflicts that landed everyone in the tenuous circumstances they occupy today, although the definition of "tenuous" is very much a matter of perspective, and closely tied to the color of the perceiver's skin. And the history and process involved in the Tribe's loss of this land are never fully explored on the show, although glimmers of resentment surface from time to time when modern Tribal leaders and Tribal members talk about the Duttons and "their" land.

Although viewers are not treated to this part of the story, Tribal citizens at some point stopped using the Dutton ranch lands, either voluntarily or forcibly. For their descendants, who still hold connections to this land, the strength of the modern relationship to it seems to depend on the strength of their relationships with the mercurial Dutton patriarch, who holds the proverbial keys to this vast kingdom. For Dutton's daughter-in-law Monica, who is one of these Tribal descendants, access to the ranch lands is easier, although in passing, Monica frequently makes comments about her conflicting feelings toward the ranch and her role in preserving the "family legacy" of this land. For the Tribal governmental leaders, it seems to be somewhat of a political gamble to get too close to Dutton, although it certainly makes life easier for any Tribal member to have a powerful white ally like him on their side, especially when he runs for Governor and handily wins the election in Season 4.[3]

The grasses of the Yellowstone Ranch are not exactly the stars of the show, although they are typical of those found throughout the western region that is the focus of this book. Unlike the grassland ecosystems of regions like the Great Plains, in and among the mountainous terrain of the arid West, grasses have fewer opportunities to take root and thrive, as they tend to be nestled in pockets of terrain that are otherwise inhospitable to many plants. Dutton works with this reality by rotating the pastures that his cattle have access to, which is also typical for the region. Moreover, when the summer sun and grazing cattle and wildlife finish doing their work, the remaining grasses turn brown, and the wind blows dust through the air. Sometimes, fall comes earlier than expected when the summer rains stop early, and Dutton has to supplement his cattle's feed and water using baled hay and diverted or pumped water.[4] Like so many others in the region, the fictional Dutton ranch is highly dependent on not only the weather and the climate, including annual precipitation content and form, topography, and access to land and other resources, like surface and groundwater sources, but also other influences, like law, policy, race, class and social status.

The fields of natural resources and public lands law and policy treat the subtext of the scenarios depicted in "Yellowstone" using a unique vocabulary. The terminology used to discuss land changes is distinct and steeped in history. For instance, where a scientist might use the words "ecosystem" or "habitat", natural resources lawyers might select "range" or "rangeland," even though all terms relate to the same land.[5] Range and rangeland are terms that are used to signify lands used by ranching operations, which, in the West, is sometimes a blend of federal land, state land, and private property. Similarly, where the scientific term species might describe a grass plant, natural resources law uses the term "forage," or in other words, grass and other vegetation that feeds domestic livestock. And finally, while scientists might view public lands as a source of biodiversity, natural resources law describes the public lands as "resources," which have derived their modern value based on their economic value to certain groups of people.

3 Bryan Alexander, *Kevin Costner Talks Ruling as "Yellowstone" Montana Governor and Real Politics: "I'm disappointed,"* USA TODAY (Nov. 10, 2022), www.usatoday.com/entertainment/.

4 NOAA Nat'l Centers for Environmental Information, State Climate Summaries 2022: Nevada (last visited Dec. 16, 2023), https://statesummaries.ncics.org/chapter/nv/.

5 Rasband at 367, 1013.

The following chapters analyze the development of this terminology through the stories of individual and communal agricultural operations. Using the stories of real ranchers, like John Dutton and others who are quite different, the historical evolution of law and policy becomes more relatable and understandable, and the "real-life" consequences of the laws and policies designed by and for the "lords of yesterday" become clearer. Also, the consequences of other social influences will be explored, such as the Indigenous calls for "land back" to redress genocide and land divestiture, and the impact of the social justice movement that spread throughout the country after the tragic murder of George Floyd by Minneapolis police officers in 2020. Floyd's murder spurred a series of conversations about the need for a comprehensive national reckoning with police brutality, systemic racism, and intergenerational trauma. The effects of Floyd's death were felt beyond African American communities, with women, Latinos, Indigenous Peoples, and other marginalized peoples galvanized by the global attention that Floyd's death and subsequent protests received, demanding justice, standing against racism, and organizing to spur long-desired change.[6] For Indigenous Peoples in particular, George Floyd's death and the protests that followed resonated with aspects of their own history, marked by similar challenges with policing and law enforcement, systemic racism, colonization, boarding schools, and the resultant intergenerational trauma.

The stories of the ranches and other agricultural operations in the following chapters echo many of the themes of "Yellowstone," although they depict a reality that is much more complicated, legally, financially, and otherwise, than what the millions of viewers would understand from watching the show. These stories tell a more complete picture of the evolution of agricultural practices in the West, exploring the relationship between Indigenous Nations, historically and at present, with the lands that became these ranches, and the role of European, Mexican, and European American settler colonizers, together with the laws they created to fortify their exclusive use and access to these lands. The following chapters will use the stories of these ranches to illustrate less visible aspects of the larger arc of this region over time, to illustrate how the rule of law influenced the establishment of the operation, how the owner's race impacted the trajectory of the operation historically and today, the manner in which its grass (and grass-dependent) species changed as a result of these earlier laws and uses. The chapters will also explore the regulatory framework governing and restricting operations today.

The grasslands of what is now the western United States have experienced relatively rapid social and sociopolitical changes in waves. One well-known wave is

6 Jason Silverstein, *The Global Impact of George Floyd: How Black Lives Matter Protests Shaped Movements around the World*, CBS News (June 4, 2021), www.cbsnews.com/news/george-floyd-black-lives-matter-impact/.

documented in a "Yellowstone" prequel, which follows the first Duttons across Texas, Colorado, and Wyoming as they made their way toward "open" land to homestead, like so many other Europeans and European Americans of the 1800s. But that was not the first. The first Europeans – Spanish explorers – arrived via Mexico in the 1540s, well before the British established the first European settlement at Jamestown. In the ensuing years, the Spanish presence grew, particularly in the regions now comprising the southernmost states of the intermountain West – Arizona, New Mexico, Colorado, and Utah. Indigenous Nations were subjugated to Spanish rule when their lands and resources were needed to support the expanding Spanish empire. As the Spanish presence and their need for land and water grew, so did tensions with Indigenous governments seeking to defend their citizens and their lands. During the centuries of colonization that flowed from these initial European forays into the intermountain West, the grasslands were both the allure and the anchor point for the immigrants. They were a necessary element of immigration, whether as fuel for the animals bearing loads for human occupants in their travels or as food for people once they arrived and decided where to settle down and stay.

Today, the western grasslands bear the scars of these waves of colonization, use, and overuse. In many places, soils are unstable due to overgrazing and other surface-disturbing activities, surface and groundwater has been depleted, while native grasses have in many places been replaced by more resilient invasive species. The grasslands are also now heavily impacted by urban growth and suburban and exurban development, because they are still the most habitable places in the West. Physical modifications by past and present settlers have made many grassland areas highly susceptible to fire and drought. Legal and policy modifications adopted to address problems resulting from these modifications have created a complex patchwork of laws and regulations that provide imprecise and, sometimes, counterproductive authority. Finally, while it has become clear to ecologists and climate scientists that grassland biomes will be a critical component of a national strategy to combat climate change, the laws and policies created to solve resource problems in times of scarcity now frequently hinder efforts to use them for this purpose.

As noted above, there is also the complicated role of race in the tableau of modern agriculture in the West. The famous rap artist Kanye West, whose ranching story is the focus of Chapter 8, echoes the stories of the Dearfield homesteaders in Chapter 4. Through the stories of these farms and ranches and their owners in the chapters that follow, a deeper understanding will emerge: one of law dividing a region and allocating its resources using race as an unspoken criterion, which affected land tenure rights, access to water and land, and so many other factors that position a farm or ranch for success in this region. The white ranchers and their successors, whose title is derived from the white ranchers who homesteaded these lands, own their property in fee simple, which is the strongest form of title recognized in the United States. The Indigenous rancher in Chapter 3, by contrast, does not own his land in fee; his ranch is a patchwork of parcels of land to which he has legal rights akin to tenancy. He must, literally, obtain the permission of the Bureau of Indian Affairs (BIA) to do anything on his land that produces a profit, because of archaic laws that were developed during a time in which federal policy dictated that Indigenous Peoples were incapable of managing their land and financial affairs. Tribal and individual member legal rights in these lands are subordinated to the paramount rights of the United States federal government by operation of the legal doctrines explored in Chapters 1 and 2, and the rancher's land use is subject largely to the regulatory approval and oversight of the BIA. The differences between the respective circumstances in which white ranchers, and white-owned corporate ranchers, operate, and those in which Indigenous and Black farmers and ranchers operate, is often stark. The stories explored in the following chapters will bring much of this history from the relative shadows into the light.

The patterns that emerge elucidate themes that play out, time and again, throughout the West. Considering these themes in the larger context of federal law and policy is essential given the public interest in federal public land, public waters, and wildlife species. Analyzing the ecological costs and values associated with the conversion of these grasslands during and after the population waves discussed below is also necessary for any effort to restore the relationship of people to land and wildlife that is necessary to achieve true justice for Tribal Nations and others whose lands were taken to achieve the goals of Manifest Destiny. For these hundreds of Indigenous Nations, whose cultural and physical survival depended upon their relationship with, and understanding of, the ecological interactions of water, land, grass, wildlife, and other species throughout the seasons and from year to year, the severing of that relationship has caused intergenerational trauma, disease, death, and other consequences. In recent years, ecologists, archaeologists, and ethnobotanists have proven what Indigenous Nations have documented in their own languages and histories for centuries and longer, which is that their ancestors throughout the regions that eventually became the United States had widely curated different ecosystems to suit their needs, using fire to cultivate grasslands that would lure bison and antelope, cultivating plants like wild rice to ensure that the genetic constitution of the plants would survive and thrive in adapted wetland ecosystems, and cultivating many other plant species, including those that would currently be labeled as "crops," such as beans, peas, and maize.[7] Even in the driest and most arid regions of the southern Rocky Mountains, Indigenous Peoples used agriculture and resource stewardship practices that allowed vast populations to survive and thrive for hundreds of years.

7 Jules Janick, *Development of New World Crops by Indigenous Americans*, 48 Journal of Horticultural Science 4, 406–07 (2013); Baldes, Jason. Native Memory Project, "Native Fire Management" (last accessed Oct. 16, 2024), https://nativememoryproject.org/voice/native-fire-management/.

Post-contact historical accounts of non-Indigenous explorers, such as European fur trappers and traders, reveal evidence of the tremendous agricultural productivity of Indigenous Nations across the continent.[8] Indigenous crop production in and near the Great Lakes region and along the Missouri and Red Rivers sustained the fur trade and thereby contributed to broader regional economies.[9] Individual Indigenous Nations navigated far-reaching trade routes to leverage their agricultural productivity and these networks sometimes required extensive travel. People traveled to trade for items that were not available in their immediate area,[10] seeking supplies to use in ceremonial dress, such as feathers or shells, but also those that became incorporated into their diet.[11] Precontact, people and entire nations moved, changed, innovated, and responded to intertribal pressures, enticements, and conflicts, adapting their environments along the way.

There has been some momentum recently galvanizing around attempts to reincorporate Indigenous stewardship of land and resources into federal, state, and even private land management frameworks. Yet, these efforts are still in their early days. To avoid repeating the mistakes of the past, it will be important to thoroughly understand what happened in the past, and what has come of those changes and challenges. It will also be essential to understand the people who used, changed, and in some cases, dominated these lands over time, including the role of race in shaping the resultant laws and policies. These laws and policies impacted, and were also informed by, ownership, use, and access rights, which were, in turn, influenced by race – the race of those creating the laws and the race or races of those affected (and often, excluded) by them. The chapters that follow will therefore explore the foundations of the rules of law that established ownership and use rights over time, using various policy approaches. Through this lens, it is possible to gain a more comprehensive picture of how law, policy, and race shaped the region's grassland ecosystems.

In recent years, studies like the ones documenting the agricultural history of Chaco Canyon have changed the common understanding of the North American continent before the arrival of significant populations of Europeans. As Western scientific research has revealed more of the complex picture of Indigenous Nations and their agricultural practices, broader awareness of the nuances of Indigenous societies, including their languages, horticultural practices, and their laws and customs regarding ecological stewardship, has grown, giving scholars and policymakers substantive guidance to replace the previous narrative of North America as an untouched wilderness prior to European arrival. While Indigenous Nations and communities have

8 D. G. Kapayou, E. M. Herrighty, C. G. Hill *et al. Reuniting the Three Sisters: Collaborative Science with Native Growers to Improve Soil and Community Health.* 40 Agric Hum Values 65–82, p. 66 (2023), https://doi.org/10.1007/s10460-022-10336-z.

9 *Id.*

10 Peter Iverson, When Indians Became Cowboys: Native Peoples and Cattle Ranching in the American West, p. 6 (University of Oklahoma Press 1994) (Iverson).

11 *Id.* at 7.

documented these historical events and passed them down through successive generations internally, their knowledge base was not always mirrored, much less recognized, by that of non-Indigenous scholars, historians, and other experts in fields like natural resources, agriculture, and ecology.[12] In recent years, interdisciplinary research has demonstrated the extent to which that Indigenous Peoples throughout what became the United States have been cultivating plants for thousands of years pre-contact.[13] Some Indigenous Nations had been actively engaged in what non-Indigenous cultures would recognize as "agriculture" on a large scale, cultivating crops that supported vast population bases.[14]

This book will not analyze every law that contributed to changes in the ecological constitution of grasslands in the West, nor assemble a complete list of those that must be changed to restore plant species like Indian ricegrass. It will not propose to abolish entirely the structures of colonialism that permeate federal and state law and policy, although these structures are sometimes obvious impediments to ecological restoration. Instead, it will explore key laws and policies that were adopted to solve problems that no longer exist, or that have changed in the ensuing years since these rules of law were established, and outline the ways that these laws no longer serve the ecosystems or their modern human stewards, whether they are ecological, social, or political. This book will also propose certain reforms to these laws, which if adopted, could result in significant progress toward creating a more just, diverse, and climate-resilient West. The laws in these chapters are, in a sense, the low-hanging fruit of the national ecological and social reckoning and reconciliation that should occur in the American West. Once this begins, the changed landscape of the agricultural system will be better positioned to provide for the American West of the twenty-first century and beyond.

The existing literature on grazing and the law of grazing, more specifically, is often dichotomous, characterizing agriculture as the friend or foe of grassland ecosystems. This is frequently echoed by the media sources that cover these issues in the West. Yet, emerging scientific research is replete with evidence that the existing structures of law and policy relating to grazing fail the ecosystems and human stewards of those ecosystems, most critically with respect to Indigenous stewards. The nascent body of social and racial justice literature largely has not entered the dialogue surrounding public lands and natural resources management, and the aim of

12 Interview with Gary Tso, Second Mesa, Hopi Nation (Oct. 21, 2023) (recounting Hopi migration story from northern regions near Bears Ears National Monument to present location of Hopi reservation).

13 Aurelien Bouayad, *Wild Rice Protectors: An Ojibwe Odyssey*, 22 Environmental Law Rev. 27, p. 34 (2020); Jules Janick, *Development of New World Crops by Indigenous Americans*, 48 Journal of Horticultural Science 4 (2013).

14 Andrew D. Cliburn & Hillary M. Hoffmann, *Coming Home Again: Inherent Tribal Sovereignty, the Tribal Wildlife Grant Program, and Their Potential for Endemic Wildlife Reintroduction*, Ariz. Journal of Envt'l Law & Policy (Jan. 2022), available at https://papers.ssrn.com/sol3/papers.cfm?abstract_id=3895078.

this book is to begin to fill some of that void with concrete, tangible analyses and recommendations for a path forward.

Carving the path forward requires an understanding of the history of the American West, including through the stories of the people who used and occupied this region over time, while reexamining back some of the narratives surrounding the so-called settlement of the West to evaluate more critically how factors like race, ethnicity, and social status and influence impacted land ownership, use, and access rights. Through this deeper exploration of the relationship of people to place, using the lens of the rules of law, a more holistic and accurate picture of the evolution of agriculture in the grassland regions emerges. It becomes apparent, for instance, that European-Americans established rules of law to colonize and then displace Indigenous Peoples and divest them of their lands, largely for the purpose of furthering their own agricultural interests.[15] It also becomes apparent that when a series of laws failed to achieve their objectives, successive efforts were frequently undertaken to "double down" on the initial investment. Included in these layers of developing law and policy were incentives or mandates for Tribes to convert from their traditional agricultural lifeways to ones reliant on cattle, sheep, and horses, instilling the once-foreign value of domestic animal agriculture in some Tribes that continues today.[16] Slightly different tactics were employed to target Black and Latino farmers and ranchers and incorporate them within the western agricultural tableau, and the result of these compounding layers of law and policy was a system incorporating structural racism that tied access rights, land tenure rights, water rights, and other valuable preferences to the color of a person's skin.

The chapters that follow will explore the systems that arose to support agriculture in the West under the European and European American model, placing those systems in the broader context of Indigenous stewardship and the legacy of past laws that have permanently changed the relationship of Indigenous Nations to their lands and their stewardship of traditional knowledge and traditions.[17] They will also explore the history of Black and Latino farmers and ranchers and their experience with some of these same laws. These historical analyses will reveal correlations

[15] There were other drivers, too, such as the pursuit of mineral-bearing lands, but this book argues that the agricultural need was in some ways greater, fulfilling colonization and settlement of a much greater portion of the continent, using both general and specific laws.

[16] The book will not offer normative commentary on this change but will explain the legal rules that arose to ensure that individual tribal members cannot engage in agriculture to any significant degree on certain types of tribal lands without seeking the approval of the Bureau of Indian Affairs and subjecting their operations to continuing oversight and "management" by the Bureau, including the problematic financial arrangement the Bureau has set up, which requires all agricultural lease payments to be submitted to the Bureau, which deducts administrative fees before remitting the balance to the tribal allottee.

[17] Beth Mitchell, *Plant Species Richness at Bears Ears Reveals Archeo-ecosystems, and Implications for Public Land Management*, Natural History Museum, University of Utah (May 17, 2021), https://nhmu.utah.edu/articles/2023/05/ecological-legacy-bears-ears.

between law and policy and access to resources like water and grass, and describe how so many endemic species like Indian ricegrass faced extreme tests with the combined effect of removing Indigenous Peoples and their stewardship practices and the surge in non-Indigenous agricultural operations.

The latter chapters will reveal a change in collective consciousness around wildlife, public lands, and public sentiment, and the resulting pressures these changes placed on ranchers. More recent tensions between ranchers and wildlife conservation efforts will be explored, including Kanye West and Wyoming laws and policies protecting sage grouse habitat, and the famous standoffs between the Bundy family and the federal government in Nevada and Oregon. Chapter 9 will explore the causes and circumstances leading to a Bundy ally, Lavoy Finicum, being shot and killed during a roadblock set up by the FBI and Oregon State Police following his participation in the occupation of the Malheur Wildlife Refuge in eastern Oregon.

Each of the following chapters illustrates who benefits from the existing framework of laws related to agricultural use of land in the West, and the resulting cost.[18] Each also explores the intersection of law and policy with this power and ecological structure of the West. The common thread is that grass, land, and other resources in the West are still viewed as "gold" by not only ranchers, but also wildlife, the federal government, state governments, Tribal governments, and for profit and nonprofit corporations. These are finite resources, and the choices that were made in the chapters that follow illustrate the collective cost well.[19] The system of laws, incentives, and other policies that grew up around these choices still permeates critical policy debates today about land use, conservation, and critically, climate change. Therefore, the book will conclude with observations and suggestions for law and policy reform that could benefit western grassland ecosystems and the people and wildlife who rely upon them, without perpetuating the classism, racism, and other problematic values of the past.

[18] Bradley J. Gentner & John A. Tanaka, *Classifying Federal Public Land Grazing Permittees*, 55 J. Range Mgmt. 2–11 (Jan. 2002).

[19] Caroline Fraser, *The Crucial Role of Predators: A New Perspective on Ecology*, 360 Yale Environment (Sept. 15, 2011).

1

Spanish Land Grants and the Cielo Vista Ranch

Five miles east of San Luis, the oldest postcolonial town in Colorado, lies the Cielo Vista Ranch, which sold for $105 million to an undisclosed buyer in 2017.[1] The ranch is near the Colorado-New Mexico border, closer to Albuquerque than Denver. The famous San Luis Valley, which encompasses the town of San Luis and the Cielo Vista Ranch, is approximately 122 miles long and 74 miles wide, stretching from the Continental Divide of Colorado on the northwest rim of the valley into New Mexico on the south. It is what geologists refer to as a high-elevation depositional basin, with an average elevation of 7,664 feet above sea level. The valley is well known in Colorado and New Mexico for its stark beauty, appearing as a relatively fertile oasis nestled amongst strikingly tall mountains, within a proverbial stone's throw of some of the most arid, desert country in the nation. The valley is drained by the Rio Grande River flowing south into New Mexico, and although its climate is cold and dry, there are year-round surface and groundwater sources capable of sustaining seasonal farming activity during the months of the year in which it is possible to farm.[2]

Cielo Vista Ranch is one of the crown jewels of the San Luis Valley. Previously known as the Taylor Ranch, and stretching across 3,000 acres of the valley floor, the ranch also includes portions of the flanks of the stunning Sangre de Cristo mountains and 14,047-foot Culebra Peak.[3] The varied topography of the ranch has always offered good hunting and fishing, as well as meadows for grazing livestock and ample supplies of timber for firewood and building material. One of the ranch's previous owners, John Taylor, was well versed in the timber

[1] Sylvia Lobato, *Unidentified Purchaser Buys Taylor Ranch for $105 Million*, Conejos County Citizen (Aug. 16, 2017), https://conejoscountycitizen.com/article/unidentified-purchaser-buys-taylor-ranch-for-105-million.

[2] Karin Deneke, *Old and New Methods of Agriculture in the San Luis Valley*, Countryside Mag. (Feb. 25, 2019), www.iamcountryside.com/growing/old-and-new-methods-agriculture-in-san-luis-valley/.

[3] Kate Perdoni, *Costilla County Commissioners Reach Settlement with Cielo Vista Ranch*, Rocky Mtn. PBS (Nov. 15, 2022), www.rmpbs.org/blogs/rocky-mountain-pbs/costilla-county-commissioners-reach-settlement-with-cielo-vista-ranch/.

business, having run a massive timber company in North Carolina before moving west to Colorado's poorest county in the 1960s.[4] Soon after Taylor acquired the ranch, he began to build a fence around his property line, sealing off his newly acquired jewel from any interlopers.

The land on which the Taylor – and later Cielo Vista – Ranch was established was not ordinary fee land, though – meaning that it was not completely private. It carried communal use rights, which had been exercised for hundreds of years prior to Taylor's arrival. After his fence went up, the holders of these rights, all of whom are descendants of Spanish and Mexican families that emigrated to the San Luis Valley in the 1800s, were excluded from their traditional hunting, fishing, grazing, and gathering areas. Their rights to use the ranch lands derived from an 1844 Mexican government land grant promising their ancestors access to and use of the land in perpetuity, as a commons. The allocation of use rights in this commons was documented in historical records, which marked it as perpetual. The document creating these was sometimes referred to as the Sangre de Cristo Land Grant, or simply "the Grant."

The use of this area as an agricultural commons predated the Sangre de Cristo Land Grant by centuries, and possibly millennia, though. In a dry, dusty basin 230 miles southwest of Cielo Vista Ranch is Chaco Canyon National Historic Park. Within the Park boundaries are structures and other evidence offering proof that this area was once the center of an empire.[5] Although the canyon itself is relatively small, archaeologists now know that the empire spanned an area the size of Ireland that crossed the modern boundaries of four states: New Mexico, Arizona, Colorado, and Utah.[6] The Greater Chaco region, as the larger circumferential area is known, once contained a network of settlements, villages, and storage structures that either served the nerve center at Chaco Canyon or were served by it, or perhaps both. Archaeological records reveal that the Chacoan empire may have emerged because previously disparate populations settled in more urban patterns and the cities, towns, and isolated outcroppings emerged from this consolidation, in a pattern that lasted approximately 500 years. Remnants of the outer edges of this civilization are visible today in Mesa Verde National Park in Colorado, Hovenweep National Monument on the Utah-Colorado border, Bears Ears National Monument in southern Utah, Canyons of the Ancients National Monument in Colorado, and Canyon de Chelly National Park and Navajo National Monument in Arizona. The sites these reserves have been created to protect make up what is often referred to as this continent's

4 James Brooke, *In a Colorado Valley, Hispanic Farmers Try to Stop a Timber Baron*, N.Y. TIMES (Mar. 24, 1997), www.nytimes.com/1997/03/24/us/in-a-colorado-valley-hispanic-farmers-try-to-stop-a-timber-baron.html.

5 Childs at 14.

6 Paul F. Reed, *Chaco's Legacy: Discerning Migration and Emulation along the Middle San Juan River*, 20 ARCHAEOL. SOUTHWEST 1, 4 (Winter 2014).

"Cradle of Civilization."[7] Archaeological records indicate that the outlier communities in these areas of protected public lands – such as Hovenweep National Monument and Bears Ears National Monument – were possibly ancient suburbs to which the urban residents of Chaco Canyon fled, with the archaeological records indicating that they were occupied for a time after the buildings in Chaco's urban center. Some of these outliers are also found in the Sangre de Cristo mountains, not far from Cielo Vista.

A typical Chacoan community was focused around the "unit house," essentially a family dwelling structure with anywhere from six to fifteen adjacent rooms that served as living areas, storage, and ceremonial space.[8] The community consisted of several unit houses loosely clustered near one another and always oriented in rows from east to west, facing a central open plaza.[9] Some of the communities also contained multistory dwelling structures and kivas, the round ceremonial rooms used for prayer and other ceremonies.[10] Great houses, as the multistory structures are known, reached four or five stories in height and sometimes contained hundreds of rooms. The main urban hub at Chaco was a large city even by today's measure, occupying over 100 square kilometers, and its buildings were the tallest in the area that became the United States until steel skyscrapers built in Chicago in the nineteenth century surpassed them.[11]

The workmanship at Chaco is extraordinary; the number of individual stones used to build the Chacoan great houses is estimated in the millions.[12] The great houses also contained rooms with eight-foot ceilings, some weighing upward of ninety tons.[13] Supporting these heavy structures required a combination of adobe-like clay and timber, and their construction required laborers transporting hundreds of thousands of timbered beams over distances of more than fifty miles without the benefit of livestock. Construction of a complex, large great house could take several decades. But these great houses were likely not houses at all – rather they seemed to be public buildings, probably used for public gatherings, ceremonial purposes, and for similar reasons that public buildings exist in urban centers today.[14]

7 John W. Ragsdale, Jr., *The Rise and Fall of the Chacoan State*, 64 UMKC L. Rev. 485, 487 (1996) (Ragsdale I). The precise purpose of Chaco Canyon's buildings, streets, and ceremonial centers is not known, but it was important to those living in the outlier communities throughout the region, which bore its architectural and agricultural characteristics.

8 *Id.* at 489.

9 *Id.*

10 Annalee Newitz, *Conservatism Took Hold Here 1,000 Years Ago: Until the People Fled*, The Washington Post (June 1, 2018), www.washingtonpost.com/news/speaking-of-science/wp/2018/06/01/conservatism-took-hold-here-1000-years-ago-until-the-people-fled/.

11 Cody Cottier, *Cahokia and Chaco Canyon: The Ancient Cities That Flourished in North America*, Discover Mag. (Mar. 10, 2021), www.discovermagazine.com/planet-earth/cahokia-and-chaco-canyon-the-ancient-cities-that-flourished-in-north-america.

12 Ragsdale I. at 489.

13 Childs at 14.

14 *Id.* at 15.

They also may have been symbolic – built to demonstrate the power of the Chacoan center and perhaps as a show of wealth and force that outlying communities should emulate.[15]

Those outlying communities bear similar hallmarks, including multistory dwelling structures and kivas, along with a similar planning style with respect to the orientation of the buildings and their proximity to one another. They may have served for a time as agricultural hubs, as the necessity of importing food and especially water into the narrow canyon that housed the urban center is clear from the still visible earthen and masonry dams of a few feet in height and the remains of storage structures for grains and other crops. These hubs were part of a network of thousands of smaller villages, remote settlements, and agricultural lands that were connected by roads still visible using Light Detection and Ranging (LiDAR) technology.[16] Although the exact nature of the relationship between the main urban centers and the outlier communities is unclear, archaeologists agree that the settlement and road patterns indicate a planned, rather than spontaneous, effort. The archaeological records also reflect that people from far-flung regions likely were drawn to Chaco, leaving traces of their migration toward this urban center along the roads that can be seen from orbiting satellites today, dotted with shattered pottery they likely used to transport food, water, and possibly ceremonial items or trade goods.[17]

By the year 1000, the Chacoan settlements had expanded to virtually all the arable land in the 100-mile-wide San Juan Basin of northwestern New Mexico, and the carrying capacity of the basin was stressed to what must have been close to its maximum.[18] Agriculture was essential, and needed to support the population that swelled into the thousands by AD 1100. This required some creative farming techniques in the canyon itself, but also required imported grain and maize grown in farther-flung regions, as the canyon was too small to cultivate the quantities of maize and grains that were needed to sustain the population.[19] Several studies have revealed agricultural secrets of Chaco, including that

[15] Newitz.

[16] Sean Field, *Lidar-Derived Road Profiles: A Case Study Using Chaco Roads from the US Southwest*, 11 Adv. Archaeol. Pract. 2, 184–97 (2023). doi:10.1017/aap.2022.31.

[17] Childs at 17; David E. Stuart, The Ancient Southwest: Chaco Canyon, Bandelier, and Mesa Verde, p. 77 (2009). The road network that connected Chaco Canyon to the greater region is so vast that only a small fraction of it has been thoroughly inventoried or documented. Ragsdale I at 514. In the 1980s, the BLM initiated the most comprehensive survey of these roads to date, cataloguing approximately 1,500 roads radiating outward from the San Juan Basin. *Id.* The longest road segments measure up to fifty kilometers and appear to connect outlier great houses with urban great houses. *Id.* Main roads were approximately twenty-seven-feet wide and smaller, spur roads were roughly ten-feet wide.

[18] John W. Ragsdale, Jr., *The Aboriginal Land and Water Rights of the Jemez Pueblo*, 24 U. Denv. Water L. Rev. 109, 117 (2021) (Ragsdale II).

[19] Larry Benson, John R. Stein, & H. E. Taylor, "Possible Sources of Archaeological Maize Found in Chaco Canyon and Aztec Ruin, New Mexico" (2009). USGS Staff – Published Research. 748.

remnants of corn found among the Chaco canyon dwelling structures were imported from places like the Chuska mountains, over sixty miles away.[20]

The archaeological record, combined with the histories of the descendants of those who lived and traveled through the canyon, reveals that the urban hub was positioned to import agricultural products from producers scattered across a region of astonishing size – approximately 40,000 square miles in total.[21] At the time that Chacoan leaders were determining how to feed the thousands of people that converged upon the urban center in the heart of the canyon every year, the applicable rule of law they would apply to solve this problem would have taken the form of Traditional Ecological Knowledge, norms of behavior based on information passed down from one generation to the next. As is reflected in descendant communities today, hunting, gathering, farming, and plant cultivation followed rules that were tied to families or clans, and other cultural markers, like gender.[22] Families cultivated crops or harvested wood in certain areas, the jurisdictional limits of which were dictated by history, practice, and language.[23] Resources were shared, even if access to land was delineated and more restrictive, to ensure a food supply for the entire community.

Sometimes, the internal rules of law did not translate to other nations, and the need to access resources resulted in intergovernmental negotiations to resolve the resulting disputes, or outright warfare, especially when resources were scarce. There is evidence in the Chacoan record to support the argument that the people who lived in Chaco Canyon may have abandoned their city due to this type of intertribal conflict. Some archaeologists theorize that residents of Chaco fled to the north in fear of a military assault from the south, or perhaps directly after an invasion.[24] Skeletal remains excavated from Chaco and dating to the post-1100 AD period could support the latter theory, with indicia of violent deaths resulting from severe, human-inflicted injuries, and mass graves indicating that armed conflict may have included massacres.[25]

Approximately 400 years after the collapse of the urban center at Chaco Canyon,[26] the Spanish arrived in this region, exploring it with the messianic zeal that was their trademark throughout the world at this time. They arrived astride horses, armed with guns, and bearing the blessing of the Pope in the form of a rule of positive

20 *Id.*

21 Ragsdale II at 117.

22 Univ. of Arizona, Indigenous Resilience Center, "The Man Working to Sustain Hopi Dry Farming in Arizona" (Sept. 2, 2022), available at https://resilience.arizona.edu/news/man-working-sustain-hopi-dry-farming-arizona.

23 *Id.*

24 George Johnson, *Scientist Tries to Connect Migration Dots of Ancient Southwest,* N.Y. Times (June 29, 2009), available at www.nytimes.com/2009/06/30/science/30chaco.html.

25 Newitz, www.washingtonpost.com/news/speaking-of-science/wp/2018/06/01/conservatism-took-hold-here-1000-years-ago-until-the-people-fled/.

26 Ragsdale II at 127.

law called the Doctrine of Discovery.[27] This Doctrine, which will be explored in more detail in Chapter 2, served as a religious and legal justification for the violent takeover of Indigenous populations the world over, including Puebloan people in northern New Mexico in the sixteenth and seventeenth centuries. The Catholic Church and the secular governments of the Mexican territory, backed by the army, consolidated to repress and control the Pueblos and their land, using techniques such as forced tribute slavery, religious persecution, and executions.[28] These brutal but effective strategies, combined with imported diseases that the immune systems of the Pueblos could not fight, brought the entire Puebloan population to the brink by 1680.[29]

Despite the deadly efficacy of the initial Spanish colonization effort, the descendants of the Chacoan occupants in the Pueblos did not yield their lands without a fight. In August of 1680, the Puebloan Nations consolidated their force and ejected the Spanish, not only their clergy, government functionaries, priests, officials, but the families of settlers, including women and children, in what later became known as the "Pueblo Revolt."[30] The resulting independence they secured lasted only slightly more than a decade before a force of 800 Spanish soldiers, settlers and priests began to retake Puebloan lands and communities in 1692. Having possibly learned a lesson from the experience of the pre-Revolt occupation, the new Spanish leadership colonized in a "lighter" fashion – allowing greater political, economic, and religious autonomy among the colonized nations.[31] The heart of this policy shift was a recognized minimum entitlement to land under Spanish law, which applied to the Pueblos as a population colonized by the Spanish government. The Spanish called this concept the "Pueblo Leagues," which is still reflected in the twenty-first century rules of law defining land grant rights.[32]

During the Spanish and Mexican conquests of the Puebloan and Chacoan regions, both foreign sovereigns used land grants to distribute rights to land

[27] *Id.* at 127.

[28] *Id.*

[29] *Id.*

[30] *Id.* at 137.

[31] *Id.* at 128.

[32] Richard W. Hughes, *Pueblo Indian Water Rights: Charting the Unknown*, 57 NAT. RES. J. 219, 222 (2017), n. 7. The Spanish governors also gave Pueblos additional land grants to be used as a grazing commons, which represented the first iteration of the grazing commons that this region would experience under post-contact colonial rule. Under Spanish colonial law, the Pueblos were considered wards of the Spanish Crown, and the Crown forbade all other Spanish citizens to live on Pueblo lands. This system endured from 1692 until 1821, for over 120 years. The jurisdictional framework altered slightly for the Pueblos in 1821, when Mexico achieved its independence from Spain, and the Mexican government notified the Pueblo tribes that their members would be recognized as citizens of Mexico and their title to their lands would be recognized by the new sovereign colonial power. Ragsdale II at 128.

and other resources, like water and timber.[33] These systems reflected values of shared property rights and common control over land and resources.[34] Under both systems, one individual, usually wealthy and powerful, would receive a grant from the regional Governor, guaranteed by the wealthy grantee's promise to lure settlers to the granted lands to establish a visible footprint of occupation and productivity throughout the Spanish and Mexican territories. As these settlements spread, they would serve as a warning to other governments that the colonizing sovereign behind them claimed these lands and intended to stay.

To encourage the settlers to move to the grants, the grantee would promise them land for home sites, cultivation of crops, grazing of livestock, and for hunting and other subsistence purposes.[35] Families would therefore move, usually to remote areas, in reliance on the promises of perpetual access to the commonly held resources of the grant.[36] Some grantees would record their promises and permissions with regional or local authorities, detailing the settlers' rights to access common resources on the granted lands, containing more detailed provisions for organizing life on the grant, including "the use and care of the water, regulation of roads, land for churches, location of mills, and pasturing of animals."[37] Some recorded documents included clauses guaranteeing the "enjoyment of benefits of pastures, water, firewood and timber," provided that the settlers and their descendants did not take more than their fair share.[38]

Under Spanish, and later Mexican, law, land grants were property rights; fully alienable, transferrable, and hereditary. The original Spanish land grant system depended upon a hierarchical structure, under which a Lord, or Patrón, was given authority by the Spanish Crown to allocate land located in a claimed territory. In exchange, the Crown expected each Patrón to ensure that grantees made productive use of the area within the Grant and paid taxes. To build a solid tax base, the Patrón would recruit individuals and families to come live on the land and organize cooperative farming communities, like the one in San Luis, Colorado. The Patrón would then divide his land into individual parcels – known as varas – and reserve a portion to be used in common.[39] The varas were narrow strips of land adjacent to a river or stream, and the Patrón allocated pastures or parcels within the vara to settlers in fee simple, giving them exclusive

33 Ryan Golten, *Lobato v. Taylor: How the Villages of the Rio Culebra, the Colorado Supreme Court, and the Restatement of Servitudes Bailed Out the Treaty of Guadalupe Hidalgo*, 45 NAT. RES. J. 457, 459 (2005).

34 *Id.*

35 *Id.* at 460–61.

36 *Id.* at 461.

37 *Id.*

38 *Id.* at 461–62.

39 Richard D. Garcia & Todd Howland, *Determining the Legitimacy of Spanish Land Grants in Colorado: Conflicting Values, Legal Pluralism, and Demystification of the Sangre De Cristo/Rael Case*, 16 CHICANO-LATINO L. REV. 39, 41 (1995).

rights to use and occupy their delineated areas. Areas nearby, outside the boundaries of the vara, but either unsuitable for farming or inaccessible by existing irrigation methods, were either held in common by the settlers of the vara; or, under private land grants, were available for use by the settlers for a variety of nonagricultural purposes.[40] The Grants also contained corollary rights: communal grants and private grants to individuals.[41] Recognition of each right codified a resource management system that took into account the aridity of the region and its limited water resources, requiring users to share.

Because land grants were themselves property rights, Patróns could sell them, which sometimes resulted in dramatic changes to the terms of the bargain that settlers had struck with the original grantee, especially if the terms had not been recorded. Under the prevailing legal system in which non-property owning individuals and families engaged in farming to benefit the community as a whole, use rights to the commons were perquisites that lured people to the arrangement – giving them access to land for farming, hunting, and other activities that they otherwise could not attain. This system made sense in the San Luis Valley because individual varas did not usually have the capacity to produce enough crops to sustain single families, let alone the entire community.[42] Moreover, areas like the flanks of 14,000-foot Culebra Peak were not suitable for farming – but they could be set aside as common hunting grounds and for harvesting valuable timber. And the settlements established by those who created communities like San Luis gave notice to neighboring Tribal Nations and other foreign governments that the Spanish crown claimed this land. The arrangement had echoes of the communal experiment to the south, in Chaco Canyon, half a millennium prior.

Ultimately, Spanish dominion over the area did not last, and the Mexican system that supplanted Spanish law changed the land grant framework. Instead of granting lands to Patróns, who were entitled to these benefits by virtue of their heredity, Mexican land grants were awarded to entrepreneurs who demonstrated the potential to generate tax and other revenue from the lands.[43] Mexican land grants were also conditioned on some reciprocal service promised to the central government – such as establishing a visible footprint of colonization and settlement, or Christianizing the Indigenous population. By contrast to the Spanish grants, the Mexican grants included additional incentives for grantees and settlers that reflected these national values in collective land use and access. Unlike the more feudal Spanish system, the Mexican grantees were permitted to retain one-third of the grant in fee, as long as they distributed the remaining two-thirds of the grant to settlers within twenty years.[44]

40 *Id.*
41 *Id.* at 40.
42 *Id.* at 41.
43 *Id.* at 42.
44 *Id.*

Interestingly, the Mexican government also made many grants to groups of settlers, creating autonomous pluralistic communities with private and communally held lands.[45] But Mexico struggled under this system to establish itself as an autonomous nation, at the same time the United States was also expanding and permanently establishing its territorial boundaries.

The American model of settler colonialism did not use a land grant system, in keeping with the American preference to eschew the land baron model of Europe, and particularly feudal England. In the 1800s, fast-moving American settlers were encroaching upon Mexican lands in what is now southern Colorado and northern New Mexico – which of course were once the lands of Puebloan people descended from the Indigenous occupants of the Chacoan empire.[46] Into this quilt of legal frameworks for allocating land and water rights, the American legal system was also beginning to develop around a very individualistic model of land ownership and resource control. While United States courts favored exclusionary, individual rights to land and disfavored communal access rights like those of the people who lived on or used the grants, Mexican law continued to value and recognize communal land use, especially for agricultural purposes. These contradictory values toward land and resources were never reconciled, and United States courts made little effort to explore or reflect the Mexican values underlying these legal rights when adjudicating cases involving land grants, even after the United States had acquired nearly half of Mexico following the Mexican–American War.[47]

The Cielo Vista ranch traces its title to a Mexican grant issued in 1844, during the height of the tension between Mexico and the United States. The Sangre de Cristo Land Grant conveyed rights to approximately 1,000,000 acres of land to Stephen Luis Lee and Narcisco Beaubien, two entrepreneurs who had promised to develop and reap financial rewards from this land for the benefit of the Mexican government.[48] After Lee and Beaubien were killed in 1847 in the Taos Rebellion, one of many battles of the Mexican–American War, Beaubien's father, Carlos, inherited his son's half-interest in the grant and purchased the remaining half-interest from Lee's estate.[49] Carlos moved quickly to satisfy the terms of the grant, recruiting over 1,500 settlers from Mexico to establish farms and put down roots by 1860. This included the founders of the town of San Luis, Colorado.

Meanwhile, the United States had emerged victorious from the war, and forced Mexico to cede the territory including this grant and so many others to the United States in the 1848 Treaty of Guadalupe Hidalgo. It was this war, and this treaty, by

45 *Id.* at 42–43.
46 *Id.* at 42.
47 *Id.* at 54.
48 *Id.* at 44.
49 *Rael v. Taylor*, 876 P.2d 1210, 1213 (Colo. 1994); Lobato, https://conejoscountycitizen.com/article/unidentified-purchaser-buys-taylor-ranch-for-105-million.

which the United States took over half of Mexico's territory, including the sovereign lands of so many Indigenous Nations.[50] The present states of Utah, as well as portions of Colorado (including the lands of Cielo Vista), New Mexico, Arizona, and Wyoming, were carved out of that 529,000-square-mile acquisition from the Republic of Mexico – the largest by the United States since the Louisiana Purchase. The 1848 Treaty of Guadalupe Hidalgo protected the rights of Mexican citizens living on and using grants, though, noting that "Mexicans now established in territories previously belonging to Mexico … shall be free to continue to reside, or remove at any time to the Mexican republic, retaining the property which they possess in the said territories…."[51] Moreover, the treaty acknowledged that Mexican citizens living on the lands subject to the treaty possessed property rights "of every kind," which would be "inviolably respected" by the United States.[52]

Operating under the premise that this treaty would protect the rights of those living on his grant, Carlos Beaubien executed and recorded a document memorializing the permanent regulations, rights, and privileges of the Sangre de Cristo settlers.[53] Recorded in 1863, this document provided that certain lands within the Grant would "remain uncultivated for the use of the residents of San Luis, San Pablo and the Vallejos, and other inhabitants of said towns, for pastures and community grounds, etc."[54] It also allocated waters of the Rito Seco river to "the said inhabitants of the town of San Luis, and those on the other side of the Vega, whose lands lie in the vicinity and cannot be irrigated by the water of the Rio Culebra."[55] Three acres of land within the Grant were dedicated to the local Catholic Church, and the remainder was "deeded for the use of the inhabitants of this town and of the others up … the Vallejos Creek and also for the benefit of those who may in the future, settle on the Gregorio Martin Creek."[56] Finally, the Beaubien document stated that "no one shall have a right as they might have thought, to place any obstacles or hindrances to interfere with the rights of others," and "regulations as to roads shall be also observed so as to allow every one [sic] to have access to his farm lands" and water.[57]

For more than a century thereafter, the community members of San Luis enjoyed exactly what was guaranteed by the 1863 Beaubien document – undisturbed communal use of this land and access to water for the purposes specified therein. An anthropologist who researched these communities found that they supported themselves

[50] Christine A. Klein, *Treaties of Conquest: Property Rights, Indian Treaties, and the Treaty of Guadalupe Hidalgo*, 26 N.M. L. Rev. 201 (1996).

[51] Treaty of Guadalupe Hidalgo, Feb. 2, 1848, U.S.-Mex., 9 Stat. 922.

[52] *Id.*

[53] Garcia & Howland at 45.

[54] *Id.*

[55] *Rael v. Taylor*, 876 P.2d 1210, 1213 (Colo. 1994).

[56] *Id.*

[57] *Id.*

from "a mixed economy of irrigated river agriculture on the valley floors, pastoralism with seasonal migrations of flocks between the highland mountain meadows in the summer and valley-bottom pastures in the winter," and free hunting and fishing rights year-round.[58] Their usufructuary, or use, rights were respected by their neighbors in Colorado, including landowners whose lands they had to cross or use to exercise them.

All of this changed in 1960, when Taylor purchased the 77,500-acre tract then known as "the Mountain Tract," which was communal land subject to the 1863 Beaubien document and within the boundaries of the Sangre de Cristo grant. The North Carolina-born lumber baron paid seven dollars an acre for that land, and a nearby parcel, which thereafter became known as the Taylor Ranch.[59] Upon purchasing this land, Taylor immediately began fencing it off, preventing the descendants from exercising their rights to access and use it. The conflict that followed Taylor's 1960 purchase ultimately generated one of the longest title disputes in Colorado history. The legal and factual issues were complex, but the core legal issue in each case was whether Taylor's attempt to exclude descendants of the Beaubien beneficiaries from the lands within the Ranch boundaries was lawful, or whether the beneficiaries still held the legal rights memorialized in the Beaubien document.[60]

Although unacknowledged in the litigation, the threads that wound through every case were race, class, and ethnicity – the Beaubien beneficiaries were Mexican American, Spanish American, or Indigenous Mexican-Americans, while Taylor was white. Taylor was also rich, and the Beaubien beneficiaries were poor, living in a county that in the 1990s recorded a per capita income average of only $7,057.[61] Taylor's original action, filed under the Torrens Act, asked a Colorado court to invalidate any legal rights claimed by the Beaubien beneficiaries, due to the fact that Taylor had purchased the land in fee simple absolute and (allegedly) not subject to any conditions imposed by foreign governments. Taylor's claims were belied by the Beaubien beneficiaries' lived history on this land and their descendants understanding of the legal basis under which they had done so for generations, though, despite his legal arguments that he and "his predecessors in title have maintained continuous possession of the subject land and have exercised complete dominion over it since the issuance of the original grant from the Mexican government."[62]

58 Garcia & Howland at 45 (quoting Marianne L. Stoller, Preliminary Manuscript on the History of the Sangre de Cristo Land Grant and the Claims of the People of the Culebra River Villages on the Lands, 4–5, 46–47 (1980) (unpublished manuscript, submitted as an affidavit to the District Court of Costilla County)).

59 Brief of Petitioners, p. 6, *Rael*, 876 P.2d at 1213.

60 *Rael*, 876 P.2d at 1212.

61 U.S. Dept. of Commerce, Economics and Statistics Administration, Bureau of the Census, 1990 Census of Population – Colorado, Social and Economic Characteristics, Table 3, p. 35, www2.census.gov/library/publications/decennial/1990/cp-2/cp-2-7.pdf (noting that statewide average at that time was 50 percent higher, at $14,821).

62 *Rael*, 876 P.2d at 1216.

Although Taylor could prove he had "continuously paid the taxes on said land and … maintained sole and exclusive use and occupation thereof," the beneficiaries offered significant evidence to the contrary – that they and their forebears had used these lands for hunting, fishing, grazing, and other purposes dating back to at least 1863.[63]

The trial court and the Colorado Court of Appeals both concluded that Taylor had demonstrated that any use rights of the Beaubien beneficiaries to the Taylor Ranch had been extinguished, reasoning that "neither the Beaubien document nor the agreement between his [Beaubien's] heirs and Gilpin evidenced a clear intent to establish or recognize a 'dedication' of the usufructuary 'privileges' the defendants sought to establish."[64] The appellate court affirmed the trial court's legal determination that none of the individual descendants possessed any legal rights to use the Taylor Ranch lands and affirmed the lower court's judgment awarding full title, in fee simple absolute, to Taylor. This ruling effectively removed any "cloud", or claim, on Taylor's title and affirmed a legal right to leave his fence up and pursue trespass actions against the Beaubien beneficiaries should they or their livestock set foot on the Ranch property.[65]

The beneficiaries did not give up, though, despite the money, power, and leverage of Taylor and his legal team. Fourteen years after the appellate court's ruling on the original Taylor lawsuit under the Torrens Act, they filed suit in a Colorado state court alleging that the Torrens Act ruling had violated their constitutional rights to due process of law under the Colorado State Constitution. The basis of their claim was that they "were … heirs or successors in interest of the original settlers of the Sangre de Cristo Grant" and that the Taylor Ranch lands had been "historically subject to the community rights and uses of the [petitioners] for grazing, lumber, fire, wood, water, pasturing, hunting and recreational uses."[66] They argued that the court's ruling in the earlier Torrens Act cases had taken their property rights without the minimum due process required by the state constitution. The trial court rejected these arguments, dismissing the claims on a motion from Taylor and the other defendants arguing that this litigation was nothing more than a repackaging of the issues resolved in the earlier Torrens Act litigation. The beneficiaries appealed, initially suffering another defeat in the Colorado Court of Appeals, but they appealed and requested a review by the Colorado Supreme Court. The highest court affirmed the lower court's rulings and it appeared that Taylor had emerged victorious again, although the appeal was limited to the procedural issue of whether Taylor had given adequate notice to all of the Beaubien beneficiaries with claims to the Taylor Ranch.

63 *Id.*
64 *Id.*
65 *Id.*
66 *Id.* at 1217.

Because this issue involved questions of fact, which are outside the scope of the supreme court's jurisdiction to resolve, the supreme court remanded the case back to the trial court for a rehearing to determine which of the beneficiaries had received adequate notice. The trial court ruled that some of them had, but critically, others had not. For the latter group, the supreme court required the trial court to hold a trial on the merits,[67] and following that, the court issued a finding that the beneficiaries and their predecessors had "grazed cattle and sheep, harvested timber, gathered firewood, fished, hunted and recreated on the land of the defendant from the 1800s to the date the land was acquired by the defendant, in 1960."[68] In addition, the trial court found that the beneficiaries had always known the Taylor Ranch lands as their shared space, and that prior to Taylor's purchase in 1960, they had never been denied access to this land. Finally, the court noted that there was no dispute "that the settlers could not have survived without use of the mountain area of the grant."[69] Yet, despite these findings, the lower court ruled that Colorado law did not recognize the type of property rights that the beneficiaries were asserting – communal use rights to the Grant, which was now the Taylor Ranch.

The beneficiaries appealed to the Colorado Court of Appeals, where they lost again, but they appealed the Court of Appeals' decision to the Colorado Supreme Court. By then, nearly forty-two years had passed since Taylor first bought the Cielo Vista Ranch and built his fence. Yet, by contrast to its earlier decisions, this time the Colorado Supreme Court appeared finally ready to consider whether Colorado law recognized their communal use rights to land derived from Spanish and Mexican land grants. After analyzing the claims, the court concluded that they were recognizable as a form of easement and that Colorado law had long accommodated easements held by more than one individual. Notwithstanding the difficulty inherent in "attempting to construe a 150-year-old document written in Spanish by a French Canadian who obtained a conditional grant to an enormous land area under Mexican law and perfected it under American law," the court nevertheless determined that it had to apply modern principles of Colorado law regarding the interpretation of source documents that create easements to the facts of this case and the Beaubien document.[70] The court found that "Beaubien wrote this document … in an apparent attempt to memorialize commitments he had made to induce families to move hundreds of miles to make homes in the wilderness," and held that "[i]t would be the height of arrogance and nothing but a legal fiction for us to claim that we [could] interpret this document without putting it in its historical context."[71]

67 *Lobato v. Taylor*, 71 P.3d 938, 944 (Colo. 2002).
68 *Id.*
69 *Id.*
70 *Id.* at 947.
71 *Id.*

That context showed that the Beaubien beneficiaries' ancestors would have never moved to the San Luis Valley to settle permanently without an understanding that the incentives Beaubien offered were permanently available to them, and to their children and grandchildren. If they lacked permanent access to the communal areas of the grant, those without varas could not survive, and even those with varas needed the supplemental acreage to support various subsistence activities, including hunting, grazing livestock, procuring water, and cutting timber for firewood.[72] Their survival depended on access to these resources, and the limited supply required that they be shared. Therefore, the supreme court concluded that the rights Beaubien established in the 1863 document "ran with the land," meaning that they were permanent and could not be extinguished by passage of time, transfer of title, or by Taylor's fence.[73]

The 2002 Colorado Supreme Court decision memorializing this rule, *Lobato v. Taylor*, was a landmark decision in that the court recognized the claims of a powerless majority of plaintiffs who were people of color and whose land and resource rights derived from a foreign government's colonial settlement laws. Yet, only a small group of Beaubien descendants emerged from that forty-two-year battle with use rights – those who had not received adequate notice of Taylor's 1960 Torrens Act case. In this way, the ruling fell short for the entire class of beneficiaries. Taking a broader view, though, the *Lobato* decision is a good place to begin any discussion about race, power, and access to resources in the West. It contains every theme that characterizes land ownership and use throughout the region: people of color with communal values and shared principles around agrarian and other resource use and stewardship, colonized by white settlers who wanted exclusive rights to use their lands and attempted to extinguish their legal title. The white settlers succeeded in excluding the people of color, for a time anyway, and the fight to retain the communal use rights wound its way through a state court system for over forty years, forcing a tremendous financial and resource burden on people who were already under-resourced and underprivileged. The legal system itself reflected and embraced the white privilege that permeated the litigation, and only began to reconcile that legacy in the early years of the twenty-first century.

Furthermore, the power, privilege, and value set of Jack Taylor and others in his position changes not only the relationships of people to land that have developed over hundreds of years, but complicates modern conservation challenges facing the West, including the climate crisis and the task of ensuring climate justice for all people living in this region, not just the wealthy or the non-Hispanic white. From the earliest agricultural eras in this region, starting with the farmers who supported the settlements in Chaco Canyon and continuing through the twentieth century with the Spanish and Mexican settlers living on the land grants, farming and ranching activities

72 *Id.* at 944.
73 *Id.*

were supported by the resources that existed on the land and there were sufficient resources for all who were recognized within the system, at least for a time. But, the repeating patterns starting with the Chacoan Phenomenon and most recently, with disputes over land and water similar to those that arose in *Lobato*, have shown that this region has never been capable of sustaining sufficient agricultural productivity or ecological health for more than a few centuries without experiencing a crisis that leads to a form of legal "reset."

The reset in *Lobato* could portend further upheaval in the system of allocating resources and users in Colorado, and perhaps in other states with land rights derived from Spanish or Mexican land grants. It calls into question the security of the fee title of other ranchlands located within this grant, and within other grants, throughout the region that was once Chaco, then Spain, then Mexico, and is now the United States. It provides arguments for other land grant beneficiaries and descendants to use in pursuing legal claims based on their own usufructuary rights guaranteed by the Spanish or Mexican governments, and this could potentially include Tribal Nations, such as the Pueblos. These implications will be discussed in more detail in Chapter 10, but for now, it is time to journey south to New Mexico, to another famous land grant ranch.

2

The Doctrine of Discovery and Vermejo Park Reserve

From the South comes a blue mare. Changed into a maiden. She comes to me.
– Diné (Navajo) Song of the White Bead Woman.[1]

In the heart of northern New Mexico, among the southernmost peaks of the Rocky Mountains, lies the largest ranch in the country: Vermejo Park Reserve. Roughly the size of Rhode Island, the ranch spans over 500,000 acres of grasslands, forests, lakes, and rivers near the Colorado border.[2] Like Cielo Vista, Vermejo Park traces its title to a land grant, known informally as the Maxwell grant.[3] Also like Cielo Vista, Vermejo Park has a wealthy owner, although this one is more widely known. Vermejo Park's owner is Ted Turner, the founder of Cable News Network (CNN), who is legendary throughout the West for the zeal with which he purchases large private ranches and land. He is most often associated with these activities in Montana, but he has been actively scooping up vast portions of other states too, including New Mexico. He is not dependent on his ranches or properties as a source of income and uses the business entities that own and run his ranches to reduce the financial risk associated with off-ranch income, specifically his extensive investment income. Ranching is not necessary for Ted Turner to feed his family and he does not engage in this business as part of any inherited family legacy; he is running what is essentially a giant experiment in private landownership as a means of restoring land and ensuring sustainability, as he understands both terms.

The business entity that Turner uses to hold and oversee the ranches is Turner Enterprises, Inc (TEI).[4] According to testimony that Turner's son, Beau Turner,

[1] Iverson at 9–10.

[2] April Reese, *Drilling Done Right?* High Country News (Jul. 19, 2004), www.hcn.org/issues/278/14862; https://tedturnerreserves.com/vermejo/.

[3] U.S. Dep't of the Interior, National Park Service, *et al.*, *Study of Management Options: Vermejo Ranch*, p. 4 (Jul. 1979), http://npshistory.com/publications/proposed-parks/nm-vermejo-ranch.pdf.

[4] *Baker v. Turner Enterprises, Inc.*, Mem. Opinion & Order Granting Defs.' Mot. for Protective Order, at *3 CIVIL NO. 10–1089 DJS/LFG (D.N.M. May 10, 2011).

provided in litigation, TEI manages Ted Turner's "business interests, ranches, land holdings and investments, including the oversight of ... two million acres in twelve states and in Argentina, as well as the 50,000 bison herd" that Turner runs on Vermejo Park and various other ranches.[5] Forbes Magazine puts Turner's net worth in 2023 at $2.5 billion, and noted in an article that year that he has not dropped below the $2.1 billion mark for over a decade.[6]

Vermejo Park is notable for many reasons, but among wildlife biologists, it is perhaps best known for its bison herd, although bison are but one of the 60 species of mammals, 200 species of birds, 33 species of reptiles and amphibians, and 15 species of fish sharing this landscape and its lakes, rivers, and streams with paying ranch guests.[7] The Castle Rock bison herd is distinguished for its genetic purity, and for having one of the most secure, private open ranges in North America: the vast acreage of Vermejo Park. The ranch staff rotate the herd seasonally, from the high country in the spring, summer, and fall to the lower elevation prairies in the winter. The high country pasture area consists of pinyon-juniper and oak shrubland and alpine tundra, measuring approximately 500,000 acres in total. During the winter, the herd is moved to the ranch's five lower elevation short-grass prairie pastures, consisting of approximately 60,000 acres.[8] The herd was originally transplanted to the area between 1920 and 1940 from Yellowstone National Park and despite interbreeding with two other "outside" herds, the herd is negative for mitochondrial cattle DNA, which is rare among North American bison.

Vermejo Park has also been a cattle ranch. At one time, up to 19,000 cattle grazed the same pastures where the bison range today, although that herd size was at some point determined to be excessive and harmful to its soils, grasses, and riparian areas.[9] A healthier herd size was estimated by the US Department of the Interior in a 1979 study to be around 4,000 cattle year-round, with perhaps an additional 1,000 during the May–November grazing season.[10] Historical cattle grazing on the Ranch has contributed to significant erosion, formation of gullies, and has affected endemic vegetation and soil quality, which may be why there are no longer any cattle grazing Vermejo Park.[11] Turner's public mantra for the ranch has been one of conservation and restoration ever since he acquired it in 1996.

5 *Id.*
6 Forbes Profile, *Ted Turner* (Nov. 17, 2023), www.forbes.com/profile/ted-turner/?sh=32593f2d50db.
7 *Study of Management Options: Vermejo Ranch* at 52.
8 *Id.* at 68. The herd got its name from the unique castle-like geological feature on the ranch and the surrounding area, which has been home to the herd since at least the 1920s.
9 *Id.* at 75.
10 *Id.*
11 Nina Boys, *A Day with Vermejo's Last True Cowboy* (Aug. 12, 2019), https://tedturnerreserves.com/blog/a-day-with-vermejos-last-true-cowboy/#:~:text=Even%20though%20there%20are%20no,Sheep%2C%20and%20other%20native%20wildlife.

The scope of Turner's landholdings in New Mexico alone is so vast that it is hard to imagine for those who have not experienced a tour, and these are only some of the properties in his immense portfolio. Like the fictional John Dutton in "Yellowstone," Turner is a modern land baron, with a measure of privacy and control over land, water, and other resources that most could not imagine. As New Mexico journalist Dave Herndon explained in a 2015 article covering Turner's landholdings within the state, when driving south on Interstate 25, just south of Bosque del Apache, it takes a long time to drive across Turner's properties in New Mexico. He owns mountain ranges, lakes, various homes, historic lodges built by the founders of Vermejo, and "vast sea[s] of high-desert grassland that wash[] up to distant mountain shores."[12] The ranches he owns in this region of New Mexico have names recalling a bygone era – Vermejo Park, Armendaris, and the Ladder Ranch. By the time one has traversed Armendaris and Ladder alone, they have been driving through "Turner country" for approximately sixty miles.[13]

Truth or Consequences, New Mexico is a small town of about 6,000 between the Armendaris and Ladder Ranches, where Turner owns a hotel, the Sierra Grande. Local restaurants purchase Turner's bison meat, so visitors may end up experiencing Vermejo Park by eating a bison burger or consuming the beef produced by another of Turner's ranches. Much of the well-traveled Interstate 25 corridor from Denver to Albuquerque passes through or near Turner's property, although there are no signs or other indicia that one individual owns so much land nearby. Even though it may be hard to tell from the road, the region is now "a rich man's domain."[14]

Turner's Vermejo Park, like Cielo Vista, is a product of the Mexican land grant era.[15] Before that, Vermejo was Indigenous land, home to the Apache people. The Apache once called all 1.7 million acres of land that were deeded in the Maxwell Land Grant home.[16] Archaeological evidence reveals that the Spanish first made contact with them and with other Indigenous Nations of what is now New Mexico and Arizona in 1539, with the first "famous intruder" to the region being Francisco Vásquez de Coronado, who brought cattle with him on his expedition north.[17] In 1598, Juan de Oñate brought domestic livestock into the Rio Grande Valley, which marks their first documented appearance in the territory that ultimately became the United States. These expeditions needed horses to herd their imported cattle, and for transportation, in regions where alternatives would not become available for centuries to come.[18]

12 Dave Herndon, A *Turning Point in Turner Country*, NEW MEXICO MAG. (Apr. 29, 2015), www.newmexicomagazine.org/blog/post/a-turning-point-in-turner-country-91138/.
13 *Id.*
14 *Id.*
15 *United States v. Maxwell Land-Grant Co.*, 121 U.S. 325, 357 (1887).
16 *Id.*
17 *Id.*
18 *Id.*

Post-contact, Indigenous networks and travel patterns were disrupted as these Nations faced challenges of massive and unprecedented dimensions, forcing them to accommodate changes to a degree many had never experienced.[19] Warfare and disease presented sometimes insurmountable obstacles to the social, political, and physiological adaptations that Indigenous Nations had utilized to their advantage precontact. Other aspects of the introduced culture were easier to adopt and adapt to, especially when facing these obstacles. One of these was domestic livestock.[20]

For Spanish, Mexican, and Indigenous Peoples alike, cattle were a food source and horses were necessary "equipment" to herd the cattle from place to place. By the late 1500s, Spanish and Mexican expeditions were routinely bringing cattle into the area that is now the American southwest to feed their large expeditions, and within a few short decades, Indigenous Nations had begun to acquire horses through trades for their own purposes.[21] Horses quickly became a part of some Indigenous cultures and lifeways, and many have documented this moment in their history through Traditional Indigenous Knowledge passed down through generations.[22] Following the Indigenous acquisition of horses by Tribes like the Comanche, Apache, Navajo, and Ute, other Tribal Nations that did not migrate with game followed suit, especially those occupying the same towns and villages year after year. Even for Tribes that had traditionally migrated following herds of elk and other game species like bison, sedentary cattle ranching held some appeal. Through either route, many Tribes in the region of what is now Texas, Arizona, and New Mexico acquired their own herds by the late 1600s, along with other livestock the Spanish and Mexicans introduced, such as sheep and goats.[23]

Yet, Tribes like the Apache ended up being removed, divided, and ultimately allocated to reservations where they now share use rights in common with each other and with the federal government as their trustee. Many no longer have sovereign rights to the lands that became ranches like Turner's, while Turner, as a single individual, owns half a million acres, sharing ownership rights with no one other than the corporation he created to hold and manage them. The federal laws that divested the Apache of their lands and allowed Turner to buy them did not develop in a vacuum. Eighteen years before the Republic of Mexico issued the Maxwell Land Grant, the fledgling United States Supreme Court issued an opinion designed to facilitate the removal of Indigenous Nations like the Apache, to essentially clear the way for non-Indigenous settlement of their lands.

[19] *Id.* at 7.

[20] *Id.* at 8.

[21] *Id.* at 9.

[22] Southern Ute Tribe History, *Early History* (last visited Oct. 9, 2023), available at www.southernute-nsn.gov/history/#:~:text=Around%201637%20Ute%20captives%20escaping,as%20early%20as%20the%201580s.

[23] Iverson at 12.

This opinion, *Johnson v. M'Intosh*, announced a new rule for American common law that was based on the common law system of government coopted from the British, with elements of other European laws and customs added in where convenient. The British by that point had significant experience in colonizing Indigenous-occupied lands in far-flung locations across the globe, and it had expeditious options enabling it to move millions of Indigenous Peoples "out of the way," so British immigrants could settle and lay permanent claim to their lands. Some of these options were more appealing to the United States than others, based on the American desire to reject a monarchical form of government in favor of a democratic one. Thus, there would be no royal charter allowing the President of The United States to seize Indigenous lands, such as the ones that had issued from the British Crown in the seventeenth and eighteenth centuries. But another tool, based on a Catholic religious tradition, would suit the federal government's purposes well, according to the newly established United States Supreme Court under the leadership of its first Chief Justice, John Marshall.

This tool, the Doctrine of Discovery, came from Spanish law,[24] and Marshall's selection of it in *Johnson v. M'Intosh* became perhaps the most devastating legal precedent for Indigenous Nations in American history.[25] The dispute at the heart of *Johnson* consisted of facts that belied the significance of its holding, involving a seemingly mundane property dispute. The dispute was filed as an ejectment action – a lawsuit designed to "eject" one party occupying or claiming land, in favor of another, based on the latter's stronger claim. In this case, the lawsuit was filed by a lessee of Johnson and Graham to validate the lessee's claim to 11,560 acres of land in the State of Illinois against Thomas M'Intosh, who believed he was the true owner.[26] Johnson and Graham's lessee had acquired a legal interest in this property from a common ancestor, Thomas Johnson, Jr., who coincidentally, was a former Associate Justice of the United States Supreme Court.[27] Thomas Johnson, Jr., in turn, had acquired the property through a deed from the Piankeshaw Tribe, which once occupied portions of what is now Indiana and Illinois.

Thomas M'Intosh, had purchased the same 11,560 acres claimed by Johnson and Graham's Lessee from the United States government more than forty years after the Piankeshaw had signed the deed conveying the land to Thomas Johnson, Jr.[28] The United States government had acquired its title through a deed conveyance from Virginia in 1784, and Virginia traced its title back to Great Britain, acquiring the title

[24] 21 U.S. (7 Wheat.) 543 (1823).

[25] Walter R. Echo-Hawk, In the courts of the Conqueror: The 10 Worst Indian Law Cases Ever Decided, p. 57 (Fulcrum Press 2010).

[26] Brief for the Appellant, *Johnson and Graham's Lessee v. William M'Intosh*, Kan. J. L. & Pub. Pol'y, p. 852, 858 (Summer 2000).

[27] *Id.*

[28] The Tribe conveyed the lands to Thomas Johnson, Jr. by deed poll on October 18, 1775, and the United States conveyed the lands by patent to M'Intosh on July 20, 1818. *Id.*

when Virginia declared its independence from Great Britain in 1778.[29] So, on the one side, the Johnsons acquired the title directly from the Piankeshaw Nation, and on the M'Intosh side, the title was acquired through *de jure* transfer of title (first by Great Britain, then Virginia, then the United States) by a distant sovereign government, without notice to, or knowledge of, the Piankeshaw Nation.[30]

In the opinion, authored by Chief Justice John Marshall, the Supreme Court ruled in favor of M'Intosh.[31] The Court based this ruling on several factors. For one, the justices concluded that the Piankeshaw Nation lacked a full fee interest in the disputed lands, so the Tribe had no interest to convey to Johnson's ancestor. The interest of the Piankeshaw in these lands, was instead an occupancy right, which was conveyable only to the United States.[32] Both of these legal realities were, in the Court's view, necessary consequences of European discovery of North America. According to the Court, "[o]n the discovery of this immense continent, … the potentates of the old world" found it necessary, "in order to avoid conflicting settlements, and consequent war with each other, to establish a principle, which all should acknowledge as the law by which the right of acquisition, which they all asserted, should be regulated as between themselves."[33] In the Court's words, "this principle was, that discovery gave title to the government by whose subjects, or by whose authority, it was made, against all other European governments, which title might be consummated by possession."[34] Two corollary rights flowed from this rule of law. First, "the exclusion of all other Europeans necessarily gave to the nation making the discovery the sole right of acquiring the soil from the natives…."[35] Under this reasoning, Johnson's ancestor (as a *citizen* of the nation making the discovery) had no legal right to purchase Indian lands – that right being reserved to his own government exclusively.

Second, "[i]n the establishment of" the relations between the discoverers and the native people, the Court held that "the rights of the original inhabitants were … impaired. They were admitted to be the rightful occupants of the soil, with a legal as well as just claim to retain possession of it, and to use it according to their own discretion;" but the Europeans asserted "ultimate dominion…."[36] The Supreme Court relegated the Tribal Nations to a legal status of "occupants," who were legally incapable of transferring more than they owned ("ultimate title," in the Court's words) to anyone else.[37] Put another way, the Piankeshaw Nation lost the underlying fee title to its lands upon a claim of the conquest of

29 *Id.*
30 *Id.*
31 *Id.* at 852, 859–60.
32 *Id.*
33 *Johnson v. M'Intosh*, 21 U.S. (8 Wheat.) 543, 572–73 (1823).
34 *Id.* at 573.
35 *Id.*
36 *Id.*
37 *Id.*

those lands by "discovery," even if they had no knowledge of the act of discovery and even if the act of discovery did not take place anywhere near their lands. It was more or less bad luck that their lands happened to fall within the bounds of an arbitrary charter issued by a foreign government located thousands of miles away, across half a continent and an ocean. Consequently, and although they would not know it for decades, every Indigenous Nation whose lands fell within a European charter or a subsequent area declared by the United States as "federal" territory experienced the same legal result – loss of land, resources, and power.

Losing the fee title to their lands in favor of the "Indian title" that *Johnson* created was just the beginning of the legal tidal wave that was coming for Tribal Nations in the decades to follow. This case was only the first in the Marshall Trilogy – three Supreme Court opinions penned by Chief Justice John Marshall – which established the basic framework of property rights for Tribal Nations and delineated the relationship between these nations and the United States federal government. On the heels of *Johnson*, the Court issued *Cherokee Nation v. Georgia* and *Worcester v. Georgia*, in which the Court further altered their legal status from that of foreign sovereigns to "domestic dependent nations," bringing them simultaneously under the authority of, and yet also alongside the United States federal government.[38]

The Court clarified the latter aspect of this dichotomous label in *Cherokee Nation* with its reasoning in the last case of the trilogy, *Worcester v. Georgia*, proclaiming that Tribal Nations were not akin to states, but were rather sovereign entities with their own powers of self-government and self-determination, even though they existed within the boundaries of the United States.[39] This independence had its advantages and disadvantages, though, as the seemingly extra-constitutional status of Tribes rendered them unable to avail themselves of federal judicial forums to redress harms they suffered. In other words, Tribes lacked standing to assert the sovereign rights acknowledged in the earlier cases, because they did not fall within one of the categories of Article III of the U.S. Constitution, which limits the jurisdiction of federal courts to cases and controversies "between a state or citizens thereof, and foreign states, citizens or subjects."[40]

In *Cherokee Nation*, the Tribe's attorney had argued that Cherokee Nation was a foreign state, and thus fell squarely within the scope of Article III, but the Court was not persuaded. Citing the "peculiar and cardinal" distinctions between Cherokee Nation, which as a result of *Johnson* had been declared to have surrendered its fee title to the United States, the Court found that the former was "within the jurisdictional limits of the United States," and not entirely "foreign." In short, the Cherokee Nation was more like a US territory or "domestic dependent nation," and because

38 *Cherokee Nation*, 30 U.S. at 13.
39 *Worcester*, 31 U.S. 515, 518 (1832).
40 U.S. CONST. Art. III, § 2.

Article III contained no allowance for jurisdiction over disputes involving domestic dependent nations, there was no constitutional authority supporting the Supreme Court's jurisdiction to hear the Tribe's claims.[41]

In *Worcester v. Georgia*, the Court considered another legal issue arising out of Georgia's continued incursions into Cherokee Nation's territory – whether Georgia's laws that purported to directly regulate the conduct of missionaries within Cherokee Nation were unconstitutional because they infringed on the treaties that Cherokee Nation had executed with the United States federal government.[42] The State's laws annexed Cherokee Nation lands and regulated conduct on tribal lands, ostensibly allowing the State to prosecute Samuel Worcester, a missionary from Vermont who had been proselytizing in tribal communities, for violating one of these State laws.[43] He challenged his conviction in federal court, filing a writ of *habeus corpus*, in which he argued that the state law under which he had been prosecuted and convicted was unconstitutional and therefore his conviction must be invalidated. Analyzing the Constitution and its scant references to Indigenous Nations and applying them to Mr. Worcester's situation, the Supreme Court concluded that "the acts of Georgia [we]re repugnant to the Constitution, laws and treaties of the United States."[44] The Court reasoned that, if Georgia's laws were allowed to stand, the United States would essentially be in breach of its contractual promises to Cherokee Nation to protect it from external threats, and Georgia could potentially interfere with the trade provisions and other terms of the treaties.

The rules established in the Marshall Trilogy arose from the specific circumstances that unfolded on the lands of Tribes in what is now the central and eastern parts of the United States. Yet, they became foundational rules of law that applied across all states then part of, and those that later became part of, the United States. In the ensuing decades, they provided a legal platform upon which an empire was built. They not only paved the way for two centuries of subsequent legal colonization and consolidation of European-American power over Indigenous ancestral land and resources, which have had devastating consequences for Indigenous Nations and Indigenous Peoples up to the present day, but they embedded anti-democratic and maybe even anti-American principles such as racism and religiocentrism into the bedrock of federal land disposal and natural resources laws that Congress later enacted, and which the Executive branch still implements.

The Apache were likely unaware of the early judicial opinions issued by the Supreme Court, such as *Johnson*, *Cherokee Nation*, and *Worcester*, especially given

41 Echo-Hawk, at 34.
42 31 U.S. (6 Pet.) 515 (1832).
43 *Id.*
44 *Id.*

that they were being subjected to the laws of a different sovereign during that time – the Republic of Mexico. Yet, they would feel the impacts of the Marshall Trilogy by the end of the century, given the results of the Mexican–American War and the transfer of title to their lands from Mexico to the United States in 1848. Moreover, because of the way that the Doctrine of Discovery operates, the Apache would continue to feel the impact of this *de jure* colonization up to the and during the ensuing centuries. By virtue of the Doctrine of Discovery, Apache lands became the property of the United States government once the United States signed the Treaty of Guadalupe Hidalgo with Mexico. At the same time, Court in *Johnson* had recognized that Indigenous Nations colonized by the Doctrine of Discovery possessed rights established by virtue of the Doctrine itself – the right of occupancy, which is sometimes referred to as "Indian title."[45] According to the Court, Indian title gave Tribes "a right to such a degree of sovereignty, as the circumstances of the people would allow them to exercise."[46] Indian title, unlike the underlying fee title held by the United States, was by no means secure, as Tribal Nations would come to learn. The Court had ruled in *Johnson* that the "superior sovereign" could "extinguish" a Tribe's right of occupancy through "purchase or conquest," the twin triggers of the Doctrine of Discovery.[47] Even if unbeknownst to the Tribal government, and regardless of where its citizens lived at the time their lands were purchased or conquered, the underlying title was no longer the Tribe's once the United States purchased or conquered their land.

At the conclusion of the Marshall Trilogy era, in the mid-1830s, the fate of the Apache and their land was sealed, like that of every other Indigenous Nation colonized by Spain and Mexico within the boundaries of the modern United States. The United States conquered and purchased the region that became New Mexico and southern Colorado and title to these lands would transfer to the United States, while the Indigenous Nations retained their Indian title. The United States possessed the legal right to extinguish that title and would do so in nearly every instance. In this way, the Marshall Trilogy cases provided foundational rules of law that served as building blocks for so many laws and policies to come – all of which would impact the social, political, and ecological framework of hundreds of Indigenous Nations.[48]

45 Jessica A. Shoemaker, *No Sticks in My Bundle: Rethinking the Indian Land Tenure Problem*, 63 U. Kan. L. Rev. 383, 401–403 (2015).

46 Carole E. Goldberg, *et al.*, American Indian Law: Native Nations and the Federal System: Cases and Materials, p. 47 (7th ed. LexisNexis 2015).

47 *Id.*

48 Other "trails of tears" followed in the middle Atlantic region, the upper Midwest, and in the West. *See* Jeffrey Ostler, How Many Trails of Tears Were There?, (Yale University Press Blog, May 13, 2019). The Cherokee Trail of Tears began within a short two years of the seemingly pro-tribal ruling in *Worcester*, when the US military commenced forcing Cherokee Nation citizens to march west along the Trail of Tears so named because so many people died during the thousand-mile march to the Indian Territory of what is now Kansas and Oklahoma.

As the federal government removed Tribes from their homelands using the Doctrine of Discovery, Congress and the Executive Branch established numerous reservations, which were promised to the Tribes as permanent homelands. Some of these promises – especially those memorialized in Treaties – were honored, and some were not, as most Americans who have studied this period of US history know. Yet, there was a great degree of legal nuance in the post-Marshall Trilogy era that is key to understanding the current legal and political reality of Tribes like the Apache. The federal government's primary goal for the Apache and other Tribes during the post-Marshall Trilogy era was assimilation, and agriculture was a "key ingredient" in the process of assimilating Tribal members to Euro-American lifeways.[49] Federal officials at the highest levels expressed support for Indigenous adoption of animal agriculture as a means of "settling" Indigenous Peoples in one place and reducing their "intransigence."[50] From the Cherokee, Choctaw, Chickasaw, removed on the Trails of Tears to Oklahoma, to the Pima and Papago of what is now Arizona, and the Pueblo villages of the Rio Grande valley in the southwest, animal agriculture became part of the fabric of Tribal life, even during removal and the establishment of new lifeways on reservations.[51] Cattle ranching also became a source of income for young Indigenous men trained in their own communities, who could work on large ranches owned by settler colonizers from Mexico, Texas, and points beyond. Indian vaqueros, as they were known in the Southwest and California, were instrumental in the success of the nineteenth-century ranching operations throughout the West.

The introduction of horses and cattle, along with other domestic livestock, during the Spanish and Mexican occupation of what is now the American southwest, planted the seeds for Indigenous traditions of animal agriculture and pastoralism in this region that predate those of the northern, central, and eastern European immigrants who arrived in the intermountain West in the 1800s, over two centuries after Tribes incorporated them. In southern Utah, for instance, Ute and Navajo communities had been cultivating herds of horses, cattle, sheep, and goats for two centuries before the white, Mormon immigrants from Missouri established a permanent presence in the state.[52]

Euro-American settlement came to the intermountain West in well-documented waves.[53] For the settler colonizers who opted to settle in this region, clearing fields to grow crops and raise livestock was no easy feat. The soils were ill-suited to

49 Iverson at 17.

50 *Id.*

51 *Id.*

52 Wallace Stegner, The Mormon Country, p. 172 (Univ. of Nebraska Press 1942).

53 Greg Bradsher, "How the West Was Settled: The 150-Year-Old Homestead Act Lured Americans Looking for a New Life and New Opportunities," p. 8 (2012), www.archives.gov/files/publications/prologue/2012/winter/homestead.pdf.

agricultural productivity on the scale supported in other regions, and settlers quickly discovered that some engineering was required to deliver adequate water, along with some experimentation in their selection of plant species and crop rotation to account for the rocky soils and relatively low nutrient levels. At first, customary irrigation and other previously tested practices were adequate to supply key resources, such as water, but also cleared and tilled land for grazing livestock, although the continuing emigration pressure from the East presented challenges by the end of the nineteenth century.[54]

The cattle that these settler colonizers brought or acquired to help them establish their claims to land posed problems for Tribal Nations. For one, cattle were often grazed near Tribal lands, and without fences to keep them out, they entered and devoured crops.[55] Yet, this particular conflict was somewhat short-lived, as by the late eighteenth century, the US federal government more aggressively pursued removal, reservations, and allotment policies. During this transition period, some Indigenous Nations started to change their collective opinion toward cattle and horses, from nuisances to a means of surviving reservation life and allotment. Domestic livestock sometimes allowed removed and relocated Tribes to survive not only the physical transition but the cultural and societal changes. Those changes signaled a transition in Indigenous populations that accompanied a broader mechanism of cultural adaptation to a rapidly changing sociopolitical situation beyond the Tribes' control. Importantly, it also necessitated a shift from the mutuality and relationally oriented worldview of Tribes toward animals to one that recognized animals as property that could be owned, bought, and sold. This norm was entirely new to these Indigenous Nations.[56]

At the time that Indigenous Nations of the southwest were making this transition,[57] the ranch that became Ted Turner's Vermejo Park Reserve was established. This area was a rich habitat for American bison, and at that time, the bison living on the land that became Vermejo Park were also genetically untarnished by cattle DNA. That richness would change with the arrival of that first wave of Spanish and Mexican settlement, and the result was a dramatic decrease in the region's bison herds, from the late 1600s to early 1700s. There was also significant interbreeding between cattle and bison, which changed the genetic makeup of most herds. Moreover, cattle ate the grasses that bison preferred, and throughout areas like the lowland pastures of Vermejo Park, grasses were stressed under the pressure of feeding domestic cattle, horses, and wild species such as bison and antelope. Wildlife biologists characterize bison as "generalist foragers" because of their preference for

54 Phillip Foss, Politics and Grass, pp. 3–4, 74, 77 (1960); Leshy at 795.

55 Iverson at 46–47.

56 *Id.* at 18.

57 *Id.*

a wide variety of herbaceous grasses, such as blue gramma, sand dropseed, and little bluestem.[58] Only if grasses are scarce will bison deign to eat woody vegetation and by expressing their preference for grass species in such a strong manner, bison influence prairie and grassland biodiversity, creating biological "room" for the plants they selectively avoid to thrive, while keeping grass populations healthy. In this way, grazing bison create somewhat of a biological quilt, with a pattern of grazed and ungrazed areas. This quilt pattern contains greater biodiversity than prairies or grasslands without bison, which allows greater potential for beneficial gas exchange, biomass density, and healthy plant cover. Grazing bison also create circumstances that increase the overall potential of photosynthesis because the biodiversity of their quilt pattern grazing increases light permeability and reduces competition from singular species for water and soil nutrients.[59]

Bison are adapted to areas burned by fires, attracted to the grass seedlings that first pop up in a recently burned area. They in fact flock to burned prairies, where they can gorge themselves on a bevy of grasses without the effort required to selectively avoid intermixed woody plant species that would coexist in a more mature ecosystem. The instant attraction and grazing action of the bison, in turn, help increase the biodiversity of the burned prairie because as the prairie or grassland recovers, other plant species will begin to sprout, bison will avoid them, and the quilt-like mosaic will appear. Because of their natural tendencies, grazing bison can restore even monoculture prairies, if given enough time, adequate water, and room to roam.

Tribal nations like the Apache followed bison herds as they migrated from higher elevations in the summer down to the more arid and warmer lowlands in the winter. This included areas of the Maxwell Land Grant.[60] Apache presence in many areas is hard to document using typical western data collection or research methods because they were mobile, highly dependent on hunting bison and other game species and gathering plants, with relatively small, dispersed communities.[61] Archaeologists sometimes erroneously conclude that Apache people "abandoned" an area during a given period of time because the evidence of their occupation disappears in the archaeological record and they did not discard many items as they moved.[62] Apaches are among the Athapaskan-speaking

58 National Park Serv. Biol. Res. Div., "Bison Bellows" (Mar. 24, 2016), www.nps.gov/articles/bison-bellows-3-24-16.htm?utm_source=article&utm_medium=website&utm_campaign=experience_more&utm_content=small.

59 *Id.*

60 Ryan Golten, *Translating Property: The Maxwell Land Grant and the Conflict Over Land in the American West, 1840–1900*, 43 NAT. RESOURCES J. 921, 922 (2003).

61 ADOLPH M. GREENBERG, ETHNOGRAPHIC OVERVIEW AND ASSESSMENT OF CARLSBAD CAVERNS NATIONAL PARK, p. 8 (National Park Service, Sept. 12, 1996), http://npshistory.com/publications/cave/eoa.pdf.

62 *Id.* Moreover, "a singular problem" in tracing the movement patterns and lifeways of the Apache using archaeological methods is nearly impossible because of "the fact that the Apache were making very energetic efforts not be found during the later part of their history."

people who came to dominate many areas of the southwest, including the area that is now New Mexico, where ethnohistorians have documented their presence through ties to descendant communities.[63] Apache communities acquired livestock, including horses and cattle, by raiding Spanish, Mexican, and other Indigenous communities' herds.

As these herds of domestic livestock grew, so did the pressure on bison. Bison herds usually consisted of anywhere from five to fifty animals, although anecdotal evidence indicated that herd numbers could grow into the hundreds or thousands.[64] Some early accounts of settler colonizers estimate herd sizes in the hundreds of thousands, or even more, although verifying these stories is challenging because bison were so unevenly distributed over a wide geographic range, including throughout much of the West. Early estimates put the total population of bison at sixty million at or around European contact, although more recent research indicates that somewhere in the range of thirty million animals is a more realistic figure.[65] If the herd size of these giant animals was not intimidating enough, bison also had a tendency to stampede, which would have been fear-inducing for anyone who was near enough to see or hear the phenomenon. But, this tendency also made bison somewhat easy to manipulate, and Tribal Nations like the Apache used it to their advantage, causing stampedes to herd and kill bison, using natural topographic features such as buttes and cliffs to do the work that otherwise would involve spear points and potentially dangerous close-up encounters between hunter and hunted.[66]

As Tribes like the Apache used the habits of the bison to their advantage, so too did federal officials of the United States government use the habits of Tribes like the Apache and their dependency on bison against the Tribes. It was readily apparent to federal officials that killing bison would weaken Tribes dependent upon them and assist with the federal policy of assimilation, establishing Tribes in permanent locations and ending their seasonal migratory lifeways. As part of this policy, "Army officers instigated wasteful mass killings, provided ammunition to hunters, and personally lobbied against protection measures for the species introduced in Congress, making their stance on the species and on its intimate relationship with Native people unquestionably clear."[67] One United States Army Colonel was reported to have told his troops: "Kill every buffalo you can. Every buffalo gone is an Indian gone."[68] As the policy was implemented, struggling and sometimes starving people had few options other than trying to farm or raise livestock, creating pressure on Tribal

[63] *Id.* at 11.

[64] William Holland, *The Spirit of the Buffalo: The Past and Future of an American Plains Icon*, 21 ANIMAL L. 151, 154–55 (2014).

[65] *Id.* at 155.

[66] *Id.*

[67] *Id.* at 156

[68] *Id.* This belief was not limited to the Executive branch or its emissaries to Indian Country either; in 1872, then-Congressman James A. Garfield spoke on the House floor in favor of destroying the bison to solve the "Indian question" and ease westward expansion.

governments to cede more and more land to the federal government in exchange for rations and other supplies to give to their people. The policy was incredibly effective, and federal land holdings grew exponentially in the early nineteenth century. Reflecting on this period, President Theodore Roosevelt later remarked that "[t]he extermination of the buffalo was the only way of solving the Indian question," with the crash in bison population being for "humanity at large … a blessing."[69]

Agriculture rapidly filled the void that bison and Tribes had occupied, and prairies that had once served as homes to massive herds of roaming bison were replaced with small farms, and horses, beef cattle, and sheep. Short and tall grass prairies were replaced with crops like wheat and corn. Domestic livestock decimated short grass species on the prairies, which resulted in bison starving after they arrived on their traditional summer feeding grounds and found nothing left to eat.[70] And even if settlers did not exterminate or hunt bison for food, and their livestock did not graze them out of certain regions, others traveling through the region in covered wagons on famous routes like the Oregon Trail or later, on the railroad cars that soon passed from coast to coast, shot them for sport, nearly terminating the remaining populations.

This history makes the present effort to conserve and restore bison populations even more remarkable. Whether it is Ted Turner restoring the herd at Vermejo Park, or the Confederated Salish and Kootenai Tribes curating the herd at what was once known as the National Bison Range in Montana (but is now a Tribally operated Bison preserve), private individuals and governments alike are bringing bison back from the cusp of extinction. Yet, the path to restoration of bison and "range" is not the same for all who seek to participate. Foundational legal rules like the Doctrine of Discovery impacted these efforts in the past and continue to do so well into the twenty-first century. Tribal Nations who seek to restore bison populations on their reservations do not own their lands in fee – their reservation lands are for the most part Indian Country, a legal term that generally denotes land owned by the federal government and by Tribes. Depending on the status of the land where the bison might roam, a Tribal Nation may have to secure the permission of the Bureau of Indian Affairs before releasing animals, even within a reservation. And if a Tribal Nation sought to repatriate bison to its own land by trucking them on state highways or herding them across state lands, the barriers could increase.[71]

For Ted Turner, the path is much clearer. He does have to navigate some state-law hurdles as mentioned above due to laws that were designed to protect domesticated livestock from diseases and other harms posed by wildlife. Assuming he can obtain the relevant state permissions to transport bison on state highways, though,

69 *Id.* at 157.

70 *Id.*

71 Robert B. Keiter, *The Greater Yellowstone Ecosystem Revisited: Law, Science, and the Pursuit of Ecosystem Management in an Iconic Landscape*, 91 U. Colo. L. Rev. 1, 79 (2020).

he does not need the permission of any other governmental entity before releasing them on his land. He holds all of the "sticks" in the proverbial bundle of property rights as recognized by state and federal courts across the country: the right to use his land, the right to exclude others from it, and the right to alienate the land, giving him the ability to sell it, leave it to his heirs in a will, or transfer it as part of some land swap or other commercial transaction.[72] The origin of the concept of the "sticks" in the bundle of rights was *Johnson v. M'Intosh*.[73]

By simultaneously recognizing that there are severable components of a fee simple property right, and holding that Tribes lacked at least two of those rights – the right to exclude and the right to freely alienate – the Johnson Court's adoption of Doctrine of Discovery had profound and long-lasting impacts on conservation efforts like the repatriation of bison, among others. This harm may not be able to be completely "undone" without discarding the Doctrine entirely, and for over 200 years, that idea has been a legal nonstarter. This was not because legal experts considered the Doctrine to be just or even legally valid in terms of its reasoning, but because of the seeming impossibility of convincing the United States Supreme Court to discard it. Yet, hope springs eternal in the annals of federal Indian law, and recently, a glimmer emerged from a surprising source. In early 2023, Pope Francis directed the Vatican to repudiate the Doctrine of Discovery, in response to a request from Indigenous Nations.[74] The Vatican subsequently declared that the fifteenth-century Papal Bulls, or edicts, "did not adequately reflect the equal dignity and rights of Indigenous Peoples," and should not be considered expressions of Catholic faith.[75] In response, legal scholars and Tribal leaders have called on American courts to acknowledge this repudiation under federal law and in state law property doctrines, to start the lengthy process that might begin to unravel the damage done by the Doctrine of Discovery and its legal and policy progeny over the centuries they have been part of American jurisprudence.[76]

One idea for legal reform will be discussed further in Chapter 10, which could signal, substantial changes for Vermejo Park. Turner Enterprises advertises this property as a "full service guest ranch," that "offers unparalleled opportunities to enjoy and interact with the natural world, and is one of the premier hunting, fishing and

[72] John G. Sprankling & Raymond R. Coletta, Property: A Contemporary Approach, p. 26 (West Academic Publishing 2019).

[73] *Id.* at 35.

[74] Nicole Winfield, *Vatican Formally Rejects Doctrine of Discovery after Indigenous Calls*, PBS NewsHour (Mar. 30, 2023), www.pbs.org/newshour/politics/vatican-formally-rejects-doctrine-of-discovery-after-Indigenous-calls#:~:text=VATICAN%20CITY%20(AP)%20%E2%80%94%20The,of%20some%20property%20laws%20today.

[75] *Id.*

[76] Brett Wilkins, *Vatican Rejects "Doctrine of Discovery." Used to Justify Colonial Conquest and Land Theft*, Common Dreams (Mar. 31, 2023), www.commondreams.org/news/doctrine-of-discovery.

ecotourism destinations in the West."[77] As of 2024, that offer is only open to those who can afford the $1,000 nightly rate, allowing them to bask in the glory of this property that has hosted presidents and business magnates ever since its establishment in 1909. Simply put, Vermejo Park has been the exclusive domain of the rich, the privileged, and the powerful. *Lobato*, and the land reform that might emerge from other states' recognition of land grant rights in beneficiaries, could change the nature of this place significantly. As will be discussed more in Chapter 10, these changes would impact not only Turner but also potentially the Apache descendants and land grant beneficiaries, creating a future that looks very different than the past. But for now now, it is time to travel north, to learn more about the modern legacy of *Johnson v. M'Intosh* for ranchers in Indian Country.

[77] www.tedturner.com/turner-ranches/turner-ranch-map/vermejo-park-ranch-new-mexico/.

3

Allotment Laws, Trusteeship, and Blackfeet Ranching

My savings account is the grass I saved last year. I can't afford to feed it to the neighbor's buffalo.[1]

– Danny Barcus

The bison of Vermejo Park are not the only genetically pure bison population.[2] There are others, including one that the Blackfeet Nation translocated to their reservation lands along the Rocky Mountain Front in what is now northern Montana. The restoration of this herd means more to the Blackfeet people than having a local meat supply, although this is of course advantageous to the Nation's landmark food sovereignty program. As discussed in Chapter 1, the mass slaughter of bison was one of the most devastating elements of the federal government's policy of colonizing Indigenous lands. So, restoring bison to Blackfeet lands is a form of cultural, historical, and spiritual healing for this Nation.

Blackfeet bison restoration is complicated, though, by another legal reality that stems from the federal government's colonization policies of the late 1800s, referred to in shorthand as "allotment." This term, which refers to a federal policy as well as a series of statutes passed by Congress, authorized and encouraged large-scale divestitures of tribal lands and subsequent division and differentiation of land tenure status, to mix Indian land with non-Indian land, and thereby break up the collective land base that gave Tribal Nations their sense of collective identity and for some, their power. The allotment policy was used to convert communally held Tribal lands into individually owned farms and ranches, and to attempt to assimilate Indigenous Peoples into the fold of so-called "mainstream" American society by taking away their ability to travel in search of game, fish, and plant foods and medicines.[3] The

1 Amelia Bates, *The Return of the American Bison is an Environmental Boon – and a Logistical Mess*, Grist (Nov., 2022).

2 Jason Daley, *Genetically Pure Bison Will Return to Montana After 100 Years in Exile*, Smithsonian Mag. (Mar. 29, 2016), www.smithsonianmag.com/smart-news/genetically-pure-bison-return-montana-after-100-years-exile-180958597/.

3 Vine Deloria, God is Red: A Native View of Religion, pp. 5–6 (Fulcrum Publishing 3rd ed. 2003).

foundation for allotment was the Marshall Trilogy and the rules of law established in the those opinions issued between 1823 and 1832, covered in Chapter 2. The rule from *Johnson v. M'Intosh* established the foundation, in the form of a legal rule that Tribal Nations lacked fee title – or complete ownership – of their lands. Therefore, they could not freely alienate (give, sell, or barter) their lands to any party other than the United States federal government.[4] The successor opinions – *Cherokee Nation v. Georgia* and *Worcester v. Georgia* – built upon this foundation by establishing rules of law that Tribes were domestic dependent (or colonized) nations, to which the United States federal government owed a trust responsibility, but were lacking in full sovereignty and complete independence.[5] Through these core rules of law, Tribal Nations were rendered legally vulnerable to further unilateral acts of colonization by the United States, and eventually, by states, despite the Supreme Court's recognition of Tribal Nations' sovereignty and independence from state laws in *Worcester*.

These rules also paved the way for further colonization, including settler colonialism, and consolidation of settler colonizer power over land and water, two of the most critical resources for Indigenous Nations. Within two years of the final opinion in the Marshall trilogy, the US Army began removing Tribes like Cherokee Nation, Muskogee Creek Nation, and others to the so-called Indian Territory on the infamous Trail of Tears. This removal was a result of federal acquiescence to the powerful threats of southern states like Georgia to secede from the union and permanently destabilize or fracture it if their demands for Tribal land and resources were not met.[6] Throughout this period, Tribal Nations throughout what became the United States were removed and relocated to reservations. As famed Salish and Kootenai legal scholar William D'Arcy McNickle wrote in 1949, "they all moved, the Cherokees, Choctaws, Chickasaws, Creeks, Seminoles, the Kickapoos, Wyandottes, Ottawas, Pottawatomies, Winnebagos, Sac and Fox, Delawares, Shawnees, Weas, Peorias, Miamis, Kaskaskias, Piankeshaws – all went to the land beyond the Mississippi."[7]

Despite the removals, the federal government's "Indian problem" was still not solved, whether because not every Tribal Nation was removed, and those remaining possessed either too great or too valuable a land base, or because the removed Tribes' new land base was too large, the view of the federal government or the adjacent states. The former was the case for the Blackfeet Nation, which was not

4 *Johnson v. M'Intosh*, 21 U.S. 543 (1823).

5 WALTER R. ECHO-HAWK, IN THE COURTS OF THE CONQUEROR: THE 10 WORST INDIAN LAW CASES EVER DECIDED, p. 34 (Fulcrum 2010).

6 Other "trails of tears" followed in the middle Atlantic region, the upper Midwest, and in the region that is the subject of this book. *See* JEFFREY OSTLER, HOW MANY TRAILS OF TEARS WERE THERE?, (Yale U. Press Blog May 13, 2019).

7 DAVID H. GETCHES, *et al.*, CASES AND MATERIALS ON FEDERAL INDIAN LAW, pp. 151–52 (West Acad. Publg. 2017) (quoting DARCY MCNICKLE, THEY CAME HERE FIRST: THE EPIC OF THE AMERICAN INDIAN, pp. 199–200 (Lippincott 1st ed. 1949)).

removed, but targeted for its land and resources in other ways. These included allotment laws,[8] which gave the Department of Interior the authority to survey, allocate, and open reservation lands that in the Department's estimation, were not being used or capable of being used for their greatest purpose – agriculture.[9] The predominant legal barriers to this new federal policy were the hundreds of treaties that the federal government had entered into with so many Tribes during the previous century, which often secured "permanent homelands" and guaranteed these homelands and associated rights to hunt, fish, and gather as long as the signatory Tribe or Tribes continued to exercise the treaty rights. Under the Supremacy Clause, treaties are one of the categories of delineated laws to which others must yield in the framework established by the United States Constitution.[10] Rights that Tribes reserved in treaties often included elements of traditional lifeways that Tribal leaders deemed essential to the survival of their people, socially, culturally, and historically, such as access to hunting, fishing, and gathering places.

Yet, non-Indigenous Peoples wanted those same rights, and they wanted exclusive access to those same resources and places. So, within a few decades of the final decision in the Marshall Trilogy and the Cherokee Trail of Tears, Congress began to pass laws allowing for the allotment of the reservations that were still being established in many places West of the Mississippi River.[11] In the face of the demand for land by non-Indigenous Americans and new immigrants from abroad, neither treaties nor the Supremacy Clause stopped Congress from passing multitudes of allotment statutes that legislators deemed necessary to accomplish national objectives, even though they often violated the plain terms of treaties.[12] The pattern is familiar to anyone who has any degree of familiarity with US history – the federal government enters into a treaty with an Indigenous Nation promising that if the nation relocates its people to a smaller area, demarcated legally as a reservation, the people will be protected forevermore, but then circumstances change, in that the lands within the reservation are desired for non-Indigenous settlement, or for their mineral or timber resources, and the federal government breaks the treaty promises. Although these treaty breaches were unconstitutional, that alone did not stop the federal

8 Carole E. Goldberg, *et al.*, AMERICAN INDIAN LAW: NATIVE NATIONS AND THE FEDERAL SYSTEM: CASES AND MATERIALS, p. 24 (LexisNexis 7th ed. 2015).

9 *Id.*

10 U.S. CONST., Art. VI, cl. 2 (stating that "[t]he Constitution, … and all Treaties made, or which shall be made, under the Authority of the United States, shall be the supreme Law of the Land; and the Judges in every State shall be bound thereby, any thing in the Constitution or Laws of any State to the Contrary notwithstanding").

11 Goldberg at 24.

12 *See McGirt v. Oklahoma*, No. 18–9526 (2020) (discussing congressional abrogation of Muskogee Creek treaties during allotment era) (slip op. at 9); *Lone Wolf v. Hitchcock*, 187 U.S. 553, 566 (1903) (discussing congressional power to abrogate treaties of Kiowa, Comanche, and Apache during the allotment era).

government from continuing the practice. It did not help Tribal Nations that the Supreme Court declined to opine on the matter, either. This could have created a constitutional crisis, avoided only through subsequent legal machinations by the Supreme Court, discussed more fully below. In short, though, allotment supported the federal government's acquisition policy, which required legal authority allowing the federal government to expeditiously solve "the Indian problem" by moving Indigenous Peoples out of the path of non-Indigenous settlement, while also assimilating Tribal members into non-Indigenous American society, creating a "class of assimilated, landowning, agrarian Native Americans," in the words of noted federal Indian law scholar and historian Felix Cohen.[13] Allotment was a key element of this broader plan and viewed by many federal government officials and leaders as perhaps the ultimate solution to the problem that had vexed them for the better part of fifty years.

When allotment statutes were challenged in federal courts, the Supreme Court eventually was confronted with the significant constitutional issue of whether Congress had the authority to override or eliminate treaty rights that had been promised and recognized by the Executive branch. Resolving this issue required the justices to analyze the separation of executive and congressional powers in the Constitution, as well as the Court's interpretation of the scope of Congress's Article I authority, which had scant references to Indian Tribes. In 1903, the Supreme Court resolved this constitutional tension with a new rule of law, recognizing congressional power to abrogate treaties, and not just for the purpose of the allotment policy, but for other purposes as well, provided that Congress could demonstrate "circumstances … which will … justify the government in disregarding the stipulations of the treaty…."[14] This opinion, *Lone Wolf v. Hitchcock*, gave Congress the plenary authority to eliminate – or abrogate – treaties. Reflecting on the severe consequences this new rule would have for Indigenous Nations seventy-six years later, Judge Philip Nichols, Jr. of the United States Court of Federal Claims opined that "[t]he day *Lone Wolf* was handed down, January 5, 1903, might be called one of the blackest days in the history of the American Indian, the Indians' Dred Scott decision."[15]

The legacy of the allotment laws, and of decisions like *Lone Wolf*, complicates so many aspects of modern Tribal governance and life on and off reservations. In the Blackfeet Nation, the problems it has created for Indigenous ranchers illustrate this situation particularly vividly. The present-day US homeland of the Blackfeet Nation is the northern region of what is now the State of Montana, east of Glacier National Park. The Blackfeet Nation's residents include enrolled members, who are predominantly descendants of four Indigenous Nations, the Pikuni (Piegan),

[13] 1 F. Cohen, Handbook of Federal Indian Law §1.04 (2012).
[14] *Lone Wolf*, 187 U.S. at 566.
[15] *Sioux Nation v. United States*, 601 F.2d 1157, 1173 (Ct. Cl. 1979) (Nichols, J., concurring).

Kainah (Blood), and Siksika, and the Gros Ventres, a branch of the Arapahoe known as the Falls Indians, along with people who have mixed Blackfeet and non-Blackfeet ancestry (referred to by the Tribal government as Descendants), and non-Indigenous Peoples who have moved to the reservation, like the residents of the various Hutterite Colonies dotted throughout the reservation.[16] The Blackfeet Reservation and surrounding region is known for short-grass prairies, shrublands, and mixed-coniferous forests.[17] Some of the more prolific plant, shrub, and tree species, which are also culturally significant to the Blackfeet people, are yarrow, chokecherry, blanketflower, Oregon grape, sweetgrass, Jacobs ladder, goldenrod, arrowleaf balsamroot, and wild rose, as well as lodgepole pine, ponderosa pine, Douglas fir, and cottonwood trees.[18] Animal species that rely on these plants and which are also culturally significant to the Blackfeet people, are bald eagles, gray wolves, grizzly bears, Canada lynx, bull trout, pronghorn antelope, deer, elk, prairie dogs, foxes, and one of the rarest mammals in this part of North America, the black-footed ferret.[19] The endemic grasslands of the reservation are also critical habitat for declining grassland bird species, like the greater-sage grouse and for larger species like bison, which the Tribe began to repatriate in 2016.[20]

The Blackfeet Nation has a lengthy history involving domesticated animals as well, dating back to when Tribal members began to adopt aspects of horse culture from neighboring Tribes before 1700.[21] By the 1750s, the Blackfeet had established a horse culture,[22] with an expansive land base encompassing the southern half of what is now the modern Canadian province of Alberta, parts of what is now southwestern Saskatchewan, and extending across the modern border of the United States through what is now central Montana, eastern Idaho, and northern Wyoming.[23] Unlike other Tribes to the east, the Blackfeet remained relatively insulated from the influence of white fur traders, missionaries, and permanent settler colonizers for nearly 100 years between 1750 and 1850, during which their horse culture thrived.[24] Tribal lifeways were adapted to the game species they hunted, to the climate of the region, and Blackfeet people moved throughout the year in a system of various camps that accompanied the migration routes of their primary

[16] Curt Sholar, *Glacier National Park and the Blackfoot Nation's Reserved Rights: Does a Valid Tribal Co-Management Authority Exist?*, 29 Am. Indian L. Rev. 151, 152 (2005).

[17] Univ. of Montana, Tribal Circles: Blackfeet Reservation, at www.umt.edu/native-garden/circles/.php.

[18] *Id.*

[19] U.S. Fish & Wildlife Serv., Black-Footed Ferret Recovery Plan, p. 15 (2nd rev. Nov. 2013), https://ecos.fws.gov/docs/recovery_plan/20131108%20BFF%202nd%20Rev.%20Final%20Recovery%20Plan.pdf.

[20] Tristan Scott, "Blackfeet Bring Bison Home to Chief Mountain," Flathead Beacon (Jun. 28, 2023), https://flatheadbeacon.com/2023/06/28/blackfeet-bring-bison-home-to-chief-mountain/.

[21] Wissler, Clark, *et al.*, Amskapi Pikuni: The Blackfeet People, p. 3 (State University of N.Y. Press 2012).

[22] *Id.*

[23] *Id.*

[24] *Id.*

game species, including buffalo. This seasonal living pattern also allowed for gathering plants for food and medicine and wood for fires and dwelling structures. Because of the relative lack of settler colonial pressure, the governments of Canada and the United States did not seek treaties with the Blackfeet in the first half of the nineteenth century and Blackfeet people remained immune from the impacts of colonization that affected many other Tribes in the early years of the settler colonizers' presence in the Rocky Mountains.

Despite the lack of settler-colonizer influence in the Blackfeet Nation's lands at that time, the centralizing forces of the US federal government were institutionalizing a framework of legal colonization that would affect the Blackfeet and other similarly situated Tribal Nations dramatically in a short time. Although the term had yet to be coined, the essence of the federal government's policy was Manifest Destiny, or the pursuit of the sea to shining sea imprint of Christian, Euro-American farms and towns, reminiscent of Europe but translated on a grander scale across the newly "discovered" North American continent. And it began quite early in the nineteenth century.[25] To accomplish these ambitious goals, it was necessary to remove and relocate Indigenous Peoples, their communities, and acquire their lands, to make way for non-Indigenous settler colonizers.[26]

Their forays would come in waves. As discussed in Chapters 1 and 2, at the conclusion of the Mexican–American War in the 1840s, one wave of settler colonizers arrived in the southwest, to establish farms, ranches, and communities in the lands that were eventually firmly established as United States territory. The California gold rush in 1849, the Mormon migration to the Great Salt Lake valley in the 1840s, and the end of the Civil War in 1865 brought additional waves of non-Indigenous settler colonizers. These waves were supported by large herds of domestic livestock that accompanied and fed the migrants along the way and were instrumental during the early years of establishing non-Indigenous homesteads and towns. During the 1800s, there was very little in the way of "regulation" of this settlement from the federal government, except in the form of statutory incentives from Congress that aimed to "dispose" of federal landholdings rapidly, like the famous land grants to western states and the early homesteading laws.[27]

This period, which is the heart of what is referred to in federal public lands law as the "disposition," or "disposal" era, was distinguished by the transfer of federal land (which was once Tribal land, but had been converted to federal ownership

[25] Robert A. Williams, *The Algebra of Federal Indian Law: The Hard Trail of Decolonizing and Americanizing the White Man's Indian Jurisprudence*, 1986 Wis. L. Rev. 219, 255; Robert A. Williams, The American Indian in Western Legal Thought: The Discourses of Conquest, pp. 316–17 (1990).

[26] *Id.*

[27] Leshy at 91–92.

through the Doctrine of Discovery) to states, corporations, and private individuals on a scale and at a pace unmatched during other periods of US history.[28] The purpose of this effort was to accomplish Manifest Destiny and unify the new country under a Christian God and a European-derived lifeway based on individualism, productivity, and free-market capitalism. It was essential that disposal should be deliberate and purposeful, in a fashion that would allow for documented, uniform transfers that allocated the greatest number of parcels for the benefit of the greatest number of individuals or families, while occupying the greatest physical footprint on the land.

The disposal laws demanded surveys to help ensure that land was divided in a way that allowed each claimant some measure of capacity to farm, or to extract valuable natural resources such as timber and minerals. One of the earliest acts of the US Congress was the 1785 Land Ordinance, which established a rectangular survey system that divided the former homelands of so many Tribes into square "townships" of thirty-six identical sections, each of which was precisely 640 acres.[29] These square-shaped sections, replicating the pattern of a checkerboard writ large across the landscape, created "[a] uniform invariable shape" that looked good and orderly on a map, but that "that took no account of springs or hills or swamps," let alone immense natural features like the Black Hills, the Rocky Mountains, or the Grand Canyon. The tricky topography of the West often flummoxed the surveyors employed by the General Land Office, but their decades of dutiful survey work created marketable titles that were more easily appraised given their known size and acreage.[30]

Congress was not writing these disposal statutes on a blank slate, though, and before they could be implemented, people who lived in these places had to move or be moved. This is where allotment played its insidious, but effective role, which is key to a thorough understanding and explication of the twenty-first-century situation of Tribes like the Blackfeet, especially with regard to ranching. In general, the allotment laws were a method that Congress invented to "open" Tribal lands to non-Indigenous settler colonizers, states, and corporate interests without the consent of the Tribe whose lands were being "opened," even when the Tribe or Tribes had negotiated a treaty that prevented this type of unilateral federal action. Meanwhile, allotment statutes divided reservations into smaller areas that were often noncontiguous.[31] Thus, not only did the Tribe lose acreage and a percentage of the land base that may have been guaranteed or promised in a treaty, it also lost contiguity because of the mechanism used to open the lands.

[28] *Id.* at 58.

[29] *Id.*

[30] *Id.* at 59; Jessica A. Shoemaker, *No Sticks in My Bundle: Rethinking the Indian Land Tenure Problem*, 63 U. Kan. L. Rev. 383, 401–403 (2015).

[31] Judith V. Royster, *Mineral Development in Indian Country: The Evolution of Tribal Control over Mineral Resources*, 29 Tulsa L. J. 541, 548 (1994).

Congress created the a reservation for the Blackfeet on October 17, 1855, pursuant to a treaty and the authority recently recognized by the Supreme Court.[32] Following years of tensions, and sometimes, outright warfare, between the Blackfeet and other Tribes, and between the Blackfeet and the United States, the treaty attempted to strike a peace to "cultivate good-will and friendship" between Blackfeet bands and to maintain "peaceful relations" with the surrounding Indigenous Nations and settler colonizers.[33] The 1855 treaty also established the Blackfeet Reservation and marked the moment at which settler colonizers could begin to prevent Blackfeet people from moving or residing outside the reservation's boundaries to follow and hunt roving herds of bison and other game species and move between summer and winter homesites, even as the federal government purported to protect those same rights. The 1855 treaty reserved to Tribal members the legal rights to "enjoy equal and uninterrupted privileges of hunting, fishing and gathering fruit, grazing animals, curing meat and dressing robes."[34] This arrangement was not effective from either party's perspective, though, and citizens of both the United States and the Blackfeet Nation continued to clash in their pursuit of land, wildlife, and water.

Thereafter, subsequent treaties were made, each one further reducing the size of the reservation and the Blackfeets' access to game species, plants, and other traditional food sources located outside of the Tribe's new jurisdictional boundaries.[35] Political pressure also escalated in Washington, and Congress responded by abrogating the 1855 treaty, diminishing the reservation by "agreement" on February 11, 1887, and ratifying the agreement on May 1, 1888. This agreement and the accompanying legislation reduced the Tribe's homeland to the grasslands just east of the Rocky Mountains and cut off the Tribe's access to the mountains themselves, except for a slender strip of land located on the Rocky Mountain Front in what became Glacier National Park.[36]

Even these subsequent cessions were not enough to satisfy the non-Indigenous greed for Blackfeet lands, and they were not effective solutions to this particular "Indian problem" because the Blackfeet, like so many other Tribal Nations, fought for and would not cede their remaining lands. So, in 1907, Congress passed another allotment act, which authorized a survey of all of the lands within the reservation and directed the Commissioner of Indian Affairs to "cause allotments of the same to be made under the provisions of the allotment laws of the United States."[37]

32 Sholar at 154.
33 *Id.* at 153.
34 *Id.* at 154.
35 *Id.* at 153.
36 *Id.* at 154. This area is now referred to by Blackfeet people as the "Ceded Strip."
37 *Glacier Cnty. v. United States*, 99 F.2d 733, 734 (9th Cir. 1938) (citing 34 Stat. 1035).

Following the initial survey, the Secretary of the Interior recommended a division of lands into sections (in the range of 100–300 acres) using the grid method that supported the Jeffersonian surveys of federal lands under other statutes, and a population survey of the Tribe. The Department of Interior, through the Commissioner of Indian Affairs, then apportioned sections to each family head, or single adult male, for a period of twenty-five years. This period was referred to as the "trust period," and during this time, the federal government continued to hold the land in trust, as it was held prior due to the authorization from *Johnson*, but for the benefit of the individual or family, not the entire Tribe.[38]

If the total number of tribal heads of household or single adult males was less than the total number of sections, the additional lands were marked as "surplus," and according to the statute, they could be sold or deeded directly to settler colonizers under any number of homesteading laws. For those lands that were allocated to heads of household, the allottee received what was essentially a right of first refusal for the fee title to their allotment. The parcel would be held in trust for twenty-five years and patented in fee if the allottee could "prove up" the homestead by building a house and establishing a permanent homestead with recognizable agricultural pursuits on the surrounding acres.[39]

If the allottee proved up, the federal government would issue an unencumbered patent in fee at the close of the twenty-five-year trust period, transferring title outright to the individual or head of household. The General Allotment Act further provided that citizenship would be unilaterally conferred on the allottee at the end of the proving up period. Also, the transfer of title in fee had the legal effect of subjecting the allottees to state laws, including property tax laws, and state jurisdiction. So, if allottees obtained a fee simple title, the reward included a yearly tax bill, which some allottees were not willing or able to pay. Judicial opinions from this era illustrate the complexity of allotment laws for the Blackfeet, particularly for those who were not willing to accept the terms of these federal bargains. In one instance, within two years of receiving fee title to their allotments, patents had been issued to several allottees, but the allottees did not want the patents, or likely the legal status that came with them, and attempted to reject the federal government's offer.[40] Litigation ensued, and extensive federal court proceedings followed. The parties agreed that fee title was granted to the allottees without their having applied for it and without their consent. From there, they disagreed about what could happen next. The tribal allottees wanted to reject the patents and had asked for assistance in doing so from the federal agency overseeing the transfer. In a letter written on April 24, 1918, from the office of the Commissioner of Indian Affairs to the special superintendent on the reservation, the Commissioner noted that the federal

38 Goldberg at 26.
39 Royster at 548.
40 *Glacier Cnty.*, 99 F.2d at 734.

government had "the right to issue these patents, and if they [the tribal allottees] refuse to accept them, you [the superintendent] are directed to have the patents recorded and after recording same, to sent them to the patentees by registered mail and retain the receipt cards for the files in your office."[41]

Pursuant to this letter, the patents were sent by registered mail and the lands were subsequently placed on the tax rolls of Glacier County. The county then levied taxes against the Blackfeet allottees – now fee owners of this land – according to state law. Some of the allottees paid the taxes every year, and others made partial or intermittent payments. Between 1927 and 1932, the Department, under authority of a statute that had been passed on February 26, 1927, canceled the fee patents of all but one of the allottees, on the basis that "they had been issued without application or consent."[42] This, the court concluded, eliminated the forced fee ownership, and its associated state tax liability, including interest that Glacier County had sought on the unpaid property taxes in this case. The result of the case, therefore, was that the Blackfeet landowners who had received fee simple title to their allotments were successful in rejecting the patents, and the underlying fee title land reverted to the federal government to hold in trust for the allottees under the framework established in the Marshall Trilogy.

This case illustrates the Hobson's choice that allotment created for Indigenous People whose lands were targeted for allotment. They could play by the rules of the allotment act, but the prize for doing so was a form of assimilation, and that came at a cultural and financial cost. If they declined to play by the rules, their land remained Indian Country, subject to the jurisdiction of the Tribe, but because the Tribe was a domestic dependent nation and subject to the plenary power of Congress, this probably did not feel like much of a victory either. Writ large, the allotment era resulted in the largest wholesale transfer of remaining Indigenous lands in the history of US-tribal relations and a corresponding increase in federal claims of legal power to govern Indian country and the persons and property of Indian tribes.[43] This plenary power must have seemed and felt all-encompassing in the worst of so many ways.

Today, in the legal shadows of this era, Danny Barcus and his wife Alcinda run cattle on the Blackfeet reservation, where they navigate one of the most complex land tenure and regulatory frameworks in the country as they work to keep producing beef each year.[44] This framework emerged from the legacy of federal allotment of the Blackfeet Nation's land in the early part of the twentieth century. In addition to challenges that many ranchers face, from the cost of the non-native wheat grass

[41] *Id.*
[42] *Id.*
[43] *Id.*
[44] Pls.' Compl. ¶17, *Wellman v. Orcutt*, No. CV-21-30-GF-BMM, 2022 WL 169696, at *1 (D. Mont. Jan. 19, 2022).

they grow to supplement the herd's diet, to the pressure of the Tribe's growing herd of buffalo breaking through their fences, to sometimes years-long droughts, they also face the byzantine regulatory mess that allotment left behind.

To understand these challenges, it helps to contextualize ranching in northern Montana grasslands. Most ranching operations in this region utilize additional land, beyond that owned by the rancher in fee simple, to provide enough forage for the herd throughout the year. The system of utilizing federal public lands to supplement private grazing pastures will be discussed more thoroughly in Chapters 6 and 7, but for the purposes of understanding allotment and its legacy, one only needs to know that ranchers in the West often need more land than they own to graze their livestock, usually due to the aridity, but sometimes based on other complicating factors, such as access to water and grazing wildlife. On Tribal lands, one might assume that a Tribal member would be subject to Tribal laws and regulations in any given aspect of a grazing operation, and perhaps some federal laws that would regulate any ranching operation, including any that protect federal interests in private and hybrid private–public ranching operations. This assumption would be a safe one, but it only provides the barest glimpse into the realm of law and policy affecting ranching on Tribal lands. Indigenous ranchers like Barcus and his wife are also subject to pervasive and complex federal, and to a lesser degree, state laws that have encroached over time into the Tribal lands through the laws discussed in Chapters 1, 2, and in the previous sections in this chapter. As a result, regulatory complexity burdens these ranchers much more significantly and pervasively than the operations of white ranchers or farmers, even though the Indigenous ranch and the non-Indigenous ranch are neighboring operations within the same reservation.

To understand this system and how it produces such incongruous legal burdens, it is necessary to understand the history of these lands and allotment of the Blackfeet Reservation. The present-day reservation encompasses nearly 1.5 million acres and serves as home to approximately 56 percent of the Tribe's members.[45] Reservation lands like these are defined legally as "Indian Country."[46] This term invokes a legal distinction between the area that a Tribe regulates under its sovereign authority and the area or areas that the Tribe cannot regulate, according to rules developed by the Supreme Court in the wake of the Marshall Trilogy. Under these rules, if lands are legally defined as "Indian Country," they fall within a Tribe's regulatory authority, jurisdiction, and civil adjudicatory authority.[47] For the Blackfeet Nation, the reservation consists of some lands legally defined as Indian Country, but a significant amount that is not. The lands

[45] Donald R. Wharton, *Organization and Structure of Tribal Governments*, 23A ROCKY MTN. MIN. LAW INST. 2 (1989).

[46] *See Oklahoma v. Castro-Huerta*, 142 S.Ct. 2486, 2493 (2022) (defining "Indian Country" include, among other things, "all land within the limits of any Indian reservation under the jurisdiction of the United States Government.").

[47] Goldberg at 312 (citing *Montana v. United States*, 450 U.S. 544 (1981)).

falling outside the purview of Indian Country are those that were allotted and transferred to individual Tribal members in fee or to nonmembers who were allowed to homestead them when they went "unclaimed" by any Tribal heads of household or single adult males. As a result, 67 percent of the land base of the reservation is Indian Country, which the Tribe can regulate, and the remaining land base is fee land, subject to state regulatory authority and presumptively excluded from Tribal regulatory authority. Moreover, because of allotment, the trust and fee lands are not contiguous, but rather alternating and sometimes scattered, creating another patchwork quilt of federal, Tribal, and state-regulated land across the reservation.

This framework and the challenges it created for the Tribal government, and for individual ranchers like the Barcuses, are part of the legacy of allotment, a legacy that makes ranching on the reservation much more complicated for Blackfeet ranchers than for anyone else. The Barcus Ranch is in this way, and in many ways, symbolic of the modern realities facing Tribal ranchers operating on allotted reservation lands across Indian Country. So, despite the non-Indigenous American perspective that allotment was a legal key that unlocked the West, the changes in the land tenure status of these lands in fact accomplished the opposite goal throughout Indian Country. Tens of millions of acres of land were converted from "Tribal" to "federal" ownership because the number of tribal members able to occupy the allotted lands was small, and the number who could prove up under the onerous and alien requirements of these statutes was smaller still.[48] During this period, which lasted from the passage of the Dawes Act in 1887 until Congress ended it in the Indian Reorganization Act of 1934, Indigenous Nations lost approximately two-thirds of their land base, including many lands protected by earlier treaties. In total, some ninety million acres of Tribal trust land passed into fee ownership in two ways: fee patents to allottees and the sale of the "surplus" lands to nonmembers.[49] During these five decades, the federal government issued thousands of patents in fee to Indian allottees. This had the legal effect of removing all restrictions on alienation and encumbrance of the land, such as those imposed by operation of the Doctrine of Discovery and other subsequent rules from the US Supreme Court covered in earlier chapters. However, this came at a cost that would not be appreciated or acknowledged by federal and state policy makers until decades had passed.

As discussed in judicial opinions that attempt to sort out the legal mess that allotment created, Tribal ownership of fee land was not the panacea that it was marketed to be. This change in land tenure brought with it property tax obligations that many

[48] Goldberg at 24.

[49] Judith V. Royster, *Mineral Development in Indian Country: The Evolution of Tribal Control over Mineral Resources*, 29 TULSA L. J. 541, 550 (1994).

Tribal members did not have the means to fulfill, and many Tribal members who were fee owners sold their land voluntarily, or lost it to involuntary tax sales.[50] In total, approximately twenty-seven million acres of allotted lands were sold to nonmembers by Indian allottees, likely for various reasons but certainly including among them the prohibitively high tax burdens. This had implications beyond surface use, as well, because if the allottee sold the fee-patented lands without reserving mineral rights, the mineral rights underlying the fee lands transferred to the non-member purchaser along with the surface area.[51] The same result occurred following the tax sales. Also, through the allotment process, significant Tribal mineral holdings passed into individual fee ownership, and sometimes into the hands of multi-national mining companies, who would seek to develop them as history revealed massive mineral resources underlying so many reservations, including under Indian allotments.[52]

Of the ninety million acres Tribes lost during the allotment years, approximately sixty million were opened and offered for sale by the federal government to non-Indian homesteaders.[53] As noted above, the purpose of these allotment acts was "to break up the reservations into private ownership, with the underlying belief that individual ownership would turn the Indians from a Tribal life to one of agriculture, Christianity, and citizenship."[54] So, in other words, it was not entirely about opening land to poor, destitute, and land-hungry non-Indigenous settlers, as many films and novels about this time would lead one to believe, including the Paramount hit "Yellowstone" and its prequels, which document the Dutton family's struggles as they cross the central plains in search of "open" land to settle and build their family dynasty. Allotment was also about assimilating Tribal members to a non-Indigenous way of life, one that was much less communal and more individual. This is part of the reason for using the grid system to open sections of land, because the resulting land tenure pattern, even within a reservation, would be an alternating checkerboard of Tribal sections and non-Tribal sections, forcing Tribal members to be neighbors with the white farmers and ranchers they were supposed to emulate.

As the US Supreme Court noted in a 1987 decision, *Hodel v. Irving*, allotment nonetheless also proved to be "disastrous" for individual Tribal members in other ways.[55] The monetary proceeds generated by the sale of fee lands did not last long, and Tribal allottees often leased their allotted lands to non-Indigenous farmers and ranchers rather than using them for farming or ranching. As successive generations of Tribal members and descendants were born, they inherited rights to the allotted parcels, and soon the parcels became "splintered" legally into multiple interests,

50 *Id.*
51 *Id.*
52 *Id.* at 551.
53 *Id.* at 550–51.
54 *Id.* at 548.
55 481 U.S. 704, 707 (1987).

which could not be severed by any single allottee.[56] Parcels routinely ended up with dozens, and sometimes hundreds of Tribal owners, and because by law the allotted lands could not be alienated (due to the Doctrine of Discovery) or partitioned, the fractionation problem grew exponentially over time. As the number of owners grew, the relative share of profit from leasing diminished, creating a situation where, sometimes, allottees were owed as little as one cent per month in lease revenue.[57] Allotments that contain more than one allottee are referred to as "fractionated" allotments, and in some corners of Indian Country, the mere mention of that word will send interested lessees immediately running toward the hills, given the complexities attendant with the property interests involved.[58] The Bureau of Indian Affairs (BIA) is charged by law with administering leases of allotted lands, which encompassed everything from producing the lease to overseeing its signing, then collecting the revenue from the lessee and holding it in trust for the allottee or allottees, distributed according to a schedule set by the Bureau, and with accrued interest, including for fractionated interests.

Although the allotment policy itself ended in 1934 with the passage of the Indian Reorganization Act (IRA), its legacy looms over the Blackfeet Reservation.[59] Allotment and the Tribal tradition surrounding horse culture created circumstances that led to more individual farms and ranches than would be true for other Tribal Nations. Unlike Tribes like the Hopi, for instance, who did not adopt a horse culture and were not subject to allotment, and to the present day do not operate individual farms and ranches, many Blackfeet people do. According to the Tribe, agriculture has become "a pillar of the local economy, and potential engine for economic development."[60] As of 2017, there were a total of 645 farms on the reservation, 478 of which were Blackfeet-owned or operated.[61] The alternating pattern of fee lands owned by nonmembers, including the colony of seventy-five Hutterite families in the northeastern corner of the reservation, and trust land owned by the Tribe, with trust allotments owned by individual Tribal members, complicates every aspect of ranching life.[62] As a result of allotment, the reservation's population of over 8,000, 95 percent of which consists of enrolled Blackfeet members, contains 1,525,712 acres, yet only 67 percent of this land base is allotted

56 *Id.*

57 *Id.*

58 Goldberg at 1114–15.

59 Royster at 551–52.

60 Blackfeet Nation Agricultural Resource Management Plan 2022 (Blackfeet ARMP), p. 10 (noting that in 2017, "the market value of agricultural products was approximately $122,000,000. Crops accounted for $59,000,000 of the total, while livestock and poultry products accounted for approximately 63,000,000.").

61 *Id.*

62 Edward P. Kleinsasser & Daniel E. Wipf, *Report: Big Sky Colony Public Water System PWSID # MT0001647*, p. 3 (prepared for Montana Dep't of Water Quality, Dec. 2021), https://deq.mt.gov/files/Water/WPB/NRISReports/MT0001647.pdf.

individual trust land or Tribal fee land, and the Tribe controls only 12 percent of the surface estate.[63] Moreover, the Department of the Interior, through the BIA, controls the use of trust and Tribal fee lands, and this is especially problematic for agricultural uses of those lands.

The BIA's role in managing the agricultural uses of Tribal trust lands and individual allotted lands has not changed much since the days of the Indian agents installed on tribal reservations to ensure that Tribal members and Tribal governments were adhering to the edicts of the President, Congress, and the agency itself. In those days, the BIA sent agents to permanently reside on reservations, to oversee daily life and ensure that Tribal members were speaking English, cutting their hair, going to church, and otherwise adhering to the regulatory or policy mandate of the time. Today, some of the regulatory and policy mandates are different, but the BIA's function is largely the same. One of the roles of the local BIA agency in Browning, Montana, is to oversee agricultural leases, such as the ones that Danny Barcus uses to operate his ranch. Danny and his wife, Alcinda, hold title to their lands in trust, and they need more acreage to pasture their herd than what they own or control, so they lease additional pasturage.[64] The leasing of allotted lands differs depending on the land tenure of the lessor and the land status of the allotment under the framework discussed earlier in this chapter. If the land to be leased is Indian Country, it is partially owned (and controlled) by the federal government, although that ownership is supposed to be exercised in a manner that benefits the Tribe or Tribal members who hold corollary rights to the land.[65] If the lessor is non-Indian, there are fewer restrictions on the leasing arrangement, as the Supreme Court has held that Tribes presumptively lack direct authority over non-Indians outside specifically delineated categories.[66] If the lessor is "Indian,"[67] the general rule is that the BIA must approve the lease agreement, as well as administering any lease payments and proceeds, if the land is held in trust (meaning, title was not perfected during the allotment era, transferring the status from trust to fee). This means that there is no money that exchanges hands between lessor and lessee after the lease is signed – the BIA approves the contract, the BIA invoices

63 Wharton.

64 *Wellman*, 2022 WL 169696, at *1.

65 American Indian Agricultural Resource Management Act, 25 U.S.C. §§ 3701–3746 ("the United States has a trust responsibility to protect, conserve, utilize and manage Indian agricultural lands consistent with its fiduciary obligation and its unique relationship with Indian Tribes").

66 *Montana v. United States*, 450 U.S. 544, 564 (1981) (noting that the "exercise of tribal power beyond what is necessary to protect tribal self-government or to control internal relations is inconsistent with the dependent status of the tribes, and so cannot survive without express congressional delegation.").

67 The term Indian is considered offensive to many Indigenous People of what is now the United States; however, it has legal significance in many contexts relevant here, in matters such as Tribal jurisdiction, Tribal regulatory authority, and eligibility for certain federal programs enacted for the benefit of Tribal members. The term is used here to explain the relevant law and as it is used in federal law.

the lessee, and the BIA collects the lease payments from the lessee and provides them to the lessor, along with any interest that might accrue in the interim.

The BIA has done an abysmal job of administering this program for the Blackfeet, and so many other Tribes and the "interim" can sometimes stretch into absurd lengths of time, upwards of decades. The agency's most grievous errors included failures to document the number and names of allottees, and the amounts owed, along with accrued interest, especially for fractionated allotments. The mismanagement was suspected or known by Tribal lessors for a very long time, but it did not formally come to light until the 1990s when the federal government attempted to transfer the responsibility of administering the trust assets from one division of the Department of Interior to another. As part of an audit conducted during that process, the Department discovered that the records BIA had "maintained" for up to a century prior were missing, inaccurate, or insufficient to document the amounts owed to individual allottees for income derived from leasing and developing their allotments.[68] In a famous class action lawsuit brought by Blackfeet allottee Eloise Cobell, an accountant, in which the class was estimated to include over 500,000 individual allottees and billions of dollars in damages, federal district court Judge Royce Lamberth described the Department of Interior's administration of this system as "fiscal and governmental irresponsibility in its purest form."[69] Over the course of two decades, in a series of lawsuits, the Department resisted the plaintiffs' requests for an accounting at every turn, resulting in multiple citations of contempt of court against the Secretary of Interior, the Assistant Secretary of Indian Affairs, and others in the Clinton and Bush administrations.

Ultimately, this lawsuit was successful, although Mrs.Cobell did not live to see the benefits of the $3.4B judgment she secured for Indian Country, dying of cancer within five months of the court issuing its final judgment and before any funds were disbursed.[70] The judgment reflected a settlement agreement between the parties, which the plaintiffs and the federal government announced on December 8, 2009. Under this agreement, the government promised to establish a $1.4 billion fund to settle historic trust mismanagement and erroneous accounting claims by allottee claimants and create a $2 billion fund to support Tribal "buy backs" of fractionated allotments. The settlement also guaranteed that up to 5 percent of the value of a fractionated interest sold by an allottee would be directed into a college scholarship fund of up to $60 million for enrolled Tribal students.[71] The Blackfeet Nation received two rounds of offers under the *Cobell* buy-back program, in 2016 and 2019, and used the funds to

68 Goldberg, p. 607.

69 *Id.*

70 Valerie J. Nelson, *Eloise Cobell Dies at 65: Native American Activist*, L. A. Times (Oct. 7, 2011), www.latimes.com/local/obituaries/la-me-elouise-cobell-20111018-story.html.

71 Goldberg at 621–22.

purchase 323,513 acres of formerly fractionated land, restoring them to Tribal trust status and rebuilding some of the contiguity of the Tribal land base lost during allotment.

The Tribe is also working on leveraging another federal law to its advantage in the arena of agricultural development, the American Indian Agricultural Resource Management Act, or AIARMA. This statute was passed to support Tribes in developing their own agricultural resource management plans (ARMPs), which would replace those of the BIA and possibly alleviate some of the longstanding tension with federal management of agricultural operations.[72] Passed in 1993, AIARMA's purpose is to "carry out the trust responsibility of the United States and promote the self-determination of Indian tribes." Under AIARMA and the Indian Self-Determination Act, the BIA's Bureau of Agriculture and Rangeland Development "provides support for tribal agricultural programs under tribal contracts and direct implementation, covering over forty-six million acres of Indian land used for farming and grazing by livestock and game animals." Although management responsibility of funded projects under AIARMA largely rests with the BIA, there seems to be a consensus that the statute strengthens tribal control over the use and management of fractionated agricultural landholdings.[73]

Yet, rather than yielding federal authority and oversight to the Tribe and respecting the Tribes' inherent sovereignty to accomplish agricultural goals in a manner that suits their needs, customs, culture, and values, AIARMA, like so many other attempts by Congress to solve "Indian problems," instead continues to perpetuate some of them. AIARMA has lofty goals, like making "better use" of Indian agricultural land through management plans. The statute also demonstrates Congress's aims "to enhance the capability of Indian ranchers and farmers to produce crops and products from such lands; to affirm the authority of the Indian tribal governments in the management and regulation of Indian agricultural lands; and to enhance educational opportunities for Indian students in the management of Indian natural resources."[74] But it does not come without a cost, financial or otherwise, and these goals themselves may be out of reach for Tribes that are not financially or otherwise prepared to jump through the various congressional hoops of AIARMA, such as creating an Agricultural Resource Management Plan and finalizing it within three years, then revising it every ten years.

The Blackfeet Tribe completed an ARMP pursuant to AIARMA, which was approved by the Tribal government on April 12, 2022. The vision statement for the

[72] Darla J. Mondou, *The American Indian Agricultural Resources Management Act: Does the Winters Water Bucket Have A Hole in It?* 3 DRAKE J. AGRIC. L. 381, 388–92 (1998).

[73] Julia Guarino, *Tribal Food Sovereignty in the American Southwest*, 11 J. FOOD L. & POL'Y 83, 103–104 (2015).

[74] § 3:10. Farm leases, American Indian Law Deskbook § 3:10.

Blackfeet ARMP states that the Blackfeet Tribe envisions itself as "fully engaged, informed, and actively involved in the development of holistic agriculture resource management for the economy, the environment, and the health of the people, land, flora, fauna, and water," by 2028.[75] The Tribe's goal is to work together to use "natural laws, values, and relationships based on respect, trust, and healing," to establish "reciprocal partnerships among producers, businesses, and landowners to increase the profitability and sustainability of agricultural production for current [sic] future generations."[76] This will ensure that Blackfeet youth will have "mentoring opportunities to learn from elders, producers, and leaders to contribute their voice to a quality Blackfeet way of life."[77]

According to the ARMP, ranching is the "dominant land use" on the reservation and a "critical economic engine" for the Tribe.[78] The total land base dedicated to ranching is over one million acres, and as of 2017, when last surveyed, these lands support roughly 112,000 cattle, 5,000 horses, 4,000 bison, and 600 sheep. Enrolled Tribal members constitute over half of the 906 ranchers operating on the reservation, and revenue from grazing leases and other permitting represents a "significant source of revenue" for the Tribe and individual member allottees. In 2019, leases generated $1,462,845 for the Tribe and $778,288 for individual allottees.[79] The Blackfeet Nation allocates grazing using two main land designations – range units and pasture units. Range Units are defined as of "groups of tribal, allotted, and fee parcels leased to ranchers for grazing" and as of the date of the ARMP's adoption, there were 480 Range Units.[80] Pasture Units, by contrast are "single tract plots of tribal and allotted land that are leased for shorter time periods than Range Units," which unlike Range Units, may contain planted species like alfalfa.[81]

As for the leasing oversight, AIARMA does not release the authority of the BIA, nor replace its role as trustee manager.[82] Although it provides that agricultural leases can be negotiated by the landowner, each lease involving allotted land is ultimately subject to the approval of the Secretary of the Interior.[83] Moreover, AIARMA relegates Tribes to the role of lessors and does not account or provide for other types of arrangements that would give them the flexibility to address modern-day complexities

75 Blackfeet ARMP, p. 8.
76 *Id.*
77 *Id.*
78 *Id.* at 16.
79 *Id.*
80 *Id.* Range Units are further divided and allocated as follows: An Allocated Range Unit is a range unit allocated for the purpose of grazing livestock owned by enrolled members of the Blackfeet Tribe. A Bid Unit is a range unit that is utilized for grazing livestock that is awarded on a competitive basis.
81 *Id.*
82 United States Senate, Committee on Indian Affairs, American Indian Agricultural Resource Management Act Report to Accompany H.R. 1425, the American Indian Agricultural Resource Management Act, p. 11 (Nov. 18, 1993).
83 *Id.*

of administering heavily allotted reservations. The leasing gap in AIARMA is a significant barrier to agricultural producers across Indian Country, given the reality that by the early 2000s, over 70 percent of trust lands that could serve as croplands or "range" for grazing livestock by Tribal members, their families and their businesses, are leased to non-Indians.[84] Under AIARMA, Tribal owners of trust and restricted-fee allotments (a unique legal status in Alaska) may also apply to the Secretary for "owner-manager" status. With this status, owners can issue leases for "agricultural purposes" for up to ten years without Secretarial approval. Otherwise, the approval of the Secretary, by way of the local BIA office, is required.[85] However, for fractionated allotments, AIARMA respects the ownership rights of allottees with an interest in fractionated allotments, unless the Tribe enacts a law that defines "highly fractionated undivided heirship lands" and establishes an alternative means of allocating the attendant rights. Doing so, however, could prove politically unpalatable to Tribal governments representing constituents with an interest in fractionated allotments, even if the interests are considered small by outside standards.

Then there is the matter of the Blackfeet Nation's version of Ted Turner, a billionaire who has been buying vast tracts of fee land inside the reservation. And like Jack Taylor at Cielo Vista, as soon as he purchases a parcel of Blackfeet land, he puts up a five-foot fence, excluding people, domestic livestock, and wildlife alike. Joe Ricketts' wealth stems from founding the financial services firm TD Ameritrade. His ranch, which in 2023 totaled approximately 32,000 acres, constitutes roughly 2 percent of the entire reservation. Because the ranch lands are fee lands, alienated from Tribal control during or as the result of allotment allotment, the Tribe presumptively cannot regulate Ricketts or his ranch through the ARMP or any other mechanism of Tribal law. Adjacent ranchers and residents allege that Ricketts is a "terrible neighbor," completely unwilling to work with the Tribal agencies charged with protecting wildlife on the reservation.[86] Ricketts' focus is likely directed externally though, given that he has been working for decades to establish himself as a national bison producer. His company, High Plains Bison, sells meat on the national market.[87]

The Blackfeet Nation attempted to buy Ricketts' ranch, which used to be Blackfeet land prior to allotment, when it last went on the market in 2019, using funds from the *Cobell* buy-back program. The Tribe wanted to establish this open land as a bison range for the herd it has been repatriating, but Ricketts' offer was accepted and the Tribe's was rejected. Now, the Tribe's options have narrowed

[84] Royster at 110–11 (citing Harvard Project on American Indian Economic Development, The State of the Native Nations: Conditions under U.S. Policies of Self-Determination, 167 (2008)).

[85] § 3:10. Farm leases, American Indian Law Deskbook § 3:10.

[86] Sierra Cistone, *The Billionaire Blocking Off Montana's Wildlife: "Like Fencing People Out of Walmart,"* THE GUARDIAN (Jun. 29, 2022), www.theguardian.com/us-news/2022/jun/29/joe-ricketts-bison-ranch-fences-blackfeet-reservation.

[87] *Id.* (noting that High Plains Bison does not sell its meat locally).

because the only governmental entity with definitive authority to regulate Ricketts and his fences is the State of Montana. Even though the fences block migrating wildlife and violate the Tribe's fish and wildlife code, the Tribe is powerless to enforce them against a non-Indian like Ricketts or his company without amending existing Tribal laws and regulations to assert this authority. Even if it could do so, it is unclear whether any challenge that Ricketts might bring to this assertion of Tribal authority would persuade a federal court judge. The contrast of Ricketts' circumstances with those of ranchers like the Barcuses is even more striking when set against the legal backdrop of the Ricketts' ranch. The Barcuses and their ranch are subject to Tribal laws and the administrative oversight of the BIA. Danny Barcus cannot sign a pasturage lease with his neighbor (or anyone else) without securing BIA approval, and *all of the* allottees if the allotment is fractionated. Ricketts, by contrast, does not have to worry about the Tribe's ARMP, its wildlife laws, or fractionation because those laws as of yet do not apply to him, as a non-Indian resident of the reservation.

This comparison illustrates the inequities that federal law has created for ranchers like Danny Barcus, as compared to non-Indigenous ranchers like Ricketts. The legal rules and restrictions that apply to the Barcus ranch are more onerous and more restrictive than those that apply to Ricketts and his bison company, illustrating very clearly how allotment continues to impact Indigenous farming and ranching operations in Indian Country, even in the twenty-first century. AIARMA provides some glimpses of a different future, but there are limits to its impact, given the narrow criteria in the statute related to land tenure status and a narrow focus of Tribal regulatory authority – over agricultural leasing only. The continual failure of the US federal government to fulfill its legal obligations as a trustee to individual allottees further limits the appeal of AIARMA and other one-time changes, as does the reality of navigating leases and other transactions involving fractionated ownership interests. These limitations, when combined, may outweigh any potential benefits offered by AIARMA, and for individual producers like Danny Barcus and his wife, who do not control whether their Tribe opts into a program like AIARMA (or any other), it leaves them in much the same circumstances as in decades prior – one in which their race and ancestry limit their operation's potential in ways that do not similarly affect or apply to a rancher like Ricketts. Reforming the law in a way that repairs the damage done by allotment will have to go further than AIARMA, though, as the Ricketts' Ranch situation on the Blackfeet Reservation and others that will follow illustrate so well. As we travel south to Colorado in the next chapter, and back in time, the impacts of law and policy on other ranchers and farmers of color will become even clearer, as will the corresponding need to reckon with this problematic framework.

4

Black Homesteading and the Dearfield Colony

[I]t is time … to desert the State and seek homes elsewhere where there may be fruition of hopes inaugurated when by the hand of Providence the shackles were stricken from the limbs of four million men, where there may be enjoyed in peace and happiness by your own fireside the earnings of your daily toil.

– Robert H. Knox

Settler colonization of the North American continent significantly altered the continent's grasslands, perhaps most famously during the allotment era and the years leading up to the Dust Bowl of the 1920s and 1930s.[1] Understanding the causative factors that produced the Dust Bowl years of the 1930s, particularly in terms of the racial challenges of non-white Americans during the homesteading era, along with the power dynamic that flowed from the systemic and societal racism cultivated during the slavery era, are key to better understanding of the modern framework of race, law, and land ownership in the West. These years, and the role of Black homesteaders, are also worth exploring given the intermingled social and ecological tragedies that occurred during this time, especially given that there is a strong correlation between the social and ecological crises of the twenty-first century, and the exact factors that contributed to the Dust Bowl phenomenon in the 1930s.[2]

While the Dust Bowl has been the subject of many historical and scientific analyses, the role of law and race during this time has not been as heavily examined, especially in the fields of public lands law, property law, and natural resources law and policy.[3] It is clear now that the homesteading and public commons system of "regulating" farming and ranching in the grassland regions of the Great Plains and

[1] National Drought Mitigation Center, "The Dust Bowl," University of Nebraska; Alexander Koch, *et al.*, *Earth System Impacts and the Great Dying in the Americas after 1492*, SCIENCE (March 2019).

[2] IRMA S. RUSSELL, THE USE AND PRESERVATION OF GRASSLANDS: THE LOGIC OF HARD LESSONS, pp. 359, 365 (Kan. J.L. & Pub. Pol'y, Summer 2017).

[3] *Id.*

beyond caused the circumstances that exacerbated the drought conditions leading up to the Dust Bowl, which were documented by policy analysts in the early 1920s and in congressional reports by the late 1920s.[4] It is also clear that the federal government did not respond quickly enough to calls for federal regulation to stem the tide of westward-moving homesteaders, using farming methods unsuited to the region, and the result was economic and social devastation.

In the decades prior to the Dust Bowl's nadir, though, there was a great deal of hope on the horizon for homesteaders moving West, or in some cases, northwest from the former slave states of the south. On the plains of northeastern Colorado, a communal homesteading experience emerged from this hope, born of the ingenuity of an African-American entrepreneur who sought to create a community for Black families wishing to actualize their version of the American Dream. The experience of the people who moved to this place, known as Dearfield, or the Dearfield Colony, is similar to that of many homesteaders in some ways, but distinct in others due to the particular challenges that these homesteaders faced by virtue of their race. Their experience is the African-American homesteading experience of this time, shared by several communities that sprung up throughout the Great Plains and Rocky Mountain states after the Emancipation Proclamation was signed in 1863.[5]

The experience of the Dearfield homesteaders illustrates how race played an outsized role in forming the agricultural fabric of this region, starting in the early twentieth century and continuing until the present day. It also provides a lens through which to examine African Americans' use of the homesteading laws discussed in Chapter 3 to participate in the great federal settler colonial experiment in the late nineteenth and early twentieth centuries. Finally, the community established at Dearfield illustrates the experience of Black homesteading and Black land and resource control, which are important themes in the overall story of settler colonialism in the West, and which have not been salient themes in the literature and legal scholarship analyzing the disposal era.[6] Those stories have largely been told from the perspective of the white settler colonizers, with a recent focus on incorporating more of the elements of the Indigenous experience and relationship to land. But legal scholarship has not focused on the Black experience with farming and ranching in the West, nor integrated it fully into the scholarship analyzing the disposal era.

Unlike most of the locales that provided a backdrop for Chapters 1–3, the homesteading experience at Dearfield, Colorado in the early 1900s was not a ranch, nor a farm, nor a singular livestock operation, but rather a communal agriculture

4 *Public Lands Council*, 529 U.S. at 731–32.

5 Sylvia A. Law, *White Privilege and Affirmative Action*, 32 AKRON L. REV. 603, 610 (1999).

6 Thomas W. Mitchell, *Destabilizing the Normalization of Rural Black Land Loss: A Critical Role for Legal Empiricism*, 2005 WIS. L. REV. 557, 559 (2005).

cooperative that appeared in, then disappeared from the landscape of eastern Colorado in the first half of the twentieth century. Although the community and its cooperative structure held great promise even through the devastating years of the Great Depression, no African American farms associated with Dearfield lasted into the twenty-first century, which is not true of so many other farming and ranching homesteads in the intermountain West, including many in Indian Country.[7] Historical records reveal the brutal context in which the founders of Deerfield tried to build their agrarian community. Between 1863 and 1939, some 1.5 million households received 246 million acres of land by homesteading. Scholarly estimates put the total number of Black homesteaders at 3,400, and when their family members are included, the total number of African Americans who participated in homesteading could have been as high as 26,000.[8] If true, this would mean that less than 0.02 percent of homesteaders were Black. If the assumptions underlying these statistics are even close to accurate, only a miniscule percentage of homesteads were declared by African American heads of household. As will be discussed in the case with Dearfield, it is also likely true that more Black farmers than white farmers were forced to ultimately sell or abandon the lands they homesteaded.[9]

Dearfield provides an intriguing window into the Black homesteading experience, given how extensively it has been studied by archaeologists, historians, and social scientists. The community was the brainchild of Oliver Toussaint Jackson, an entrepreneur who wanted to create the agricultural equivalent of Tulsa's Black Wall Street on the high plains of eastern Colorado, near the modern city of Greeley.[10] First established in 1910, Dearfield eventually became the largest and best known of the Black homesteading settlements in Colorado and was among the six largest Black homesteading communities in the country.[11] Inspired by white settler colonizers who adopted a communal agricultural model in Greeley, seventy miles north of Denver, Jackson formed the Negro Townsite and Land Company to serve as a holding company for the homesteaded parcels at Dearfield.[12] He had experience

7 Luke Runyon, A *Forgotten Piece of African-American History on the Great Plains*, NATIONAL PUBLIC RADIO (Apr. 12, 2017), www.npr.org/sections/thesalt/2017/04/12/521800847/a-forgotten-piece-of-african-american-history-on-the-great-plains.

8 Edwards, Richard, *et al.*, *"Canaan on the Prairie": New Evidence on the Number of African American Homesteaders in the Great Plains*, 39 GREAT PLAINS QUARTERLY. 3, 224 (2019), www.jstor.org/stable/26757616.

9 *Id.* at 242 Shoemaker at 1718.

10 National Park Service, "Dearfield Agricultural Colony: Written Historical and Descriptive Data," Historic American Landscapes Survey; Jacob K. Friefeld, *et al.*, *African American Homesteader Colonies in the Settling of the Great Plains*, 39 GREAT PLAINS QUARTERLY. 1, 15 (Winter 2019), www.jstor.org/stable/26643048.

11 Jacob K. Friefeld, *et al.*, *African American Homesteader Colonies in the Settling of the Great Plains*, 39 GREAT PLAINS QUARTERLY. 1, 12 (Winter 2019), www.jstor.org/stable/26643048.

12 National Park Service, "Dearfield Agricultural Colony: Written Historical and Descriptive Data," Historic American Landscapes Survey.

forming collectives and cooperatives to advance Black land ownership and community goals, having founded the Colorado chapter of Booker T. Washington's National Negro Business League, which drew its inspiration from Washington's 1901 biography "Up From Slavery."[13] Yet, Jackson's dream was quickly challenged by drought, the Great Depression, and the Dust Bowl, which combined with devastating effect to eliminate so many ranches and farms of the Great Plains and Rocky Mountains in the 1920s and 1930s.

The southern states that had legalized slavery had a distinct perspective on the disposal era, opposing federal homestead laws due to fears that they would increase the power of the states that had banned slavery. Despite opposition from the former, Congress passed the Homestead Act midway through the Civil War, which would be the law that would allow for the greatest degree of privatization of federal public lands in the nation's history.[14] As detailed later in Chapter 5, this law created a right for any person over the legal age of majority (or a head of household), a citizen of the United States or a person intending to become one, to claim ownership of 160 acres of the federal domain. Upon living on and cultivating the land for the statutory period, the homesteader would obtain a patent to the land, establishing fee simple absolute property rights, for the nominal cost of filing the original claim.

At the time Congress passed the Homestead Act, enslaved African Americans did not have citizenship and were ineligible to file applications for homestead claims. As slaves, they were not allowed to acquire private property in this way, and were legally the personal property of their owners. By the point when the Homestead Act took effect, President Lincoln had signed the Emancipation Proclamation and former slaves were legally eligible to apply.[15] However, most freed slaves did not immediately jump at this opportunity. It is likely that some did not possess the resources to move West, or lacked information they would need to determine where to go. By the time many freed slaves obtained the resources and information they needed to plan their moves, and ultimately arrived in states like Kansas and Oklahoma, much of the arable land had been claimed.[16] This presented the Black homesteaders with

[13] *Id.*

[14] Law, at 614.

[15] Tom I. Romero, II, *A Brown Buffalo's Observations on Color (Blindness), Legal History, and Racial Justice in the Rocky Mountain West*, 2022 Utah L. Rev. 751, 757 (2022).

[16] Law at 612. Kansas, which was not considered a true Southern State (except by some pro-slavery groups before the Civil War), was a "much simpler and less expensive" goal than California or the other far western territories and states. But even getting to Kansas was challenging for most Black immigrants. Romero, at 761–62. ("For those coming from many parts of the South, a boat or train ride to St. Louis was the real beginning of their journey to Kansas. While conditions on these boats and trains were never ideal, riding in any form was certainly preferable to walking. Many arrived in St. Louis with little idea how they would get across Missouri and into Kansas. They must have felt, however, that whatever hardships they faced on that leg of the journey would be less significant than those left behind in the South.").

the first of many terrible choices – stop and settle on poorer quality land, usually at some distance from water sources and requiring more labor to perfect title through farming, or keep going in search of better quality grassland, likely without adequate resources for the additional journey and uncertain of exactly what lay ahead.

If they could make their way to a place that had better farmland, former slaves and their descendants had the skills to farm, and they knew how to do so successfully despite overwhelming adversity, having survived often brutal physical and psychological conditions during the slavery era, along with the intergenerational trauma these conditions imposed upon their families. They had in fact been doing both – farming and overcoming adversity – since well before the formation of the United States.[17] But freed slaves and their descendants did not have access to the same resources as their white counterparts and competitors in the western land rush, although Oliver Jackson stands out as a seeming exception to this general rule. Born in Ohio in 1862, the same year that the Homestead Act was signed into law, Jackson moved to Colorado with his wife, Minerva, in 1887. Over the course of his life, he was a newspaperman, a restaurateur, and an entrepreneur. In Colorado, he served as a messenger to the governor, which gave him access to political power in the capital city and a window into a different life, and Booker T. Washington inspired him to dream big about the future he wanted to create in Colorado.

Washington wrote and spoke of the need for freed slaves to bring themselves "up" in society by working in every available profession and occupation, including those that incorporated manual labor similar to the work that many had done prior to emancipation, even though for understandable reasons, these might not have been the most enticing of the new realm of work opportunities. In his famous Atlanta Exposition speech of 1895, Washington cautioned that:

> Our greatest danger is that in the great leap from slavery to freedom we may overlook the fact that the masses of us are to live by the productions of our hands and fail to keep in mind that we shall prosper in proportions we learn to dignify and glorify common labor and put brains and skill into the common occupations of life; shall prosper in proportion as we learn to draw the line between the superficial and the substantial, the ornamental gewgaws of life and the useful. No race can prosper till it learns that there is as much dignity in tilling a field as in writing a poem. It is at the bottom of life we must begin, and not at the top. Nor should we permit our grievances to overshadow our opportunities.[18]

Federal records reveal that by 1890, close to the time that Washington issued this call, African Americans represented 14 percent of all farmers and owned

[17] Law, at 614.

[18] Booker T. Washington, "The Atlanta Exposition Address" (Sept. 18, 1895), www.nps.gov/bowa/learn/historyculture/atlanta1-1.htm.

roughly fifteen million acres of land in fee. Dearfield therefore would not have been an unreasonable dream for Jackson as a young man starting out in Colorado. According to the agriculture census, African American farmland ownership "peaked in 1910 at 16-19 million acres."[19] This was the same year that Dearfield first began to draw settlers, who eventually came in the hundreds from the South, Midwest, and the Great Plains. African Americans seeking to homestead in places like Dearfield were only 25 percent of all Black farmers in 1910, though. Most black Americans working in agriculture at this time were "trapped in the lower rungs of the [land] tenure ladder," largely working as sharecroppers on white-owned farms in the south.[20]

The lure of a different arrangement – absolute ownership of private property – was strong. In the early 1900s, the United States advertised itself as a nation of "equal opportunity and individual liberty," and private property was "the key instrument of this vision."[21] During the homesteading era, the federal government offered those individuals who wanted to make an agricultural labor investment in the land "the strongest and most complete set of property rights imagined by law: the fee simple absolute."[22] As noted property law Professor Jessica Shoemaker wrote of this time: "[w]ith fee simple title, these owners enjoyed broad rights to control, sell, lease, use, possess, develop, and exclude others from a specific bounded space on the earth's surface – into perpetuity."[23] Yet, this opportunity was not available to all, excluding Indigenous Peoples and enslaved African Americans – neither of whom were yet citizens of the United States. Although African Americans became eligible to file claims soon after the Homestead Act took effect, the forces that kept them and their ancestors enslaved for so many years were the same ones that would inhibit their success during the homesteading era.

Colorado's northern plains were alluring to all settler colonizers, including O.T. Jackson. Known to scientists as a "shortgrass" prairie, where the maximum height of grasses reach only to one's ankles, this region features a variety of endemic species, including blue grama grass, buffalo grass, western wheatgrass, and others. There is a notable absence of trees and tall grasses or shrubs in this ecosystem, due to the climate, and specifically, to lower annual precipitation numbers that do not provide enough rainfall to support larger shrubs and trees.[24] The region appears rel-

19 Jessica A. Shoemaker, *Fee Simple Failures: Rural Landscapes and Race*, 119 MICH. L. REV. 1695, 1717–18 (2021).

20 Thomas W. Mitchell, *Destabilizing the Normalization of Rural Black Land Loss: A Critical Role for Legal Empiricism*, 2005 WIS. L. REV. 557, 563–64 (2005).

21 Shoemaker, at 1697–98.

22 *Id.*

23 *Id.*

24 Colorado Department of Natural Resources, et al., "Native Plant Revegetation Guide for Colorado," p. 15 (October 1998) (citing Galatowitsch 1988; Mutel and Emerick 1984) (noting that glaciers never

atively flat compared the dramatic Rocky Mountain front less than fifty miles away, but upon closer inspection, the topography reveals itself as more varied, including gently undulating hills, with the occasion dramatic bluff, butte, or shallow canyon. These features help buttress the soils against the winds, which are another dominant feature of the northern Colorado shortgrass prairies. The grasses historically attracted large herds of deer, antelope, elk, and buffalo.[25] Seeing these large mammals grazing on the abundant grasses must have inspired visions in the Dearfield colonists of livestock doing the same.[26] And if the wild grasses could grow, surely crops could too.

The early years of the Dearfield colony were tough; Jackson noted that the first winter saw most residents struggling to make it through without wooden houses, living in dugouts or other makeshift canvas tents. Dugouts were a type of earthen dwelling that many homesteaders built if they could not afford lumber – they were dug by hand out of the ground, as the name implies, with a subterranean entrance and no windows. Only two wooden houses had been built before the brutal winds and cold temperatures of the first northern Colorado winter arrived in Dearfield. The six horses that the homesteaders brought with them were left to the elements and only three survived the coldest months. Of this time, Jackson wrote: "Ours is a prairie country and there was no nearby timber – [b]uffalo chips and sagebrush were our chief fuel."[27] But the earliest residents nonetheless persevered through that first winter and several more, in a testament to their physical and mental fortitude and their desire to make a new life on the Colorado plains.[28]

made it as far as the Colorado plains, but "their presence was felt east of the mountains." The plains rivers, including Arkansas and South Platte, "were swollen with melted ice and ground-up rock and spread a blanket of sand and silt far beyond the current floodplains").

25 U.S. Dep't of Ag., Forest Service, "History of the Pawnee National Grassland," (last visited Mar. 26, 2024), www.fs.usda.gov/Internet/FSE_DOCUMENTS/fseprd501692.pdf. These herds are what drew Indigenous People to the region as well, and the Tribes with present and past ties to the area are many. They include members of the following federally recognized Tribes: Cheyenne River Sioux Tribe, Crow Creek Sioux Tribe, Oglala Sioux Tribe, Rosebud Sioux Tribe, Standing Rock Sioux Tribe, Three Affiliated Tribes Mandan, Hidatsa and Arikara Nation, Crow Tribe, Montana, Eastern Shoshone Tribe, Wind River Reservation, and Shoshone-Bannock Tribes. The Indigenous presence in Colorado is documented by western archaeologists as far back as 13,000 BC, with the northeastern region experiencing many notable events throughout the colonization period by French, then Euro-American military campaigns and settlement pushes.

26 Coincidentally, this area was also the genesis of the dispute in *Camfield v. United States*, 167 U.S. 518, 521 (1897), the Supreme Court opinion discussed in Chapter 6.

27 Charlotte West, *Inside Dearfield, a Colorado Ghost Town that Was Once a Bustling, All-Black Settlement*, CBS NEWS (Feb. 28, 2019), www.nbcnews.com/news/nbcblk/inside-dearfield-colorado-ghost-town-was-once-bustling-all-black-n975716.

28 *Id.* Jackson's journals from the time noted: "We would get together in one or the other of the frame houses and sing all the louder if the wind nearly picked us up and carried us away."

By 1915, the residents of Dearfield had constructed forty-four wooden cabins on their homestead claims and built an estimated one hundred miles of fence.[29] The farms began producing crops, just as demand for food and grains was surging due to World War I. This created some initial prosperity in the community, and when word got out about the early successes, more settlers made their way north and West. In 1915, the population grew to 111 and additional homestead claims were filed – the townsite then occupied 140 acres and had a small town center, where the main street was named after Booker T. Washington.[30] In 1918, the Dearfield homesteaders made over $50,000 from the crops they brought to market, which allowed them to purchase farm equipment, acquire more livestock and make improvements to their homes. Many homesteaders also worked for white ranchers and in the town of Greeley to bring in extra income. The community began to attract businesses too, including a concrete block manufacturer, a lumber and coal yard, a rooming house, a grocery store, and a hotel. As financial returns grew, the community had the resources to create a more robust cultural life. Two churches sprung up to provide weekly services and Jackson built a community lunchroom where residents gathered for meals and to socialize. A school soon followed, and the community hosted an annual festival and carnival.[31] By 1919, Dearfield residents had received patents to 6,720 acres, representing thirty-seven individual homestead claims.[32]

At the population apex between 1917 and 1921, there were estimates of 300 to 700 residents who considered themselves part of the community at Dearfield, although the latter figure is likely on the high side, according to research by Dearfield scholar and Professor George Junne.[33] For those residents who were freed slaves, they were likely lured to Dearfield by the tempting prize of open land in a free state, which held the promise of a more and peaceful future.[34] Particularly in the years after the Civil War, the "free South" was still a hostile place for those who were not white, who had scant resources to defend themselves against the retaliatory tactics of southern whites seeking to avenge their losses

29 National Park Service, "Dearfield Agricultural Colony: Written Historical and Descriptive Data," Historic American Landscapes Survey.

30 Charlotte West, *Inside Dearfield, a Colorado Ghost Town that Was Once a Bustling, All-Black Settlement,* CBS News (Feb. 28, 2019), at www.nbcnews.com/news/nbcblk/inside-dearfield-colorado-ghost-town-was-once-bustling-all-black-n975716.

31 National Park Service, "Dearfield Agricultural Colony: Written Historical and Descriptive Data," Historic American Landscapes Survey.

32 Friefeld at 16.

33 *Id.* at 15; Charlotte West, *Inside Dearfield, a Colorado Ghost Town that Was Once a Bustling, All-Black Settlement*, CBS News (Feb. 28, 2019), www.nbcnews.com/news/nbcblk/inside-dearfield-colorado-ghost-town-was-once-bustling-all-black-n975716. "That number fluctuated as settlers bought farmland or homesteaded property in the colony area and moved their families there or sold land … and moved back out," said Brunswig, who has taken his students to excavate at the townsite as part of a summer field school.

34 Friefeld at 12.

in the war.[35] During this time, it was not uncommon for freed slaves to face white intimidation and threats, physical violence, and murder, especially after federal troops were withdrawn from the former slave states in 1877. The brutal reality of this time is reflected in the following statistic: between 1905 and 1924, white Americans were responsible for lynching an average of fifty-six Black Americans per year.[36]

But the racism that had given rise to slavery did not evaporate from white American society at the conclusion of the Civil War. Black homesteaders faced it, even in states like Colorado, which had passed equal access and equal protection laws in the early twentieth century. Despite these protections codified in law, the Colorado legislature did not create nor fund a state agency to enforce violations.[37] Meanwhile, cities and towns maintained open policies of segregation, including the capital city of Denver, which did not eliminate segregation until 1932. According to historical records, Denver's Manager of Improvements and Parks rigorously enforced a policy that "provided for certain days for '[W]hite' and other days for 'colored' people."[38] In 1932, Blacks and whites clashed over attempts to integrate a "white-only" beach at the city's popular Washington Park. In one notable recounting of a day that Black families went swimming at the Park's pool,

> Whites quickly left the water, armed themselves with sticks and stones, and advanced on the newcomers who fled towards the trucks that had brought them. When the trucks would not start, the [B]lacks were pursued and beaten as nearly a thousand onlookers watched. The police arrested 17 people – 10 African Americans and 7 [W]hites who had encouraged the [B]lacks to assert their rights.[39]

Race-based distinctions in law also cropped up in ways that impacted property ownership and agricultural enterprises for people of color during this time. Racially restrictive covenants were one of these, and their use was widespread at the time that Dearfield collapsed. These legal restraints on the alienation of property were used by white property owners to prevent non-white people from purchasing their land, homes, and other real property. A typical covenant contained language prohibiting conveyances or leases of real property to "any person not of the White race."[40] Although these covenants violated Colorado's equal protection laws, they were not successfully challenged during the years leading up to and including the Dearfield homesteading experience.

Other challenging circumstances also confronted the Dearfield homsteaders. The period following World War I was hard for every farmer and rancher in the Midwest and across most of the West, whether Black, white, Indigenous, rich or

[35] *Id.* at 13.
[36] *Id.* at 25.
[37] Romero at 760.
[38] *Id.*
[39] *Id.*
[40] *Id.*

poor. While the 1910s had been years of steady and adequate precipitation, the 1920s saw that phenomenon wane and be replaced by drought. When the decrease in available precipitation was combined with torrents of homesteaders attempting to use, or actually using, dryland farming techniques on the Great Plains and in areas like eastern Colorado, ecological disaster was almost inevitable. Farmers were quick to clear their land of its native grasses, which had adapted to the precipitation patterns and soil nutrients, and planted crops like corn, wheat, alfalfa, and sorghum, which they could use to feed their livestock or sell on the market for a profit.[41] The droughts of 1917–1921 caused enormous losses – the northern plains, for instance, lost 60 percent of its farms to bankruptcy, and 30 percent were abandoned.[42] In the southern plains, the advent of mechanized equipment, such as gasoline tractors and combine harvesters, combined with soaring prices in the early part of the decade, motivated farmers to clear, till, and plant nearly every available acre, every year. Strategies that experienced dryland farmers had advised, like crop rotation, were discarded, and when the drought came, this part of the country suffered for the mistakes in technique and equipment.

The Dust Bowl began when the chernozem soils of the panhandle area of Oklahoma, all of Texas, western Kansas, southeastern Colorado, and northeastern New Mexico were essentially laid bare by homesteaders plowing under virtually all native grasses and residual crops. Strong winds created massive clouds of airborne dust that tore through the immediate area and in parts beyond, called the "black blizzards" by those located within their path.[43] In 1932, fourteen dust storms were reported; that number would increase to approximately thirty-eight in 1933. In 1934, the most severe drought in history hit, affecting 75 percent of the nation. In 1934, the Yearbook for Agriculture reported that "Approximately 35 million acres of formerly cultivated land have essentially been destroyed for crop production.... 100 million acres now in crops have lost all or most of the topsoil; 125 million acres of land now in crops are rapidly losing topsoil...."[44] When the black blizzards finally stopped, it had been seven long years of drought, dust, financial hardship, starvation, and loss.[45] Many homesteaders in the hardest hit regions had abandoned their farms and headed further west, which only exacerbated conditions for the lands they left behind, given that no one remained on the land to till it, irrigate it, and bring the soils and vegetation back from collapse.

[41] Sarah T. Phillips, *Lessons from the Dust Bowl: Dryland Agriculture and Soil Erosion in the United States and South Africa, 1900–1950*, 4 Environ. Hist. 2, 245–66 (1999), *JSTOR*, https://doi.org/10.2307/3985305.

[42] *Id.*

[43] PBS, "Surviving the Dust Bowl: Timeline," www.pbs.org/wgbh/americanexperience/features/dust-bowl-surviving-dust-bowl/#:~:text=The%20%E2%80%9CYearbook%20of%20Agriculture%E2%80%9D%20for,are%20rapidly%20losing%20topsoil%E2%80%A6.%E2%80%9D (last visited Feb. 2, 2024).

[44] *Id.*

[45] Phillips at 256.

Were it not for the actions of the federal government and some nongovernmental entities during this time, the Dust Bowl likely would have lasted far longer, and to much greater effect. One of the efforts to reverse the catastrophic impacts was driven by social scientists who could see the proverbial writing on the wall with respect to the federal government's disposal-era policy and the capacity of the lands being homesteaded to produce what the newly minted farmers and ranchers expected. As early as the 1920s, social scientists began studying the patterns of land utilization produced by the Homestead Act and other incentive laws and compared them to the "productivity" potential of these lands, along with their soil type.[46] They determined that some lands were still capable of producing crops, but others had only "marginal" potential, and they organized and lobbied Congress to take action to remove the "marginal lands" from cultivation. Their lobbying efforts were persuasive, and in 1929, Congress passed the Agricultural Marketing Act, which authorized the Federal Farm Board to analyze farmlands for their "suitability" and remove any unsuitable lands from production.[47] As a result of these surveys, lands were identified for reacquisition by the federal government to remove them from agricultural production. Subsequent surveys called for the reacquisition of nearly seventy-five million acres of land that had been made available at virtually no cost to interested homesteaders only decades prior.

This shift in federal policy was quite remarkable when viewed against the backdrop of removal, reservation policy, allotment of Indigenous lands, and the disposal era. The motivating factor of the earlier period had been the conversion of communal property interests into individualized, private property interests. The thought had been that spurring individual private property ownership, cultivation of crops, construction of irrigation canals and infrastructure, and the raising of livestock would establish an imprint of empire across the continent, fostering badly needed economic growth. By the 1920s, the market experiment had failed and suddenly, experts were calling for the federal government to step in and help. Consistent with other themes behind New Deal-era laws and policies, the value set of the 1920s and 1930s with respect to the former public domain was that it was the federal government's responsibility – to society – to repurchase "marginal lands" and remove them from the hands of homesteaders, thus saving the homesteaders from themselves and saving society from the inevitable ecological collapse that would follow from repeated efforts to cultivate uncultivatable land.[48] In a way, this diminished the "absolute ownership" of farmers and ranchers that the disposal era had sought to encourage. By the New Deal era, the federal government had pivoted toward a trusteeship role,

[46] R. Douglas Hurt, *The National Grasslands: Origin and Development in the Dust Bowl*, 59 Agric. Hist. 2, 246–59 (1985), www.jstor.org/stable/3742388. Accessed Jan. 30, 2024.

[47] 12 U.S.C. § 1141.

[48] Hurt at 248–49.

under which it claimed responsibility to ensure that the individual farmer did not destroy arable farmland to the point that future generations could not continue to farm it. This role and value set was implemented through incentive programs, regulatory measures designed to protect soils from harmful farming techniques that caused erosion, and the federal government's "coercive power" to enforce those regulations.[49]

The New Deal era, along with subsequent legislation and federal policies to address the Dust Bowl, could fill several volumes of text and the particulars of these individual statutes and regulations are not the primary focus of this book or this chapter. Nevertheless, it is interesting to note one further outcome of the shift in federal law and policy that flowed from the New Deal era as it relates to the prairie grasslands that were so devastated during the Dust Bowl – the creation of the system of national grasslands. Following the passage of statutes like the Agricultural Marketing Act, federal government officials, social scientists, and agricultural experts from the nascent land grant universities of the plains and western states developed a model for a "Land Program," through which the federal government could not only reacquire severely damaged and otherwise unsuitable lands, but use them to study the contributing factors of the Dust Bowl. Following early enthusiasm for this model, federal agencies like the Federal Emergency Relief Administration (FERA), the Agricultural Adjustment Administration (AAA), the Resettlement Administration, and ultimately, the Farm Security Administration (FSA) shepherded the planning and acquisition of "submarginal" lands.[50] Congress transferred authority to the Soil Conservation Service in 1938 through the Bankhead-Jones Farm Tenant Act, and this agency administered the program through February 1943, the year that it ended.[51]

The objectives of this program throughout the Dust Bowl and the years immediately following were many. Purchasing the most degraded lands with no ground cover or topsoil, which were known as "blow hazards," allowed the federal government to engage in restorative cultivation techniques that would diminish the potential for blowing dust, which would further exacerbate the airborne dust problems of this time.[52] These included measures like plowing deep furrows across the dust-blown parcels, to attempt to capture as much blowing soil and precipitation as possible. Drought-resistant plants, such as black amber cane and sudan grass, were planted to form a windbreak at ground level, which would prevent the soil from becoming airborne. Federal agency staff also used weeds, like Russian thistle, because they spread and established themselves so quickly.

49 *Id.* at 249.
50 *Id.*
51 *Id.*
52 *Id.* at 253.

The federal government's Land Program also allowed it to consolidate small farms into larger parcels of land, which could be cultivated, leased, preserved, or adapted into combination of these options.[53] The scale of this program was massive, and the stakes were relatively high, given that it was the first time in American history that the federal government had attempted a land restoration project of this size and at this expense. It took decades, but by the early 1950s, the federal agencies overseeing the effort determined that some of the grassland areas that had been restored were too valuable as public resources to return them to cultivation or grazing. Some of the larger contiguous areas were protected as national grasslands and one of these preserves was established less than 100 miles north of Dearfield: the Pawnee National Grassland.[54]

Nevertheless, the Dust Bowl years were exceptionally hard on the residents of Dearfield, most of whom were forced by conditions to seek work in the city. As the population started to decline, the community's founder, Oliver Jackson, tried to rebrand the town as a "Valley Resort" for African Americans from Denver. When that plan failed, he offered to sell Dearfield to the federal government for use as an internment camp for Japanese Americans, but this plan also failed and ultimately, the homestead claims were abandoned. Most were sold, and residents left. The community, as it had existed in the 1910s and 1920s, disappeared. The idea that the federal government could save the nation from agricultural and financial ruin through the reacquisition of grasslands and the re-creation of a public agricultural "commons" that dominated the western territories only a few decades before did not reach, nor apply to Dearfield.

Part of the answer of why Dearfield did not last is no doubt economic, given the crash in the national market for agricultural products. By the 1930s, much of the so-called breadbasket of the United States was also in an extreme drought. The prices for Dearfield's crops collapsed and fewer new settlers arrived, compounding the diminishment of the annual yield in dramatic fashion.[55] Meanwhile, the Dust Bowl and its horrific conditions descended upon Dearfield and wreaked havoc with the fragile farming economy the residents had been attempting to build up. At the same time, Dearfield was surrounded by white communities, white landowners,[56] and represented by county, state, and federal government bodies consisting of white individuals who seemed entirely

53 Elizabeth Howard, *Management of the National Grasslands*, 78 N.D. L. REV. 409, 418 (2002).

54 U.S. Dept. of Ag., Forest Serv., "Pawnee National Grassland History" (last visited Mar. 31, 2024), www.fs.usda.gov/detail/arp/learning/history-culture/?cid=fsm91_058308.

55 Friefeld at 16.

56 Shoemaker, at 1718–19 (also noting that The "vast majority" of homesteaders were white households, resulting in the redistribution of farmlands taken from Native Americans and Mexican owners. Title also predominantly went to men, although some women were able to acquire title if they were "single, widowed, divorced, or deserted." Married women, however, were generally ineligible to take land in their own name as the Act was limited to the "head of [a] household.").

comfortable with the modified segregation policies and racial covenants discussed earlier in this chapter.

The federal government was passing laws at that time that theoretically should have helped the residents of Dearfield, such as the Agricultural Adjustment Act of 1933.[57] As one historian described the economic hardship that led to the passage of this Act, "prices dropped so low that many farmers went bankrupt and lost their farms. In some cases, the price of a bushel of corn fell to just eight or ten cents. Some families began burning corn rather than coal in their stoves because corn was cheaper."[58] Franklin D. Roosevelt's 1932 presidential campaign made agriculture relief a central platform, and upon winning the election, he set out immediately to secure prices for agricultural commodities, provide temporary subsidies, and otherwise relieve the financial pressure on American farmers through his New Deal initiatives.[59] One of the goals of the Agricultural Adjustment Act was "to establish and maintain such balance between the production and consumption of agriculture commodities … as will reestablish prices to farmers at a level that will give agricultural commodities a purchasing power with respect to articles that farmers buy …"[60] The substantive mandates of the statute included a number of new mechanisms empowering the Secretary of Agriculture to exercise his authority to enter into agreements in which farmers would agree to limit their production of various agricultural commodities in exchange for subsidy payments.[61] The idea was to reduce the supply of certain commodities and increase their prices, stabilizing the market.

But according to Black journalist E.E. Lewis, who expressed the reality for Black farmers in the pages of Opportunity, the magazine of the National Urban League, the Act did not benefit African-American farmers because "American agrarianism was … always explicitly coded in both gender and race." From the western expansion of the nation in the nineteenth century onward, Manifest Destiny, disposal policies, and homesteading were projects of "race-based exclusion and control, using colonialism, slavery, and other blatantly racialized tactics to ensure that private landownership emerged in the image of the white yeoman farmer ideal."[62] The beneficiaries of these laws and policies, including those of the homestead era, were almost exclusively white men, and to a lesser extent, their families.[63] As a result, the Black residents of Dearfield were facing legal and social forces that may have

57 Lawrence F. Dempsey, *Feeding the Racial Disparity in Disease: How Federal Agricultural Subsidies Contribute to A Racial Disparity in the Prevalence of Diet Related Illness*, 7 Biotechnology & Pharmaceutical L. Rev. 109, 113 (2014).

58 *Id.* at 113.

59 *Id.*

60 *Id.*

61 *Id.*

62 Shoemaker at 1698.

63 *Id.* at 1699.

simply proven too much to combat, even without the economic crisis of the Great Depression and the ecological crisis of the Dust Bowl that immediately followed.

Other forces were at work, too. Powerful railroads, which in many ways could "make or break" western communities, often declined to establish stops in Black communities.[64] Railroads marketed heavily to white immigrants, but not to African Americans. It was the official company policy of some railroads to solicit white, European immigrants by marketing directly to them, sometimes in their languages (including Norwegian, Swedish, German, and Welsh) because "these people" were "preferred to any others."[65] Railroads hired overseas agents in Europe to advertise the "railroad colonization campaign" that relied upon the bookings to fund the laying of the tracks, and ultimately catered the lines and stops to the communities where the European immigrants would settle. These corporations found that it was more profitable to encourage settlement by "colonies" that would create instant communities, and their inhabitants would provide "good neighbors, morality, security to property, comfort, and prosperity."[66] The advertising materials and word of mouth used euphemisms and tropes to lure the desired classes of settlers, advertising a transportation link to "town[s] with potential," containing "a small but desirable population," which were located "far enough from larger cities with their inferior populations," and which eagerly awaited hardworking "Anglo-saxon settlers."[67]

At the same time these advertising campaigns were targeting white Europeans and European Americans, no railroads engaged in similar marketing in the southern states. And when African Americans found their way West anyway, the region hardly welcomed them with open arms. As Kansas governor John Pierce St. John noted during his 1879–1883 term, "Indications are that we will be over run with them," referring to African American homesteaders.[68] When African American homesteaders wrote to Gov. St. John to inquire about homesteading opportunities and available land in Kansas, he did his best to dissuade them, responding that rumors about free land and livestock in Kansas were untrue and that he "would advise … that colored people not [] come to any of the Northern States…."[69]

The result is an agrarian vision that rewarded the heroic, hardworking, wholesome (and almost certainly, white) farmer. It is no accident that today, 98 percent of agricultural lands are owned and controlled by people who are white. Nor is it accidental that some of this country's most notorious and persistent regions of concentrated poverty are both rural and racialized: the farming Black Belt of the Southeast,

64 Pierce, Jason E., *The Politics of Whiteness and Western Expansion, 1848–80*, *in* Making the White Man's West: Whiteness and the Creation of the American West, University Press of Colorado, p. 145 (2016), www.jstor.org/stable/j.ctt19jcg63.11.

65 *Id.* at 161.

66 *Id.* at 162–63.

67 *Id.* at 170.

68 Pierce, at 171.

69 *Id.*

the Hispanic colonias along the southern border, and the Tribal reservations of the Southwest and Midwest.[70]

Without this effective advertising campaign by railroads and powerful white governmental officials and civic leaders, there is no doubt that more African Americans might have found their way West. Whether they could have succeeded as homesteaders is another question, but there certainly might have been more strength in numbers in places like Dearfield, which might have allowed homesteaders there to maintain ownership of their homesteads through the devastating years of the Dust Bowl. Moreover, had railroads established stops in Black communities, more economic wealth would have flowed into those communities, and it would have been less expensive for Black farmers to send their agricultural products to market. And had the residents of Dearfield been able to take advantage of the incentives provided by the AAA, there might be descendants of the original colonists still living in Dearfield and working the land.

The hard truth of this community, though, is that everyone eventually left. As of 2024, Dearfield is one of Colorado's many ghost towns, and lives on only as an archaeological site. In a testament to the construction skills of the founders, a few buildings remain mostly intact, including a gas station, a hotel, and O.T. Jackson's home, along with a sign bearing a reprinted advertisement for Dearfield in its heyday, noting that "Dearfield is the place!"[71] In 1995, the town was listed on the National Register of Historic Places, and it is now owned by the members of the Black American West Museum. When the wind blows, as it still does with vigor in this part of the world, the blue grama and buffalo grasses sway amid the remnants of the once-thriving homesteading community, visitors can stand and try to conjure up Jackson's original dream and vision using their imagination and the information on the placards that dot the remnants of the settlement.[72]

[70] Shoemaker at 1699.

[71] Monica Humphries, *See Inside the Crumbling Ghost Town that Was Once Home to One of America's Most Successful Black Farming Communities*, BUSINESS INSIDER (Oct. 23, 2021), www.businessinsider.com/colorado-dearfield-ghost-town-abandoned-photos-2021-10.

[72] National Park Service, "Dearfield Agricultural Colony: Written Historical and Descriptive Data," Historic American Landscapes Survey.

5

Treaties, the Taylor Grazing Act, and the Carpenter Ranch

Nobody in Washington seemed to know which end of a cow gets up first.[1]

– Ferry Carpenter

The Carpenter Ranch is located just outside of the small town of Hayden, Colorado, along the banks of the Yampa River, just south of the Wyoming border. The Yampa was named by the Yampuddttka (or Yamparika) Ute people, whose lands these were, before they became the ranch.[2] This 900-acre property is operated as a working ranch and conservation center by The Nature Conservancy, a multinational nonprofit conservation organization. The ranch was named for its second owner, Farrington "Ferry" Carpenter, who first visited the ranch in 1906 and later called it home until his death in 1980. The white ranch house that visitors can tour is where Carpenter lived while he crafted the regulations that would guide ranching in the West for over 100 years, as the first director of the Federal Grazing Service, the predecessor agency to the modern Bureau of Land Management.

The law and policy of ranching in the West, including those that Carpenter designed, changed the legal and ecological landscape of the entire region, from the courses of its watersheds to the very grasses that now grow on these lands. The roots of these reforms began to form during the Dust Bowl period and continued for decades immediately thereafter. This era provides incredible context regarding the modern uses and characterizations of these lands, known by many today as the western "range," a term describing land from a particular vantage point, as first mentioned in the Introduction.[3] Range is not equivalent to land – it describes land in a way that is inextricably linked to how that land is used, viewed, and valued by a distinct element of the broader population.

1 Farrington R. Carpenter, Confessions of a Maverick, p. 158 (Colo. State Hist. Soc'y 1984).

2 Uintah Basin Teaching American History Project, Ute Tribe History, www.uintahbasintah.org/utehistory.htm.

3 Rasband at 1012–13.

Range describes land that is valued and used for grazing domestic livestock, not for its value as habitat for wildlife, nor as home to medicinal plants used by Tribal Nations like the Ute. They might not describe their ancestral homelands as range or rangeland.

What Tribal members might call this land is their treaty land, or their ancestral land, or just land, without any corresponding English adjective indicating ownership. On these lands, in what is now northwestern Colorado, the rule established in *Johnson* changed the trajectory of life for the Ute, like it did for so many other Tribes subject to that decision. As of 1823, the date of the opinion, and as discussed in Chapter 2, a blanket rule was established that governed *all Tribal Nations* relative to their lands, not solely the Piankeshaw. This rule, that Tribes do not own their lands in fee, applied to every one of the hundreds of nations living anywhere within the territorial United States as of 1823, and anywhere that would later become the United States after that date, whether the land that sustained them was acquired by purchase, conquest, or congressional or judicial fiat.

In 1833, the federal government established an early outpost at Camp Carson (later, Fort Carson) along the Front Range of the Rocky Mountains, just south of the modern city of Colorado Springs. Camp Carson attracted trappers and fur traders to Colorado[4] and with them came diseases, such as smallpox and cholera, which decimated local Indigenous populations.[5] These early arrivals also paved the way for permanent settler colonizers, who found the notion of trading with or purchase supplies from white trappers and fur traders more comfortable and enticing than with the foreign, non-English-speaking Indigenous Peoples.

As was the pattern elsewhere, the trappers and traders preceded the settler colonizers, and the settler colonizers' arrival initiated a land grab. The latters' pursuit of land for ranching and farming, along with the water they would need to succeed in either endeavor, created tensions with the Ute. To resolve the tension, and cease the "hostilities" that had broken out, including the taking of hostages, the federal government initiated treaty negotiations, culminating in an 1849 treaty reserving the Ute people's rights to their ancestral homelands in Colorado.[6] In this treaty, the "Utah" Tribe acknowledged and declared that "they [we]re lawfully and exclusively under the jurisdiction" of the federal government and that they "unconditionally" submitted to its power and authority.[7] As consideration for this

4 John F. Russell, *Connections to the Yampa Valley Remain Long after Utes Forced Out*, Steamboat Pilot & Today (Oct. 7, 2020), www.steamboatpilot.com/news/connections-to-the-yampa-valley-remain-long-after-utes-forced-out/.

5 Carl Abbott, *et al.*, Colorado: A History of the Centennial State, p. 82 (University of Colorado Press 2015).

6 *Id.* at 87.

7 1849 treaty with the Utah, Art. I, 9 Stat. 984 (1850).

acknowledgment, and from the federal perspective, "to preserve tranquility," the United States promised to "establish such military posts and agencies, and authorize such trading houses, at such time and in such places as the said Government may designate."[8] For their part, Ute leaders promised to ensure that their people would stay within the territorial boundaries agreed upon in the treaty, and that they would "not depart from their accustomed homes or localities unless specially permitted by an agent" of the federal government, settling themselves "as will enable them most successfully to cultivate the soil," ceasing forever the "roving and rambling habits which [had] hitherto marked them as a people."[9] In other words, they would convert from their traditional lifeways of moving seasonally to hunt and gather and "settle" in one delineated area, like their non-Indigenous neighbors were spurred to do by the disposal era policies.

As described in previous chapters, the federal laws that would pave the way for Carpenter's dream of ranching to come to fruition were generally referred to as the "disposal laws." They took many and creative forms, and included many famous statutes that transformed the West in less than 100 years. Well-known examples are the Morrill Act of 1862, which funded higher education by selling or leasing former Indigenous lands to prospectors, farmers, and ranchers, the 1862 Homestead Act, which drew so many migrants West in pursuit of their American dream (including the Dearfield colonists), and the railroad land grants, which conveyed land to companies that promised to build rail lines to facilitate settlement.[10] Less well-known are the Preemption Act, the Stock-Raising Homestead Act, the Desert Land Act of 1877, and the Timber Culture Act.[11] Although each statute bestowed rights on distinct categories of eligible recipients, according to the purpose for which they sought to acquire the land, the results of the surveys they authorized were used by Congress not only to allocate the parcels of eligible land, but to devise creative ways to maximize the footprint of settler colonialism across the West. For instance, the railroad land grants not only deeded the acreage necessary to lay the tracks, but included extra lands within a certain distance on either side. These bonus lands facilitated timber felling for the ties that bound the tracks, but also allowed the railroad companies to sell rights to harvest the timber, or the land itself, to raise revenue that would fund construction of the tracks. Moreover, the extra acreage adjacent to the tracks was not offered in large contiguous sections, but rather in an alternating pattern of smaller square-shaped sections, creating yet another checkerboard. When the railroad decided to sell some of its "squares" on the checkerboard, the land tenure pattern became more complex, divided among three or more categories of owners: the federal government,

8 *Id.* Art. VI.
9 *Id.*
10 Leshy, pp, 92–93, 96–97.
11 *Id.* at 98–100.

railroad companies, and individuals who could afford to purchase large tracts of land at market value.

The Preemption Act of 1841 was one of the earliest of the so-called homesteading laws, which "opened" the lands that had been taken from or otherwise acquired from Indigenous Nations, making them available to settler colonizers to purchase for a below-market price.[12] The 1873 Timber Culture Act complemented the Homestead Act, allowing claimants to acquire 160 additional acres (above what was allowed by the Homestead Act) if they planted trees on at least forty acres. The theory behind this statute was that extensive tree planting would solve the problem of a lack of timber on the Great Plains. But because the forty-acre requirement was far too onerous for the average individual or family, Congress later reduced the requirement to ten acres. Ultimately, the Timber Culture Act was a modest success in terms of the total land patented – ten million acres – but it did not solve the problem of a lack of timber.[13]

The 1862 Homestead Act is perhaps the best known of the disposal era statutes because of the depictions of homesteading in popular films, television shows, and books, like "Yellowstone" and its prequels. There is a difference between the act of homesteading and the Homestead Act, though. The act of homesteading was possible under various laws, but the Homestead Act evolved under unique circumstances and was designed to achieve specific goals of the federal government during a very specific period of time – the end of the nineteenth century. The reality of this time was that the previous scheme of incentivizing settlement in the western regions, by offering lands for sale to private parties and corporations, had exhausted the supply of takers. To continue to lure people West, Congress needed a different framework, and thus, the Homestead Act's "work for land title" scheme emerged. Under this framework, as detailed in the last chapter, any citizen of the United States was authorized to enter onto 160 acres of open public land and file to establish their claim.[14] But as mentioned in the last chapter too, this incentive really was exclusive, right from the start.

For those who qualified, once entry was perfected, the land was free for the taking, if the claimant paid the minimal filing fees. After filing the necessary paperwork, the Act allowed the homesteader six months to establish residence, and after five years of settlement and cultivation, supported by an affidavit of those with first-hand knowledge, the federal government would issue a patent to the homesteader.[15] Because the system was so simple, the administrators were typically far away from the lands being claimed, and there was heavy reliance on the honor system, there were tremendous administrative problems from the outset. There were not enough

12 5 Stat. 453 (1841).
13 Leshy at 99.
14 *Id.* at 96.
15 *Id.*

surveyors to validate the claims and map the homesteaded lands, resulting in fragmented documentation and instances of fraudulent claims. Homesteading was also sometimes used as a pretense for extracting timber or other valuable resources from land that the applicant never intended to settle or make home.[16] Overgrazing also complicated the homesteading process, as settlers planned their herd sizes and ranch investments based on the availability of public lands for supplemental grazing and public water sources for watering their livestock. The Homestead Act was a success from the perspective of the federal government, and specifically Congress, though, in that it created vested private land interests across the West. Between 1868 and 1904, over 100 million acres were homesteaded and converted from public to private ownership.[17]

The 1849 treaty with the Ute did not achieve the peaceable relations that it sought, nor could it have, given the pressure that the disposal acts and their incentives imposed upon the fragile agreement. Encouraged by the promise of free land, settler colonizers kept encroaching on Ute land and the Utes were often forced to defend their land without outside assistance, sometimes using force. Violent encounters following the Treaty's signing were known as "the Ute Wars" and battles were fought throughout Ute lands, in what is now western Colorado and across the border into what is now Utah. This period of conflict lasted until 1924, when the conflict known as "Posey's war" finally ended the hostilities.

During this time, the Ute leaders and federal officials tried to use Treaties to resolve conflicts over land and other resources, and in 1868, a treaty was signed in Washington, DC, in which the Ute bands of Colorado agreed to live on the Confederated Ute Reservation, which constituted most of the westernmost portion of the State of Colorado, including the lands that are now the Carpenter Ranch.[18] This treaty resulted from the pressure that settler colonizers were applying to Ute reserved lands under the Homestead Act and from the discovery of silver and gold in the mountains, which at this point were Ute lands.[19] The 1868 agreement was known as the Hunt Treaty, and was negotiated with the leaders of seven Ute bands living in the areas that are now Colorado and Utah. It was named for one of the emissaries responsible for negotiating the treaty, then governor of the Colorado territory, Alexander C. Hunt. The circumstances

16 *Id.*

17 *Id.*

18 Ute Lands, 1868 (map), https://collections.lib.utah.edu/details?id=358609&facet_format_t=%22image%2Fjpeg%22&facet_setname_s=uaida_main&q=%28%28Ute%29+AND+%28Maps%29%29.

19 Abbott, et al., p. 88; National Park Service, FRONTIER IN TRANSITION: A HISTORY OF SOUTHWESTERN COLORADO, Chapter V: The Utes in Southwestern Colorado: A Confrontation of Cultures (last updated, Nov. 20, 2008), www.nps.gov/parkhistory/online_books/blm/co/10/chap5.htm.

under which the Ute leaders signed this treaty were what led the famous Ute leader Ouray to issue his famous proclamation, acknowledging the reality of Indian Treaties negotiated at gunpoint and under other extreme forms of duress: "[t]he Agreement an Indian makes to a United States treaty is like the agreement a buffalo makes with his hunter when pierced with arrows. All he can do is lie down and give in."[20] In the Hunt Treaty, which the Utes had no real choice but to sign, they ceded the mountain region to the federal government (allowing it to be "opened" for mineral prospecting and homesteading) and reserved most of what is now the westernmost area of Colorado as their new homeland.[21] This established the second reservation for the northern Ute bands, including the Yamparika.[22]

The peace described on paper in 1868 did not last, though, because settler colonizers, miners, and land investors poured across the mountains and into the areas that were reserved by the Utes in the Hunt Treaty. In Washington, meanwhile, Congress had ended treaty-making in 1871. This marked a significant transfer of what had been Executive power to Congress, although the Executive Branch continued to make "agreements" with Tribes after 1871. These agreements, which were ratified as Executive Orders, became the primary treaty replacement mechanism for the Executive Branch, which discovered soon that negotiations with Tribes were not ending even though Congress had proclaimed an end to the policy.[23] For the Ute leadership, an immediate need for an Executive Order presented itself regarding the boundaries of the 1868 Reservation, which had been in more or less constant dispute since the treaty was signed, because the lands reserved by the Ute were never surveyed by the Department of Interior until 1875 and non-Indigenous settler colonizers kept streaming into the reservation in search of land. At this point, the federal government learned that the lands around the White River, which had been reserved by the Ute in the Hunt Treaty, were not within the legal description of their land in that treaty.[24] To avoid further hostilities, the Secretary of Interior advised President Rutherford B. Hayes to issue an Executive Order stating that the Hunt Treaty intended to reserve to the Ute

20 Denver Public Library, "Ute Removal and the Hunt Treaty – The Agreement a Buffal Makes When Pierced with Arrows" (Nov. 9, 2021), www.denverlibrary.org/blog/cultural-inclusivity-equity-research/dodie/ute-removal-and-hunt-treaty-agreement-buffalo-makes.

21 Tim Cooney, *Plight of the Northern Utes, Part I*, Aspen Daily News (Jun. 25, 2023), www.aspendailynews.com/news/plight-of-the-northern-utes-part-i/article_8686d45e-1344-11ee-8e54-c763f9203362.html.

22 *Ute Indians v. United States*, 330 U.S. 169, 172 (1947).

23 *Id.* at 176–77. For the Ute people, this took the form of the Brunot Agreement, which the federal government signed with the Ute Tribes in 1873, divesting them of their 1868 treaty rights to the San Juan mountains near Durango, Colorado, in the southern part of the state. Abbott at 88.

24 *Ute Indians*, 330 U.S. at 176–77.

people the disputed lands along the White River, clarifying the boundaries of the reservation as of 1876.[25] This would also help Congress direct the allocation of sections of public domain land to the new state of Colorado in its Enabling Act, which was passed on August 1, 1876.[26]

As is so often the case in Indian Country, treaty promises made, especially those regarding land, lose when they run up against the federal government's rights established by Justice Marshall's Doctrine of Discovery and the greed of a colonizing population hungry for land and resources and emboldened by the notion of the American Dream. By 1879, this greed had reached a fever pitch in the area in and around the Ute Reservation established by the Hunt Treaty, and it was aimed directly at the Ute people. That year, Colorado gubernatorial candidate Frederick Walker Pitkin ran on the single-issue platform, "The Utes Must Go."[27]

In the Meeker-Hayden area, the Department of Interior was emboldened by federal judicial rulings like *Johnson* and its progeny, as well as the relative success of the acquisition and disposal model used in the east and the central plains, and so began attempts to "remove" Ute people from lands that were coveted by non-Indigenous people for their potential as farms, ranches, and loci of businesses.[28] In 1879, violence broke out between Ute Tribal members and US Army soldiers who had been summoned by the Director of the White River Indian Agency, Nathan Meeker, to support his staff at their post near the town that now bears his name, which is about sixty-five miles west of the Carpenter Ranch.[29] This incident, which was often framed as a unilateral unprovoked attack by Ute warriors against Meeker and his agency staff, and is often described as "the Meeker Massacre," caused casualties for both sides. After Ute warriors killed Meeker's staff and took several women and children hostage, African American buffalo soldiers dispatched from the Ninth Cavalry near Steamboat Springs arrived in Meeker to defend the settler colonizers against further Ute attacks. They managed to extend the battle another four days, until an Army Colonel arrived from Wyoming with 450 additional soldiers and finally forced a surrender. Later investigations resulted in no findings of fault or punishment against the Utes, who were lawfully in possession of their reserved lands. The Army was found to have trespassed on Ute land and the Department of Interior's encroachment was unlawful from the outset.

25 *Id.* at 177, n.2 (citing Exec. Order of Aug. 17, 1876).

26 18 Stat. 474.

27 Pitkin was subsequently elected and served two consecutive terms. Russell, John F., "Connections to the Yampa Valley remain long after Utes forced out," Steamboat Pilot (Oct. 7, 2020), available at www.steamboatpilot.com/news/connections-to-the-yampa-valley-remain-long-after-utes-forced-out/.

28 Abbott, et al., p. 89. (One of the more impossible-to-believe suggestions at this time for the Ute was that they could be removed to Oklahoma, which was then known as the Indian Territory).

29 Russell.

Within a year of the incident at Meeker, Congress passed legislation to "punish" the Utes who participated in the attack on Meeker's outpost, to dispossess them of their land, through allotment and sale.[30] Like what happened to the Blackfeet Nation, Congress authorized the allotment of all Ute land within the Hunt Treaty Reservation in Colorado, and deemed unallotted lands surplus. For these lands, title would be "released and conveyed to the United States."[31] These surplus lands would then be "restored to the public domain for sale as public lands," under the Homestead Act and other federal laws in effect at that time, allowing non-Indigenous claimants to acquire title to the public domain in exchange for working the land. This statute was also a removal act, authorizing the military to remove any Ute people who remained on the reservation lands in northwest Colorado.

At the same time, the Colorado legislature passed a removal declaration, supporting the federal government's removal of the White River and Uncompagre Ute bands from Colorado and onto the modern lands of the Ute Indian Tribe on the Uintah and Ouray Reservation. By 1881, the 1,465 Ute people of the northern bands were removed from what was then the State of Colorado.[32] Yet, although the connections of the Ute people to these lands may have changed in some ways, they did not change in all ways. Even though the Ute descendants of the bands from the northern Colorado region largely reside across the border on the Uintah and Uncompahgre Reservation, many of them remain connected to these lands and view these lands as still connected to them.[33]

For the young Ferry Carpenter, these lands would become home too. As a midwesterner who spent time in New Mexico during his summer vacations in the early 1900s, word reached him that the lands formerly occupied by Ute people in northwestern Colorado were "open" and would be prime homesteading and ranching country. In the words of J.B. Dawson, a rancher who had mentored Ferry Carpenter during his youth experiences as a ranch hand on Dawson's Ranch in New Mexico:

> Colorado is a new country, and the place for a young man to go. The public domain is all open and unfenced. Any citizen over twenty-one years of age can file on a homestead and, by living on it seven months a year for five years, can get title to 160 acres of free land. The hills out there are full of deer and elk and antelope, and the streams are full of trout.[34]

30 Act of June 15, 1880, 21 Stat. 199.

31 *Id.*

32 Sean Summers, *The Utes are Removed to Reservations*, THE LEADVILLE HERALD (May 23, 2023), available at www.leadvilleherald.com/free_content/article_df32e514-1eb6-11eb-9822-5793047f06e5.html.

33 Russell.

34 Carpenter at 20.

When Carpenter got his hands on a map of northwest Colorado, it showed him that this part of the world was "a truly frontier country," designated "coal lands" and without a single town.[35]

In the summer of 1907, between his sophomore and junior years at Princeton University, Carpenter visited the area and discovered an elevated area northeast of town, with a natural spring burbling up from the ground. Upon a cursory investigation, he learned that the land around the spring had not yet been claimed and was designated as "open" land for potential prospectors or homesteaders. Carpenter followed the laws in effect at that time and filed for a homestead on the land. In 1907, he received a certificate from the land office, signifying that his application for a homestead had been received. All that had been required to obtain lawful and exclusive title to this land was a posting of public notice on the property and with the land office, and Carpenter's stated intent to make it his home. He wrote to his father to celebrate his success, "as a possessor of land claimed first by the Indians, acquired by the United States, and now to be developed by a new member of the 'Do-it-yourself-or-it-won't-get-done' club."[36]

For industrious and educated new arrivals like Carpenter, becoming a landowner under the Homestead Act was simply a matter of doing a bit of research and following the basic requirements. As Carpenter left his homestead for periods of time to continue his education, he read up on what he needed to do and found that temporary departures from the homestead were permissible, even though the Homestead Acts contained a general requirement that homesteaders spend seven to twelve months a year on their homesteads, while putting the land to continuous use. It turned out that continuing one's education was an exception to the permanent residence requirement. With the help of a neighbor and friend, who continued working on a garden and a joint irrigation canal project, Carpenter maintained the homestead despite spending the bulk of 1907, 1908, and 1909 away at college in New Jersey. During the summer after his junior year, he decided to get into the livestock business and noted in his autobiography that one attractive incentive was the free "range" that the federal government offered to those starting out in the ranching business – ranchers could graze their livestock throughout the public lands designated as open range if they were the right breed. In Carpenter's case, he was required to "furnish a bull of 18 months of age for every twenty-five head of cows," and it must be of "purebred Shorthorn or Hereford lineage."[37] Proving up on the homestead after five years would not be much of a problem either, as neighbors were interested in swapping attestations to achieve mutual goals,[38] and the Town of

35 *Id.*

36 *Id.* at 46.

37 Carpenter at 50.

38 In Carpenter's words, "the popular sentiment was, 'If you will testify for me, I will testify for you.'" *Id.* at 46.

Hayden was eager to help in any way that it could, given that the increase in private property ownership would result in a larger tax base that could help fund the construction of schools and roads.

In the late 1800s, the combination of white-owned cattle and sheep ranching operations dramatically increased on the private and public grasslands of the western territories. This was the pattern that emerged in Hayden, Colorado, and in so many other places throughout the West. The power of the white cattle ranchers was born of this early period of the common use of the grassland regions as "rangeland."[39] This period manifested as a relative free-for-all on public lands, in which anyone who could get their livestock onto the public grasslands could graze them freely, without permits, fees, or even fences. As white farmers, ranchers, and corporations snapped up allotted lands, there was tremendous pressure on limited western river systems to supply the water necessary to support these growing operations. This period was the second "wave" of livestock introduction, and quickly grew to include cattle barons, massive livestock companies, and a corresponding increase and consolidation of European-American land tenure and access rights.[40] An early 1880s surge in prices on the cattle market pushed more and more into the cattle business, and soon millions of cattle were grazing the western grasslands.[41]

As open forage and land became scarce, livestock owners sought to control their access to water, which in the arid West was a particularly effective method of simultaneously controlling vast areas of land.[42] Powerful white landowners and their political allies pressured Congress to authorize the construction of dams that often inundated Tribal lands to secure water for white ranchers and farmers. As barbed wire became more prolific, the formerly large swaths of land that had served as habitat for large ungulate and carnivore species were broken up into discrete ranching units, disrupting the grassland biome ecosystems in new and complex ways.[43] All of these trends played out at the Carpenter homestead, where Ferry and a neighboring homesteader sought to divert water from the spring on Carpenter's homestead through a ditch down to a common pasture below, where they ultimately built a

39 George A. Bowling, *The Introduction of Cattle Into Colonial America*, 25 J. DAIRY SCI. (1942), at 1.

40 *Public Lands Council v. Babbitt*, 529 U.S. 728, 731–32 (2000).

41 *Id.* (citing R. White, "It's Your Misfortune and None of My Own": A History of the American West 223 (1991) & E. Osgood, The Day of the Cattleman 83–113 (1929); W. Webb, The Great Plains 205–268 (1931)).

42 Simultaneously, the practice of grazing domesticated cattle, horses, sheep, and other species in this region rendered the grassland biomes vulnerable to weed infestations, which in some places, subsumed native and introduced grass species. Joseph Ditomaso, *Invasive Weeds in Rangelands: Species, Impacts, and Management*, 48 WEED SCIENCE 2, 255–65, (2000).

43 Robert A. McLemon, *et al.*, "What We Learned From the Dust Bowl: Lessons in Science, Policy, and Adaptation," National Center for Biotechnology Information (August 28, 2013). ("Between the US Civil War and the start of the 1930s, approximately 30% of the US portion of the Great Plains was converted to cropland, with much of the remaining grassland used for livestock grazing.").

dam to create a stock watering pond. These acts allowed Carpenter and his neighbor to acquire water rights in the spring and the creek that would survive them both, through the legal mechanisms that will be discussed in Chapter 7.

The next phase of Carpenter's evolution from an eastern transplant to a western rancher involved building up a true herd of cattle. Carpenter and his industrious neighbor, Jack White, began this phase in the summer of 1908, before Carpenter's final year at Princeton. Borrowing the money for the initial herd of bulls from Carpenter's father, Ferry and Jack established Carpenter and White with an initial herd of twenty-five purebred Hereford cattle.[44] Carpenter and White registered their cattle with the American Hereford Association in 1909, the same year that Ferry applied to and was accepted at Harvard Law School. By the time Carpenter returned to the homestead that summer, which by then he had named Oak Point, the mother cows had calved and the herd had grown. In Carpenter's estimation, they were "well launched" into their operation from that point forward.[45]

Much like what happened around Oak Point, as cattle herd sizes increased across the West, watering holes and springs were fenced off, open land was patented, and towns and infrastructure sprung up to support the new homesteads. In Hayden, a new school and hospital emerged in the decade following Carpenter's graduation from Harvard Law School, along with Carpenter's appointment as county attorney. As the occupants of this region changed and the practice of non-Indigenous ranching and farming increased, the grass itself began to change. In and around Hayden, for example, ranchers had planted fields of wheat and oats, spurred by the demands of the nation for grain crops during World War I.[46] Drawn by the new food source, so-called "Mormon crickets" migrated east to northern Colorado from Utah, and began tormenting the ranchers and their animals with their noise and predation. When Carpenter sought to help solve this problem, he and others appealed to the ranch scientists at the State Agricultural College, whose advice was to spray the crickets with arsenic and ground lime. When this failed, the ranchers brought in turkeys, who ate the crickets but soon got sick due to arsenic poisoning. As Carpenter noted at the time, "the crickets thwarted our every move."[47]

Another threat to Carpenter and the other cattlemen of the region emerged during this time too – sheep. This threat had been building since roughly 1910 and, in Carpenter's estimation, came to a head due to three compounding legal changes to the public domain in the West. First, as homesteaders settled on the

44 Carpenter at 50.
45 *Id.* at 52.
46 *Id.* at 119.
47 *Id.* at 121.

arable open land and privatized it, there was a shortage of available land for the common grazing usage of the ranching operations that up to that point had used adjacent public domain lands for free additional pasturage. In addition, in 1906, the first forest reserves were created in the northern Rocky Mountains of Colorado and elsewhere throughout the West, cutting those lands off from homesteaders and ranchers. The remaining land, which tended to be bottomland not near water sources (that land having already been settled decades before), was not "practical" to homestead until 1916 when Congress passed the Stock-Raising Homestead Act.[48] This statute incentivized dryland ranching by allowing homesteaders to perfect title to 640 acres of land, rather than the smaller 160- or 320-acre sections that could be patented under the earlier homestead laws, allocating more land, and thus, more grass and other forage to the willing homesteader. In exchange for such a large section of public domain, the homesteader did not receive fee simple absolute title, but rights to the surface estate only. Under this act, the federal government retained title to the mineral rights, creating what the law refers to as a "split estate," in which one entity owns the surface of a parcel of land and another entity owns the subsurface. The pressures imposed by the Stock-Raising Homestead Act further reduced the available open rangeland for ranchers, and, in particular, cattle companies that made their profits by running their herds mostly on public domain land.[49]

In the area around Hayden, sheepherders brought large flocks onto the remaining open rangeland from Utah, positioning their animals in direct competition with the cattle for the available forage. This upset the cattle ranchers for a few reasons, and not just because of the direct competition. They were irritated by the presence of sheep because as Carpenter described, "sheep grazed the scarce grass a little closer than cattle," and cattle were leery of herds of sheep, especially around water sources like springs and stock tanks.[50] Sheep, meanwhile, would stay in one place for longer and were not skittish around cattle. Thus, if a sheep herder brought a flock of sheep to drink at a well, the cattle would scatter, and the ranch hands and owners would have to go round them up, while the sheep stayed and drank the water. Given these tensions and the diminishing available forage, cattle ranchers took matters into their own hands and told the sheepmen to stay out. They staked out territory and claimed it their own, with no legal right to do so, but with a compelling financial reason and a healthy dose of gumption.

The sheepmen around Carpenter's homestead seemed to "obey" these commands, but as Carpenter noted in his autobiography, if they did not, "trouble

[48] 43 U.S.C. §§ 291–298, repealed by Pub. L. 94–579, title VII §702, 90 Stat. 2787 (Oct. 21, 1976).
[49] Carpenter at 129.
[50] *Id.*

followed."[51] At first, this took the form of attacks on herds, such as the one in which "five cowmen with clubs and knives killed 110 head of sheep" on a ranch west of Hayden in December 1911, but it was not uncommon for the "trouble" to escalate to threats against sheepherders, kidnappings, and even murder.[52] It did not help matters that federal prosecutors were often unwilling to prosecute these crimes, due to the large influence of cattle ranchers on juries, which only fueled the cattlemen's fire. Nor did the election of Warren G. Harding as President in 1920 help, given Harding's choice to head the General Land Office, which managed grazing on open range lands throughout the West. The man selected for the job was former Utah governor William Spry, who not only hailed from Utah, the land of the sheep, but was a sheepman himself.[53]

By 1932, Carpenter had established himself firmly on the cattlemen side of the range wars, helping his side secure legal and political victories at the expense of the sheepmen. He had also built the largest cattle company on the western slope of Colorado and started a family with his wife Eunice. That year, Carpenter took a trip to Washington, DC, to lobby on behalf of cattle ranchers in Congress, which was considering a bill proposing to make beef a commodity. This legal designation would help cattle ranchers who had found themselves nearly destitute as the Dust Bowl drought years struck and the markets all crashed. On that trip, Carpenter ran into Colorado congressman Edward Taylor, who had at that point been serving his district in Congress for over thirty years. Taylor mentioned to Carpenter, while allowing the latter free room and board in his office on the Hill, that he had been working on a bill for many years that would declare approximately eighty million acres of open public domain lands in ten western states grazing lands. When Carpenter expressed support for the bill, Taylor "marched [Carpenter] into the room where [Taylor's] grazing bill was being discussed" by the House Public Lands Committee at the urging of President Franklin D. Roosevelt's new Secretary of Interior, Harold Ickes.[54] Carpenter then found himself giving testimony in favor of the bill.

[51] *Id.* at 130.

[52] *Id.*

[53] *Id.* at 131; *see also* Adam M. Sowards, *Why Sheep Started So Many Wars in the American West*, ZÓCALO PUBLIC SQUARE (Oct. 5, 2017), www.zocalopublicsquare.org/2017/10/05/sheep-started-many-wars-american-west/ideas/essay/ ("Arizona's Pleasant Valley War through the 1880s and 1890s was one of the most famous … The Oregon Sheep Shooters Association in the 1890s organized ranchers to exclude sheep – and their herders – from the new federal forest reserves (now known as national forests) along the Cascade Mountains. Further east in that state, the Crook County Sheep Shooters told sheep herders to stay off land ranchers claimed, warning through local newspapers and in messages left on shepherds' cabins or tents: 'You are hereby notified to move this camp within 24 hours, or take the consequences.' The Sheep Shooters – 'men of high ideals as well as good shots by moonlight' – reported killing between 8,000 and 10,000 sheep in 1903 and burning down camps and corrals. Control of the range was tense, serious business.").

[54] Carpenter at 151.

This bill would be signed into law as the Taylor Grazing Act in 1934 and would transform the formerly free and open public lands used as "range" by ranchers in those ten western states. In Carpenter's estimation, it encompassed "most of the intermountain region between the Rockies on the East and the Sierra and Cascades on the West. With less than half the annual rainfall of the middle West, its agricultural use was sharply limited.... Sixty-four percent of this unclaimed land was fit only for livestock grazing."[55] It would also have impacts far beyond the intent of Taylor, Carpenter, and others who supported the bill, which was to organize grazing on the public domain and stop livestock owners from attacking and murdering one another over these lands. One of those transformative impacts was noted by Carpenter in his study of the Act: "[i]t was the first attempt by Congress to add 'grass' to the list of those natural resources that should be conserved and whose productivity should be improved."[56] The total acreage of grasslands "segregated"[57] for grazing use by the Taylor Grazing Act was 80 million acres.

Given Carpenter's education, his familiarity with ranching in one of these western states containing public grazing land, and his advocacy on behalf of the ranchers who had sought to protect their grazing interests in these lands through the Taylor Grazing Act, it was perhaps not a surprise that he was on the radar of the Department of Interior and the White House for a role as one of the early administrators of the Act. During a conversation with Congressman Taylor in his Washington, DC office, Carpenter noted that the statute's requirement for the Secretary of Interior "to cooperative with local associations of stockmen" to carry out the purposes of the Act seemed to call for the involvement of those local stockmen in the design of the framework the Department of Interior was charged with undertaking.[58] Further, Carpenter noted this as an opportunity for "local stockmen to help guide a federal grazing program in a practical way and not have all the important decisions made in Washington" by distant and disconnected career bureaucrats.[59] Of course, it did not escape Carpenter's or Taylor's attention that the term "stockmen" was an industry euphemism for cattle ranchers. And not surprisingly, much of the text of the Act protected the interests of stockmen.

Shortly after the meeting with Taylor, Carpenter interviewed with Secretary Harold Ickes for the position of Director of the Federal Grazing Service, the new agency charged with promulgating the inaugural regulations implementing the Taylor Grazing Act and carrying out Congress's mandate in the act to "organize" grazing on the public domain lands. Carpenter must have made a good

55 *Id.* at 153.
56 *Id.* at 154–55.
57 *Id.* at 155.
58 *Id.*
59 *Id.*

impression on Ickes because Ickes made him an offer the next day.[60] In his typically wry fashion, Carpenter later reflected that the modest perquisites of the new job were somewhat overwhelming to someone who had "never sought to be even a *little* bureaucrat in a small mountain town like Hayden," but now found himself "not only a bureaucrat but one with a capital B!"[61] And reality soon hit regarding the enormity of the task that he had been given. Upon asking for a map of the millions of acres that were now under his charge, Carpenter learned to his surprise that none existed. The General Land Office had surveyed the lands that became the public domain long ago, but had not documented the sales, nor the corresponding changes in land status, as they occurred. The only way to determine which lands fell under the framework established by the Taylor Grazing Act was to consult with the nineteen land offices scattered throughout the western states, which kept entries that were updated daily.

Carpenter got to work organizing these lands and the grazing use that was authorized by the Taylor Act. His first instinct was to use access to water as a "guiding principle" for the new regulations.[62] As he had learned at the little spring on his homestead, many western grazing lands were "useless to ranchers unless they had water on their property to keep livestock alive during those seasonal times when none was available on the arid grasslands."[63] He later sought the help of a seasoned Forest Service grazing supervisor, Edward M. Kavanaugh, and the former chief of wildlife and range management at the Department of Interior, Ernest Winkler. Practical life experience continued to guide his design process, though, rather than theoretical approaches. On a trip to Boston with his wife Eunice, Carpenter read on a plaque located on Boston Commons that he and other visitors were "standing on the corner of twenty-five acres" that early colonists had used to commonly graze their livestock (and train their militia), so he went to the Boston Public Library in search of the 1642 grazing regulations for the Commons. Surprisingly, the clerk returned with a copy of *Grazing Regulations on the Boston Commons* and in these Carpenter found more useful information for his federal regulations under the Taylor Act. First, seventeenth-century Boston area bureaucrats had charged a fee for commons grazing that was based on the animal type – "two shillings a week on a horse or a cow, but [] a sheep should be charged one fifth of that amount."[64] Members of the clergy were allowed to graze their "buggy horses" for free, and the regulations called this a "free use permit." It struck Carpenter that this framework bore certain similarities to what the Taylor Act had planned for the western United States, free-use

60 *Id.* at 157.
61 *Id.*
62 *Id.* at 158.
63 *Id.*
64 *Id.* at 160.

permits for ranchers to graze their livestock in the public domain, especially if their grazing needs were *de minimis*.[65]

As Carpenter's plans for implementing the Taylor Act unfolded, there were certain elements of the structure he designed that have stood the test of time, most critically, the order of precedence of grazing privileges allocated on the public range, which today is referred to as the grazing "preference." As will be discussed in Chapter 7, grazing preference became one of the most important terms that the grazing regulations would define, and this is as true today as it was in Carpenter's era. Another aspect of these regulations that emerged from Carpenter's early years as Director of the Grazing Service was the importance of base property, which is defined as the private land (or water rights) that supports public grazing. In Carpenter's estimation, base property was a prerequisite for obtaining grazing privileges under the new grazing regulations, and typically, the cattlemen had it, whereas the sheep ranchers did not. Making this a requirement to qualify to graze the public lands was a clever way to ensure that the cattlemen were given priority over the sheep ranchers in the initial allocation of grazing privileges, and because the Taylor Act prioritized historical use of the public domain in the calculus of who should continue to hold grazing privileges, this framework codified in near perpetuity the paramount rights of the cattlemen and their operations over sheepmen and theirs.

Finally, and critically, Carpenter's framework relied on the free labor of the ranchers who knew the lands within their grazing districts to administer the early regulations, although this reliance was born of necessity. When Congress first passed the Act, and Secretary Ickes gave Carpenter his initial charge of developing regulations that would implement the act, it was an unfunded legislative mandate. Carpenter had very little staff, there were no maps to work with, and he somehow had to figure out a way to develop a framework with which to allocate grazing privileges on eighty million acres of land. This left him with what seemed like "only one way to recruit an agency big enough to bring together intelligently and immediately the wisdom needed to write rules and regulations for the grazing districts" – the cattlemen and sheepmen who had "competed among themselves all their lives for use of the public lands and knew every acre of it."[66] This group also understood the critical importance of private land and water rights to the industry. In Carpenter's estimation, if he could create advisory boards for each district composed of local stockmen, their recommendations would "set the tone" for the administration of the Act, then and into the future. Further, the "prestige" of these boards would "attract the most knowledgeable and progressive stockmen."[67]

65 *Id.*
66 *Id.*
67 *Id.* at 162.

These three initial calculations, which were admittedly gambles, paid off for Carpenter in spades. Securing the free labor of the local stockmen to serve as advisory board members and incorporating their recommendations into the decision-making process endeared Carpenter to the stockmen, and vice versa. Allowing the stockmen to determine the allocation of grazing privileges also ensured that they could secure favorable permits and grazing privileges for themselves and their families, neighbors, and business partners, but in so doing, they quickly accomplished the goals of Congress and Secretary Ickes, which were to organize rapidly the eighty million acres subject to the Taylor Act's new regime.

The deficits in this framework did not materialize instantaneously, but they became quite clear by the later years of the twentieth century. The framework that Congress initiated and Carpenter implemented created what was essentially a monopoly for cattlemen, like him, who had grazed the public domain lands near their homesteads in the years leading up to and shortly after the Taylor Act was passed. The framework included sheep ranchers, but, in many ways, relegated them to a lower priority status, which has persisted in the century following the Act's passage and Carpenter's early work on the regulations. Moreover, the framework excluded those who could not or did not initially homestead, which meant that the recipients of the early permits were mostly white, European Americans. There was no accounting for treaty-protected lands of Tribes like the Ute, either, so there are no Indigenous use rights on federal public domain lands subject to Taylor Act permits, unlike in other countries that chose a different route, such as Australia and New Zealand.

In the chapters that follow, additional consequences of the Taylor Act framework that Congress and Ferry Carpenter created will become apparent, as will opportunities to reform this system in a way that allocates public lands for agricultural use more equitably and with a greater modicum of justice. In Carpenter's defense, also, it is not clear that he intended the system he designed in the late 1930s on a shoestring budget to last into perpetuity, rather he designed it with the intent that it could be quickly implemented to achieve one of the purposes of the Act, which was to restore the public domain from damage caused by half a century of overgrazing and unregulated use. To combat this, some organization was necessary, and the framework Carpenter created did indeed lend itself to more organized use of the public lands, even if that use was exclusive to a relatively insular club of cattle ranchers, and later, their descendants.

Somewhat ironically, Carpenter's legacy in Hayden now incorporates a form of environmentalism and conservation that is growing throughout the West, which is the ownership of a working ranch by a nonprofit conservation organization. In this case, for the Carpenter Ranch, the present owner is The Nature Conservancy. The organization manages this land and its buildings as a historically significant property and for dedicated conservation purposes. Carpenter's homestead, Oak Point, no longer hosts any grazing cattle. It has a small cabin, powered by solar panels on the roof, and draws drinking water from the spring. Sagebrush plants dot the hills surrounding the cabin and the occasional pronghorn antelope visits from across the border in Wyoming. The needs of wildlife will be explored in more detail in Chapter 6, using the story of a famous ranch in Wyoming.

6

Wildlife Conservation Laws and the Taylor Lawrence Ranch

Wantsi.[1]

In central Wyoming, there is an area known as the Red Rim, which encompasses parts of Carbon and Sweetwater Counties, in the heart of the Wyoming Rockies. The nearest town is Rawlins, which is home to the Wyoming State Penitentiary and proudly notes its elevation – 6,800 feet – on a sign welcoming visitors. The Red Rim is a large plateau of approximately 22,000 acres, which generally traces the southern border of the right-of-way granted to the Union Pacific Railroad in 1862 under the disposal statutes discussed in Chapters 3–5.[2] The entire region is at a significant elevation, but by the standards of the Rocky Mountains, this is a relatively low-lying oasis of riparian meadows and sprawling sagebrush uplands, interspersed with islands of shrubs and lush aspen groves.[3] The area is particularly important for large migratory wildlife species like deer, elk, and pronghorn antelope, a unique western ungulate species that could boast for decades about having a greater population than that of its human neighbors in Wyoming.[4] Pronghorn antelope migrate to the Red Rim to calve, rear their young, and build up enough fat reserves to sustain them through the winter. This is also a region where animals can return to feed in the winter because the high, windy ridges do not hold snow very well, leaving grasses and shrubs exposed and available to deer and antelope even during the coldest months.[5]

1 Antelope, in Shoshone. Shoshone Language Learning: Animals, with Elena Atkins, www.youtube.com/watch?v=omfYk2Nz_mM; *see also* Eastern Shoshone Working Dictionary (Jan. 2021), available at https://easternshoshone.org/wp-content/uploads/2021/01/eastern-shoshone-working-dictionary2.pdf.

2 *U.S. ex rel. Bergen v. Lawrence*, 620 F. Supp. 1414, 1415 (D. Wyo. 1985), aff'd, 848 F.2d 1502 (10th Cir. 1988).

3 The Wyldlife Fund, "Wildlife Friendly Fencing-Red Rim Grizzly WHMA" (last visited Mar. 31, 2024), https://thewyldlifefund.org/wildlife-friendly-fencing-red-rim-grizzly-whma/.

4 University of Wyoming, Virtual Exhibits, "More Pronghorn than People," www.uwyo.edu/ahc/eduoutreach/exhibits/pronghorn/5.html.

5 Leshy at 394.

The pronghorn antelope of Wyoming today are part of the Antilocaprinae subfamily of mammals that evolved at a time when being lightning fast and highly adaptable was a necessary survival strategy. Picture being an herbivore living on open grasslands with nowhere to shelter and hide from roaming lions, cheetahs, speedy hyenas, fast-running bears, and other dangerous predators, and the need for speed becomes quickly evident.[6] The Antilocaprinae's sprint pace is astonishingly fast, reaching up to fifty miles per hour, and herds can run, dodge, and turn in unison at speed, like earthbound swallows in a murmuration.[7] They cannot sustain their top speeds for more than a mile, but even their lower range is fast enough to outrun their predators for several miles.[8] After their ancient predators suffered an extinction event (which coincided with the arrival of a wave of human immigrants to North America), the sole surviving member of the antilocaprid subfamily, *Antilocapra Americana*, or pronghorn antelope, inherited the vast domain of North American grasslands of the Rocky Mountain region.[9] This uniquely adapted ungulate thrived until European and European American immigrants with plows and rifles appeared in the nineteenth century, and the pronghorn story since then has been one of range reduction, decline, and endless struggle to survive.

Part of this struggle is attributed to an ever-diminishing food supply. Pronghorn spend most of their time continually feeding on a wide variety of forbs, grasses, and shrubs. They carefully select specific plants or parts of plants such as leaves, flowers, and fruits, and their four-chambered stomachs contain microbes that work continuously to digest their food. Like cattle, pronghorn regurgitate and rechew their partially digested food to further break down the ingested plants into smaller fragments, before swallowing each mouthful again, maximizing the absorption of nutrients. Pronghorn adjust their foraging seasonally, moving between grassland and shrub steppe habitats to select the most desirable, easily digestible plants or plant parts available at that time of year. They choose grasses in spring, when they have a higher digestibility and protein content, and switch to forbs in the summer. In winter, they select shrubs due to their relatively high protein content during that season. This pursuit of the proper balance of protein and other nutrients is what drives the pronghorn to migrate, moving to lower elevations and windswept areas during winter where their food supply is either exposed, or they can dig beneath the snow with their front hooves to reach their food sources.[10]

6 P. J. White, *et al.*, Yellowstone Pronghorn: Recovering from the Brink of Extirpation, p. 11, www.nps.gov/yell/learn/nature/upload/download_YELLOWSTONE-PRONGHORN-BOOK .pdf.

7 *Id.* at 11.

8 *Id.* at 16.

9 *Id.* at 11.

10 *Id.* at 18.

Currently, there are about 790,000 pronghorn in Wyoming, Montana, and Idaho.[11] The most significant threat to the species as a whole is habitat loss, and the obstruction of migration corridors between seasonal feeding and calving areas. Development, mineral extraction, and climate change have presented further obstacles to pronghorn survival, with the latter compounding several impacts associated with the former. For instance, warming temperatures affect precipitation and snowmelt patterns and the frequencies and intensities of droughts and wildfires, and cause invasive annual plants to dominate native vegetation communities, in turn negatively affecting productivity and water, energy, and nutrient cycles.[12]

Pronghorn were themselves an essential food source for Indigenous Peoples who encountered them throughout their seasonal migration routes and feeding grounds.[13] Indigenous hunters herded the animals into planned ambushes, jumps, or traps and culled herds with arrows, clubs, spears, or guns. Some hunted pronghorn on horseback, and many used fire to influence the movements of game, the success of a hunt, and to regenerate habitat for hunted species like pronghorn and bison.[14] Indigenous Peoples dried meat and mixed it with berries and fat to create protein and fat-rich snacks that lasted for many months, sustaining them during their travels from their higher elevation summer hunting grounds to lower lying temperate winter homelands, and used other parts of the animal to make clothing, thread, bladder containers, glue, and bone tools.[15]

One plant that benefitted from the precontact fires set by the Shoshone and other Tribal Nations who occupied the region that became Wyoming was blowout beardtongue, or blowout penstemon, a member of the snapdragon family.[16] A small, somewhat delicate perennial herb that produces a distinct purple and white flower, blowout beardtongue can survive grazing by wildlife like pronghorn, surface soil disturbance, fire, and other stressors.[17] *Penstemon haydenii* are tiny plants found nowhere else in the world aside from the sandy dune-covered regions of Nebraska and southern Wyoming, and within those areas, only in distinct features called blowouts.[18] Blowouts are the open areas near the top of sand dunes, created by wind. As the winds blow sand from the tops of the dunes, the force creates what is essentially a vacant space on the dune, devoid of most other plant life that cannot tolerate the constantly shifting conditions.[19]

11 *Id.* at 22.

12 *Id.*

13 *Id.* at 26–27 (citing Norris 1881a, Nabokov and Loendorf 2004, O'Gara et al. 2004, Confederated Salish and Kootenai Tribes 2005, Historical Research Associates 2006a,b; Kuhnlein and Humphries 2017).

14 P. J. White, *et al.*, pp. 26–27.

15 *Id.*

16 50 C.F.R. pt. 17, p. 15929, Endangered and Threatened Wildlife and Plants; Proposal to Determine *Penstemon haydenii* to be an Endangered Species (Apr. 29, 1986).

17 www.fs.usda.gov/wildflowers/Rare_Plants/profiles/TEP/penstemon_haydenii/index.shtml.

18 www.fs.usda.gov/wildflowers/features/panels/NebraskaNFGsBlowoutPenstemonPanel.pdf.

19 *Id.*

The blowouts tend to be the windiest and driest parts of the dunes, but they provide the perfect conditions for the beardtongue, which thrives due to the lack of competition for moisture and nutrients. In fact, the blowing sand scarifies the seeds, causing them to germinate, and otherwise stimulates plant growth.[20]

Historically, fire was an important element of the penstemon's habitat, whether caused by lightning or deliberately set by Indigenous Peoples, and fires burned large areas of the plants' habitat, leaving vast open and exposed areas.[21] The fire-exposed areas created perfect conditions in which blowouts could appear. Because *Penstemon haydenii* seeks windy, sandy barrens devoid of other vegetation, and declines when other vegetation is established, active blowout cycles are essential to its survival.[22] It can take as many as ten years for these cycles to culminate in a full scale and active blowout, capable of hosting a healthy population of *Penstemon haydenii*.[23] The blowout process is started when sand is moved by wind from the slope facing directly into the wind to the side that is insulated from the direct brunt of the wind's force, and this process continues until eventually the roots of any vegetation are exposed and finally ripped out.[24] After a ten-year cycle of seasonal winds, the movement of the sand and wind creates a crater. This crater is the blowout. As a pioneer species, *Penstemon haydenii* establishes itself within the blowout, usually near the leeward side of the dune, after the sand has stabilized, but it declines once vegetation (prairie grasses and forbs) establishes and the blowout begins to cover over with other types of vegetation and more permanent soils.[25]

Blowout beardtongue is adapted to a very specific ecosystem, and historically this ecosystem involved healthy fire cycles, whether caused by lightning or set regularly and seasonally by Indigenous Peoples.[26] The fires that Indigenous Peoples set were designed to stimulate plant and tree growth, but also because traditional stewards knew that fresh greenery would attract game species that provided an important supply of food and materials, such as bison.[27] Precontact, the cycles of prairie grassland regions, and particularly those related to wind and fire, allowed blowout beardtongue to thrive in its relatively specific habitat of the regions that became western Nebraska and south-central Wyoming.

[20] *Id.*

[21] Carol A. Caha, Donald J. Lee, & James Stubbendieck, *Organellar Genetic Diversity in Penstemon haydenii (Scrophulariaceae): An Endangered Plant Species*, 85 AM. J. BOT. (12): 1704–709, (1997). https://explorer.natureserve.org/Taxon/ELEMENT_GLOBAL.2.135060/Penstemon_haydenii.

[22] *Id.*

[23] U.S. Fish and Wildlife Service (USFWS). 2022. Blowout penstemon (*Penstemon haydenii*) 5-Year Status Review. U.S. Fish and Wildlife Service, Grand Island, Nebraska. 7 pp.

[24] *Id.*

[25] *Id.*

[26] Jason Baldes, Native Memory Project, "Native Fire Management" (last accessed Oct. 16, 2024), https://nativememoryproject.org/voice/native-fire-management/.

[27] *Id.*

This all changed post contact, most notably with the removal of natural fire cycles and the introduction of intensive, European-style agricultural practices. In fact, circumstances changed so much that by the 1950s, the plant was thought to be extinct. In the 1970s, isolated patches located primarily on lands managed by the US Fish and Wildlife Service were identified, but their size and relative security rendered the plants prime candidates for listing under the Endangered Species Act, whose passage in 1973 coincided with the time period of the beardtongue's "rediscovery."[28] In the listing documents, the US Fish and Wildlife Service identified "stabilization" of the sand dunes habitat as a "range management practice" to be one of the most critical threats to the species' survival rates.[29] In other words, "range management" had to change, and by this, the agency meant the use of federal lands that are penstemon habitat by domestic cattle, horses, and other species of "stock." In plain English, the US Fish and Wildlife Service informed the public as early as 1986 in the listing documents for the blowout penstemon that the transformation of this species' sand dune habitat into pastureland for domestic livestock contributed directly to the plant's near-demise.

In the ensuing three decades since the penstemon's listing, US Fish and Wildlife has not made significant strides in recovering the species.[30] In fact, it is not clear from the agency's own records that it has been able to make any progress at all. Compounding these efforts to protect the plants and their habitat are the lack of penstemon and antelope-friendly Indigenous land management techniques, including the use of fire, which was ultimately stopped altogether in areas outside reservation boundaries. The Red Rim area, like so many other regions of the West, was opened for homesteading and other forms of disposal, and the checkerboard land tenure pattern resulted. By the 1980s, this area was heavily influenced by ranching, including on public lands, and blowouts had almost entirely disappeared because of land management practices designed to flatten or remove them, along with the removal of fire as a management technique, and the suppression of naturally occurring fires.[31]

The Grizzly and Daley Ranch is located in the heart of antelope country and partially on the Red Rim plateau.[32] Shortly after closing on the property in 1975,

[28] 50 C.F.R. pt. 17, p. 15930.

[29] *Id.*

[30] As of 2023, blowout penstemon is listed as endangered, which signifies that the plant is in danger of becoming extinct throughout all or a part of its historical range. U.S. Fish & Wildlife Serv., Environmental Conservation Online System, "Blowout Penstemon" (last visited Oct. 16, 2023), https://ecos.fws.gov/ecp/species/6172#:~:text=Blowout%20penstemon%20is%20a%20short%2Dlived%20perennial%20plant%2C%20native%20to,in%20the%20Sandhills%20of%20Nebraska.

[31] Endangered and Threatened Wildlife and Plants; Final Rule to Determine *Penstemon haydenii* (Blowout Penstemon) to be an Endangered Species, 52 Fed. Reg. 32926–01 (Sept. 1, 1987). Oddly, Ted Turner is one rancher who is trying to reverse this tide, using bison to re-establish blowouts on one of his Nebraska ranches. http://digital.outdoornebraska.gov/nebraskaland-magazine/restoring-the-blowout-penstemon.

[32] *U.S. ex rel. Bergen v. Lawrence*, 848 F.2d 1502, 1504 (10th Cir. 1988).

the ranch's owner at that time, Taylor Lawrence, constructed a twenty-eight-mile fence around the exterior boundary of the ranch. The fence enclosed over twenty-thousand acres of checkerboarded private, state, and federal lands, and for this action, Lawrence would become famous (or notorious, depending on one's perspective) in the annals of natural resources and public lands law.[33]

To more fully understand the circumstances of the Lawrence Ranch, it is helpful to revisit the disposal era, and in this case, the checkerboarding of land caused by the federal government's land grants to the Union Pacific Railroad in Wyoming and other western states during the late nineteenth century.[34] To incentivize the building of railroad tracks that would link the coasts and facilitate homesteading, Congress authorized the Executive Branch to give land to railroads, in a path that would approximate the course of the track and including a significant buffer zone on either side. In the case of the Union Pacific land grants, the buffer zone was twenty miles wide, measured from the center of the track line. The purpose of the buffer was to allocate additional land (beyond what was needed for the railroad tracks themselves) that the railroad could sell or lease to generate revenue to continue building the tracks. However, this gift came with strings attached. Within the buffer, Congress authorized the disposal of alternating sections only, resulting in a legal checkerboard pattern of federal and private land, whether owned by the railroad or a subsequent purchaser.

If checkerboarded federal lands were never sold or exchanged, the quilt-like land tenure pattern could remain in perpetuity, and that is what happened to the lands that became the Lawrence Ranch. The surveyed acreage of the ranch included alternating sections of private land, interspersed with sections of public lands managed by the Bureau of Land Management (BLM). The easiest (and least expensive) way for Lawrence to enclose his property was to build a fence around the outer perimeter of all the sections, enclosing the entire checkerboard. And this is what he did, constructing a five-foot tall, twenty-eight-mile long, woven wire fence in the summer of 1983, sealing off the public *and* private sections, and effectively doubling the size of his ranch.[35] But the reason for Lawrence's fence was different from other fences discussed in earlier chapters, like the one at Cielo Vista in New Mexico. Lawrence's goal was not to exclude human beings, it was to keep out pronghorn antelope, who competed with his livestock for precious forage available year-round on the Red Rim.[36] From Lawrence's perspective,

33 Michael J. Finn, *Storm over Red Rim: Private Property Rights Collide with the Unlawful Inclosures Act*, 21 Land & Water Law Rev. 1, 57–68, (1986) https://scholarship.law.uwyo.edu/land_water/vol21/iss1/5.

34 Leshy, at 394.

35 *Id.*

36 Cally Carswell, *Stitching Habitat Together across Public and Private Lands*, High Country News (Dec. 26, 2011), www.hcn.org/issues/43.22/stitching-habitat-together-across-public-and-private-lands.

fencing off the entire checkerboarded area, including his private fee lands, made further sense because the public lands within his fence were authorized for his grazing use under the Taylor Grazing Act and the regulations developed by Ferry Carpenter in the 1930s, which were incorporated into BLM's land management plan for this area. Under the Taylor Grazing Act's legal framework, Lawrence held the permits and the priority rights for these allotments.[37] Also, he had planted the forage – crested wheatgrass – himself.[38]

Fencing associated with cattle and other domestic livestock has a troubled history in this region. Ranchers brought livestock to the area as early as 1867, and ranches began springing up everywhere in pronghorn habitat and migration areas.[39] Initially, the industry was unregulated, and there were no restrictions on numbers, seasonal use, or type of livestock, which within a few short decades led to habitat degradation from overgrazing and soil erosion, as well as competition for forage between livestock and pronghorn.[40] The late nineteenth-century cattle boom and the decimation of open-range grasses prompted ranchers and cattle companies to buy land and build fences equipped with a new invention called "barbed wire."[41] The boom was precipitated by the 1879 completion of the transcontinental railroad, which led to an influx of livestock and additional pressures on remaining wildlife. By the mid 1880s, there were thirty-five to forty million cattle in western states and about ten million sheep in Montana and Wyoming alone.[42]

Before barbed wire existed, fencing in the West consisted of split-rail structures made of wood, or piles and rows of rock, which had been used in the Eastern states where rocks were abundant and simultaneously needed to be cleared from fields before they could be tilled or grazed. However, these methods were costly and split-rail fences required considerable upkeep, so beginning in 1868, after inventors secured patents for barbed wire, ranchers had a cheaper, relatively easy, new and expedient mechanism to fence the land.[43] Its subsequent widespread use "changed life … dramatically and permanently" in the West, as cattlemen began to buy land and build fences "to protect their investments." The dramatic and sudden increase in fenced land, combined with the still-overstocked and depleted landscape, and a bad winter in 1886–87, caused

37 *Lawrence*, 620 F. Supp. at 1415–16.
38 Dan Neal, "Free at Last," National Wildlife Federation (Feb. 1, 1992), www.nwf.org/Magazines/National-Wildlife/1992/Free-at-Last.
39 P. J. White, *et al.* at 29.
40 *Id.*
41 Colin Reynolds, *Protecting the Sublette Antelope Migration: An Analysis of the Evolution of the Legal Tools Employed to Protect the Sublette Antelope Herd from Fencing Obstructions*, 26 Lewis & Clark L. Rev. 613, 628. (2022).
42 P. J. White, *et al.*, at 29.
43 Reynolds, 26 Lewis & Clark L. Rev. at 628.

dramatic losses in livestock, estimated at over 50 percent of open-range herds.[44] Many of the deaths were gruesome – with cattle dying "piled up against … fences," unable to access more plentiful grazing lands.[45] The financial losses to these operations were staggering, estimated to be more than $20 million in Wyoming alone, causing many of the largest operations to fail entirely.

The operators that remained in business continued to fence their private lands, though, and the amount of barbed wire grew. Even for the smaller scale operators, barbed-wire fencing had tremendous benefits. It was affordable and protected livestock's access to critical forage and water. However, the fencing schemes began severely impacting wildlife, often ensnaring and killing animals as they attempted to migrate to and from seasonal habitat areas during the spring and fall.[46] By the twentieth century, ranchers and regulators alike recognized that overgrazing by cattle was decimating native grasses, and that fact, combined with the fencing schemes ranchers were using to protect the food supply for their cattle, was causing a severe decline in wildlife species like pronghorn. The early twentieth-century solution to this problem was to plant grasses that both species would eat, which may have seemed like a good solution at the time but would have disastrous consequences decades down the road.

For instance, in the Gardiner basin of southern Montana and northern Wyoming between 1904 and 1950, roughly 530 acres (215 hectares) were cleared of native vegetation and planted with non-native grasses such as oats (*Avena sativa*), smooth brome (*Bromus inermis*), clover (*Trifolium repens*), timothy (*Phleum pratense*) and crested wheatgrass (*Agropyron cristatum*).[47] Warming seasonal temperatures and high nitrogen deposited in feces and urine from pronghorn and other ungulates allowed winter annuals (including annual wheatgrass *Eremopyrum triticeum*, cheatgrass *Bromus tectorum*, and desert alyssum *desertorum*) to spread during the second half of the twentieth century, replacing crested wheatgrass and filling in the spaces between native bunchgrasses. After the introduction of these prolific and adaptable non-native annual species, it was climate change, rather than grazing, that shaped these annual grass communities.[48] By the 1980s, cheatgrass and other winter annuals often outcompeted native plants by germinating in autumn and growing earlier and more rapidly in the spring.[49]

As winter began in 1983, the Baggs pronghorn herd started moving through the Red Rim area, as was their annual custom, but that year, they ran into Lawrence's fence, which was blocking their migration route entirely. Pronghorn antelope are formidable jumpers, but they do not jump when presented with a fence, preferring

44 *Id.*
45 *Id.* at 628–29.
46 Reynolds, 26 Lewis & Clark L. Rev. at 630.
47 P. J. White, *et al.*, pp. 45–46.
48 *Id.* at 29 (citing Cahalane 1944, Whittlesey 1995, Geremia and Hamilton 2019, White et al. 2021).
49 P. J. White at 71.

to crawl or duck underneath it. However, they will only duck under a fençe if the bottom wire is smooth (not barbed), sixteen or more inches (forty-one centimeters) above ground, and not blocked by dirt, snow, debris, or vegetation.[50] Unable to jump over or duck under Lawrence's fence, and with no other accessible winter feeding grounds, the 1,600 animals of the Baggs herd milled around, waiting.[51] Their plight made national news, and reporters from both coasts covered the story as the pronghorn shivered in the cold and slowly began starving.[52] Video footage of their frozen carcasses lying piled up against the fence was released to a shocked public, and the BLM intervened, ordering Lawrence to create an opening in the fence under which the antelope could pass, allowing them access to their winter habitat. By the time Lawrence relented in December, approximately 700 animals had died.[53]

The BLM sued Lawrence in federal court, claiming that his fence violated a federal statute, the the Unlawful Inclosures Act, and rules of law established in earlier disputes of this nature, which had been resolved in the government's favor by the US Supreme Court.[54] The Unlawful Inclosures Act, passed in 1885, prohibited "enclosures of any public lands" by "any person, party, association, or corporation" lacking any claim or color of title and prohibited enclosures based on false claims, color of title, or asserted rights.[55] In an 1897 opinion applying the Unlawful Inclosures Act to circumstances identical to Lawrence's, in which a property owner who had purchased checkerboarded railroad land grant parcels fenced the exterior boundary of the private land (also enclosing the embedded public sections), the Supreme Court ruled in favor of the federal government and against the landowner, finding that the fence violated the Unlawful Inclosures Act.[56]

The property owner's sole defense in the 1897 case, *Camfield v. United States*, was that the statute was unconstitutional because it applied to fences that were constructed entirely on private property. Evaluating the merits of this defense, the Supreme Court explored the nature of property rights, public and private alike. Acknowledging that the Constitution protected the rights of private property owners, the Court noted that private property rights are not absolute, and that one cannot generally do with one's property whatever one wants, if doing so would interfere with

[50] *Id.*

[51] *Lawrence*, 620 F. Supp. at 1415.

[52] Cass Peterson, *Rancher's Private Fence Deprives Antelope Herd of Winter Food, Shelter*, THE WASHINGTON POST (Dec. 9, 1983). www.washingtonpost.com/archive/politics/1983/12/09/ranchers-private-fence-deprives-antelope-herd-of-winter-food-shelter/6f0d00fa-015d-4112-8353-1e7f673e3383/; *Gaps to be Made in Fence so Antelope Can Eat*, THE NEW YORK TIMES (Dec. 12, 1983), www.nytimes.com/1983/12/12/us/gaps-to-be-made-in-fence-in-wyoming-so-antelope-can-eat.html.

[53] Carswell.

[54] 43 U.S.C. §§ 1061, 1063; *Camfield v. United States*, 167 U.S. 518, 522 (1897).

[55] 43 U.S.C. §§ 1061.

[56] *Camfield*, 167 U.S. at 522.

the property rights of a neighboring owner. In this case, the neighboring owner was the United States, which also held property rights, some of which were unique given its sovereign status under the Constitution. The nature of these federal ownership rights included "the right of an ordinary proprietor to maintain its possession and to prosecute trespassers."[57] In this role, the United States could freely hold, use, or alienate its property, just like other property owners, and it could also defend its property against trespassers. There was no need for special legislation to protect the right. In addition, the United States held governmental rights with respect to checkerboarded lands, such as those at issue in *Camfield*, and later, in the Taylor Lawrence case. These rights are, in the Court's words, "analogous to the police power of the several states," and the "extent to which [the government] may go in the exercise of such power is measured by the exigencies of the particular case."[58] Applying this authority to Camfield's challenge to the constitutionality of the Unlawful Inclosures Act, the Court held that it was well within Congress's authority to forbid enclosures of public lands, especially in the context of checkerboarded lands, where doing so is much easier than it would be in other areas lacking this land tenure pattern.

Like Camfield before him, Lawrence tried to defend his fence by arguing that he was within his legal rights because the fence was constructed only on his own land, crossing over the checkerboard squares only at the corners of some squares. BLM standards for these "corner-crossing" barriers at that time required fences to provide a gap of at least sixteen inches at the base, using a bottom strand of smooth wire to enable antelope to crawl underneath.[59] In addition, BLM required the top wire to be no more than thirty-eight inches above the ground, to allow antelope a chance to jump the fence when snow drifts block passage underneath.[60] Lawrence's fence, as he readily admitted before the trial court, was "made of woven wire with no gap at the bottom, and [was] topped off with barbed wire at a height of five feet, making it [totally] antelope-proof."[61]

In *Camfield*, the Supreme Court held that while the defendant's fencing scheme was "an ingenious one," it was "too clearly" an invasion of the public rights to access federal public lands protected by the Unlawful Inclosures Act.[62] Therefore, "[c]onsidering the obvious purposes of this structure, and the necessities of preventing the enclosure of public lands, we think the fence is clearly a nuisance, and that it is within the constitutional power of Congress to order its abatement, notwithstanding such action may involve an entry upon the lands of a private individual."[63]

57 *Id.* at 524.
58 *Id.* at 525.
59 *Lawrence*, 620 F. Supp. at 1416.
60 *Id.*
61 *Id.*
62 *Camfield*, 620 F. Supp. at 525 (quoting 43 U.S.C. § 1063).
63 *Id.*

The question remained after *Camfield*, though, whether the public right of access secured in *Camfield* extended to wildlife, like the antelope stuck at Lawrence's fence, or whether it inured solely to the benefit of human beings. Searching for an answer in then existing federal law, the trial court in Lawrence's case found helpful language in the recently passed Federal Lands Policy and Management Act (FLPMA) which contained the following purpose statement: "the public lands [shall] be managed in a manner … that will provide food and habitat for fish and wildlife and domestic animals."[64] Combining this wildlife preservation goal of FLPMA with the still-valid provisions of the Unlawful Inclosures Act, the trial court concluded that Lawrence could not "maintain a fence which encloses public lands and prevents the lawful purpose of antelope access to their winter feeding range" and found that "[t]he fence clearly constitutes a serious nuisance which must be abated in order to avoid disastrous consequences to the antelope which use Red Rim as winter range."[65] In other words, Lawrence's fencing system violated federal law by unlawfully enclosing public lands and preventing wildlife from accessing them.

On appeal, Lawrence argued that the district court's ruling requiring him to remove the fence was an unlawful taking of his private property, essentially establishing an easement for the antelope to use his private land, which the Tenth Circuit summarily dismissed. The appeals court held that "the district court's decision did not impose a servitude for antelope, but rather, abated a nuisance proscribed by federal law."[66] Moreover, the appeals court affirmed the lower court's opinion in its entirety, which established its holding as a rule of law governing checkerboarded areas of alternating federal, state, and private lands.[67] Quoting the Supreme Court's earlier opinion in *Camfield*, the Tenth Circuit explained that,

> [t]he general Government doubtless has a power over its own property analogous to the police power of the several States, and the extent to which it may go in the exercise of such power is measured by the exigencies of the particular case. If it be found to be necessary for the protection of the public, or of intending settlers, to forbid all enclosures of public lands, the Government may do so, though the alternate sections of private lands are thereby rendered less available for pasturage.[68]

By extension, the federal government's power to forbid enclosures of public land that rendered them less available for wildlife was an equally valid exigency demanding the permanent removal of Lawrence's fence and sent a direct and

64 43 U.S.C. § 1701(a)(8).
65 *Lawrence*, 620 F. Supp. at 1420.
66 *U.S. ex rel. Bergen v. Lawrence*, 848 F.2d 1502, 1507 (10th Cir. 1988).
67 *Id.* at 1505.
68 *Id.* at 1507.

powerful message to other ranchers and private landowners who might be thinking of following suit.

Lawrence had also argued on appeal that the Unlawful Inclosures Act was limited to a prohibition of excluding human beings and did not extend to wildlife. Lawrence cited the legislative history of the Act, which was silent as to wildlife, arguing that this indicated congressional intent not to apply the enacted law to wildlife.[69] The appeals court dismissed this argument out of hand, though, holding that "[b]ecause the language of the statute is clear," there was no option of interpreting it other than according to the plain text. Moreover, the court noted precedent to enforce access for livestock, and concluded that Lawrence's argument flew in the face of this as well.[70] Applying this construction of the Act, the appeals court in *Taylor v. Lawrence* concluded that access to winter forage for wildlife was a lawful purpose of federal lands, and in fact, FLPMA required federal land managers to ensure that the public lands are managed in a way that "will provide food and habitat for fish and wildlife and domestic animals."[71] This legal mandate was a separate source of support for the conclusion that antelope access to winter feeding grounds was a lawful use of the federal lands within Lawrence's fence, thereby satisfying the precedent interpreting the Unlawful Inclosures Act in previous cases, but also reminded Lawrence (and everyone else) that federal authority to require Lawrence to remove the fence was even more powerful in the 1980s than it had been during Camfield's era.

The holding in Lawrence inspired a glimmer of hope for migratory antelope herds and the grasses upon which they feed, removing one of the many barriers facing both during the mid twentieth century. It also solidified the relationship between the newly enacted FLPMA and the previous precedent interpreting the federal government's power over federal public lands expansively. Yet, this authority would be continually challenged in the years to come, in Wyoming and other western states, where antipathy directed at the federal government was and is a popular public sentiment and political platform. Moreover, despite the Tenth Circuit's ruling, and a subsequent ruling by the court reaching the same conclusion, Lawrence did not take down his fence. For nearly ten years, the antelope herd continually ran up against it during winter migration to the Red Rim area, not knowing whether Lawrence would open a gate and allow them

69 *Id.* at 1509.

70 8 F.2d at 1509 (10th Cir. 1988) (citing *Mackay v. Uinta Development Co.*, 219 F. 116 (8th Cir.1914) (holding that livestock may not be denied access to federal lands in the Union Pacific checkerboard). In an earlier case, the Eighth Circuit Court of Appeals had concluded that the UIA "was intended to prevent the obstruction of free passage or transit for any and all lawful purposes over public lands." *Stoddard v. United States*, 214 F. 566, 568–69 (8th Cir.1914).

71 Federal Land Policy and Management Act, 43 U.S.C. § 1701(a)(8).

through, or whether it would be closed, and they would yet again face starvation and death.[72]

In 1992, the State of Wyoming bought the ranch and removed the fence, saving the herd's access through the area. Today it is managed as the Red Rim-Daley Wildlife Habitat Management Area, serving as a summer habitat for up to 200 pronghorns and a winter habitat for as many as 2,400. The area is still checkerboarded, with alternating squares of BLM-managed federal land and State-managed lands (formerly Lawrence's private lands). The BLM today manages the "range" in this area by mowing, or masticating, sagebrush and other plants, ostensibly to stimulate plant growth and thereby increase the available forage for wildlife like antelope.[73] Within the former ranchlands, the BLM and Wyoming Game and Fish Department have developed a comprehensive management regime that allows the pronghorn to migrate; however, once they leave the safety of the preserve, they encounter a checkerboard. After the Tenth Circuit's holding in the *Lawrence* case, it is impermissible for private landowners to fence the public checkerboarded lands or block the corner crossings between sections of public land, although security of passage remains an open question given that BLM often lacks adequate personnel to patrol the entirety of its landholdings along the pronghorn migration route.

Pronghorn face similar migration challenges across the State of Wyoming. The Sublette herd, which makes the longest annual migration between its winter feeding grounds in the Red Desert near Rock Springs, Wyoming, and its summer feeding grounds near the famous resort town of Jackson Hole, has been decimated in recent years by tough winters and disease. In 2022, the herd was reduced by nearly half, from 43,000 animals to 24,000, in what biologists referred to as a population "crash."[74] The herd must cross over private and public lands during its annual migration, including public lands managed by the State and the federal government. According to a recent study by the State of Wyoming Fish and Game Department, the Sublette herd faces over 19,445 "bottlenecks" along its migration corridor, where access is not dependable and external forces like heavy snowfall and colder than average temperatures can have devastating impacts.[75]

[72] Dan Neal, "Free at Last," National Wildlife Federation (Feb. 1, 1992), www.nwf.org/Magazines/National-Wildlife/1992/Free-at-Last.

[73] Wyoming Dept. of Fish & Game, Red Rim Grizzly Wildlife Management Area, https://wgfd.wyo.gov/Public-Access/WHMA/WHMA/Red-Rim-Grizzly?utm_source=Facebook&utm_medium=Social&utm_campaign=WHMA&utm_content=WHMA_PUB_111521.

[74] Kylie Mohr, *The "Unprecedented" Decline of a Wyoming Pronghorn Herd*, THE MOUNTAIN JOURNAL (Dec. 15, 2023), at https://mountainjournal.org/the-unprecedented-deline-of-wyoming-pronghorn-herd#:~:text=In%202022%2C%20population%20estimates%20placed,research%20purposes%2C%2075%20percent%20perished.

[75] Wyoming Game and Fish Department Migration Corridor Threat Evaluation Draft Worksheet: Sublette Pronghorn (Sept. 8, 2023), https://wgfd.wyo.gov/getattachment/Get-Involved/Sublette-Antelope-Migration-Corridor/ThreatEvaluation_SublettePronghorn_Final-Draft.pdf?lang=en-US.

The legal regime applicable to wildlife on federal, state, and private land complicates matters for biologists trying to save pronghorn migration corridors, as well. If wildlife species are not under threat of extinction, there is little that can be done to regulate how private landowners interact with them on private land. Wildlife passing onto private lands essentially convert from public property to private property once they cross the property line, and they can be shot, trapped, or confined, so long as the confinement does not interfere with public land management in the framework tested by Taylor Lawrence.[76] If they make it off of the private land alive, wildlife crossing onto federal public land may be protected to varying degrees, depending on the category of public land they wander onto. If they are lucky enough to wander into a national park, like some members of the Sublette herd do every year, they are protected from hunting and face minimal barriers like roads and fences. Similarly, if they wander onto a national wildlife refuge, they will likely receive a greater degree of protection from threats like fences and roads, although if they are not the species for which the refuge was established, they will not automatically receive as much attention, or protection, as the species that was identified for special protection.

If wildlife like pronghorns wander onto multiple-use public land, such as that managed by the BLM or the United States Forest Service, they are one of the "resources" that these federal agencies must "manage," but "manage" in the parlance of federal natural resources law does not equate to "protect."[77] These agencies must also "manage" timber harvests, oil and gas development, and other resources and uses on multiple-use federal lands that often interfere with, rather than facilitate, wildlife protection. Moreover, despite the promise that the *Lawrence* opinion held for pronghorn migration onto federal public land, FLPMA is by no means a wildlife protection statute. As the Tenth Circuit held in that case, wildlife management is a lawful purpose for which federal lands are managed and in the case of the *Lawrence* fence, when the BLM decides to exercise its discretion to protect wildlife in specific ways, its authority will be respected by a federal court.

Discretionary authority to protect wildlife migration is different than mandatory authority, though. Nowhere in FLPMA, the BLM's organic statute, nor the Multiple-Use Sustained-Yield Act (MUSYA), which applies to the Forest Service, does Congress require these agencies to protect migration corridors for wildlife species like pronghorn. In fact, both statutes contain language that could directly undermine that purpose. In FLPMA, for instance, Congress made a rather large concession to what western states viewed as their constitutional right to manage wildlife, *even on federal lands*. This proviso firmly establishes that nothing

[76] James Rasband, et al., Natural Resources Law and Policy, p. 384 (West Academic Press, 3rd ed. 2016).

[77] Coggins, Federal Public Land and Resources Law, p. 815 (Foundation Press 2014) (citing Multiple-Use Sustained-Yield Act, 16 U.S.C. §§ 528–529).

in FLPMA "shall be construed" as authorizing the Secretaries of Interior or Agriculture to "enlarge[e] or diminish[] the responsibility and authority of the States for management of fish and resident wildlife."[78] Although the legislative history of the statute demonstrates that this authority of the States had been traditionally limited to issuing hunting tags and fishing licenses, western Senators and Congressmen created a legislative record noting that States play a key role in managing wildlife on federal lands. Thus, even after FLPMA, and after the *Lawrence* opinion, it was legally possible for States like Wyoming to issue hunting licenses for species like pronghorn, authorizing hunting on federal and state land alike.

This federalism structure of FLPMA was immediately challenged in a case that arose from the State of Alaska's "wolf kill" program, under which the Alaska Department of Fish and Game announced a program "whose aim was to kill from aircraft 170 wolves (approximately 60 percent of the wolf population) in an area of 35,000 square miles," including federal lands managed by the Department of Interior's Bureau of Land Management.[79] The Natural Resources Defense Council, a prominent environmental and conservation organization, petitioned the BLM to prepare an environmental impact statement under the National Environmental Policy Act, which would have required the Department to take a "hard look" at this proposed action, including perhaps an assessment of its own jurisdiction over wolves targeted for culling on federal lands. The agency declined this request and took no action to stop the kill. NRDC and a group of seven other organizations whose missions included the protection of wildlife, including Defenders of Wildlife and the World Wildlife Fund, sued the Secretary of Interior and officials of the Department of Interior under FLPMA, which they argued authorized the Secretary to "prevent the killing of wildlife on federal lands and requires [them] to evaluate whether [they] must intervene if [they] are fully to serve the environmental concerns of the Act."[80]

Once the complaint was filed, the district court issued a temporary order prohibiting Alaska's Department of Fish and Game from carrying out any wolf kills on federal lands, while it considered the merits of the plaintiffs' claims. To enjoin the program permanently, the plaintiffs needed to convince the district court of four elements. One of these was that irreparable harm would befall the plaintiffs if the injunction was not issued. On this and the other elements, the district court held that the plaintiffs had provided sufficient evidence meriting a more permanent injunction and issued an order prohibiting the State from carrying out the program on federal lands.[81] On appeal, though, the DC Circuit

[78] 43 U.S.C. § 1732(b).
[79] *Defenders of Wildlife v. Andrus*, 627 F.2d 1238, 1240 (D.C. Cir. 1980).
[80] *Id.* at 1240 (citing 43 U.S.C. § 1701 *et seq.*).
[81] *Id.* at 1241.

Court of Appeals reversed the trial court's ruling and removed any legal barriers to Alaskan wolf kills on federal land. The basis for its ruling was not FLPMA, but NEPA, which requires a federal agency to prepare an environmental impact statement for any "major federal action[]" that significantly affects the "quality of the human environment."[82] The DC Circuit concluded that NEPA's trigger had not been met under the facts of the case, which involved an agency's refusal to act, rather than an affirmative action. Therefore, under a reading of the plain text of the statute, the Department's refusal to act could not trigger the need for an environmental impact statement under NEPA and the district court's conclusion of law had been in error.

With respect to FLPMA, the DC Circuit wrote separately in *dicta* regarding the interplay between NEPA and FLPMA. The district court had concluded that FLPMA imposed "supervisory duties" on the Secretary of Interior to prevent state wildlife programs that may have "significant environmental consequences," and that this was a "nondiscretionary" duty triggered by the requirement that Congress imposed upon the Secretary to "plan for and manage federal land and resources."[83] This, according to the district court, required the Secretary to "prohibit any major actions significantly affecting the human environment from occurring on federal lands until an environmental impact statement has been prepared and circulated."[84] The DC Circuit interpreted FLPMA in a way that almost diametrically opposed the lower court's conclusions. Although the appeals court acknowledged that FLPMA imposed a "general duty" on the Secretary of Interior to "plan for and manage federal resources," the court noted that Congress had "assigned the states the primary responsibility for the management of wildlife programs within their boundaries."[85] Further, the appeals court noted that States have "broad trustee and police powers over wild animals within their jurisdictions."[86] Until the federal government, through Congress, asserts the constitutional authority that the Supreme Court has recognized it possesses, the DC Circuit's opinion is that the default governmental entity with constitutional power to manage wildlife on federal lands is the State.

There have been some glimmers of hope that Congress could step in to encourage or require greater protections for pronghorn and other migratory wildlife, which would, in turn, benefit species like blowout beardtongue. In 2016 and 2018, Senator Tom Udall of New Mexico introduced a bill, the Wildlife Corridors Conservation Act, which would assert federal authority to conserve and restore habitats "that facilitate the movement of certain native or noninvasive species …

[82] *Id.* at 1243 (citing 42 U.S.C. § 4321).
[83] *Id.* at 1248.
[84] *Id.*
[85] *Id.*
[86] *Id.* (quoting *Kleppe v. New Mexico*, 426 U.S. 529, 545 (1976)).

that may be at risk due to habitat loss or fragmentation."[87] According to the congressional findings in this bill, "native fish, wildlife, and plant species in the United States are part of a rich natural heritage and an important legacy to pass on to future generations," and their protection is essential given that "the populations of many native fish, wildlife, and plant species in the United States are in decline."[88] The congressional findings include a catastrophic assessment of viability for many native species in the United States, for which scientists estimate that "1 in 5 animal and plant species" are "at risk of extinction."[89] Habitat fragmentation is cited as one of the primary threats to the survival of many native fish, wildlife, and plant species, along with climate change and habitat destruction. To ameliorate this loss, the bill proposes "the conservation of new and existing landscape and seascape corridors, through which native species can transition from 1 habitat to another," along with the "conservation, restoration, and establishment of new ecological connections to facilitate the movement of species into more suitable habitats."[90] Finally, the congressional findings include examples of states that have recognized the importance of habitat connectivity, along with the New England Governors Association and the Western Governors' Association.

The bill has not gained traction in Congress yet, despite bipartisan support, but some progress has been made through voluntary collaborative efforts on the ground.[91] In the Greater Yellowstone area, a coalition of federal, state, and private landowners was formed in the early 2000s to establish a migration corridor for pronghorn. Starting in 2002, the BLM engaged in a planning effort for the Pinedale Region, which formed a critical portion of the Sublette herd's annual migration route, but also contained the second-largest natural gas reserve in the United States, consisting of approximately forty trillion cubic feet of natural gas.[92] Pressure on the agency to protect the pronghorn migration areas from oil and gas resulted in a final plan that environmentalists criticized as being inadequate. Yet, where the BLM had fallen short, the National Park Service and the Forest Service took up the slack. The Park Service obtained a critical section of school trust land from the State of Wyoming on the northern end of the corridor, and the Forest Service amended the Bridger-Teton National Forest plan to formally designate a wildlife corridor across the lands it managed. Under pressure due to the affirmative acts of these other agencies, the BLM relented and established protected designations at the southern end

87 S. 1499, The Wildlife Corridors Conservation Act of 2019, 116th Congress, 1st Session (introduced May 16, 2019).

88 *Id.* § 2(a)(1) & (2).

89 *Id.* § 2(a)(4) & (5).

90 *Id.* § 2(a)(7) & (8).

91 Robert B. Keiter, The Greater Yellowstone Ecosystem Revisited: Law, Science, and the Pursuit of Ecosystem Management in an Iconic Landscape, 91 U. Colo. L. Rev. 1, 95 (2020).

92 David N. Cherney, *Securing the Free Movement of Wildlife: Lessons from the American West's Longest Land Mammal Migration*, 41 Envtl. L. 599, 607 (2011).

of the corridor, effectively prohibiting oil and gas development on that portion of the migration route.[93]

With respect to private ranches that lay interspersed among BLM and other federal and state lands throughout the heavily checkerboarded route, nonprofit organizations purchased conservation easements to bar migration-unfriendly development and remove and repair fences that disrupted the passage of pronghorn along the route. Not to be outdone, the State of Wyoming participated as well, building highway overpasses for pronghorn at bottleneck areas. This effort demonstrated that federal legislation is not a necessary precursor to the establishment of wildlife corridors and that public–private coalitions and partnerships can do this work without legislative authorization or specially designated appropriations.

In a similar vein, Tribal governments have long modeled habitat restoration for pronghorn, penstemon, and other grassland species. The Eastern Shoshone and Northern Arapaho Tribes of the Wind River Reservation have established a working model of connectivity just to the north of the former Lawrence Ranch. These Tribes have been working together to conserve connected wildlife habitat on the reservation since 1940, employing strategies that bolster habitat and population numbers of pronghorn antelope, which were the subject of a tribal–federal reintroduction effort in 1984. Pronghorn had been in serious decline throughout Wyoming since the turn of the twentieth century, and by the 1980s, there were fewer than 800 animals on the Wind River Reservation. In 1984, the Tribes instituted a tribal game code to regulate pronghorn hunting and simultaneously reintroduced the species on parts of the reservation. By 2021, the Tribes estimated Reservation's population had increased to 10,000.[94] Part of the management framework is the reintroduction of fire, which is a time-tested strategy informed by Traditional Knowledge passed down from generation to generation. According to Jason Baldes, Eastern Shoshone Buffalo Restoration Manager for the Wind River Reservation, "Fire we learn about as being a very important component of our lives, ceremonially, spiritually, but also as a tool. Fire as a tool promoted growth."[95]

These Tribes' efforts to reintroduce bison have received far more public attention than their efforts surrounding pronghorn and elk, but the benefits of their work with bison restoration have carried through to these other species also. For the Northern Arapaho and Eastern Shoshone, restoring bison to their reservation is a step on the path to restoring their land and its ecological integrity. Returning free-roaming bison to the reservation will require the dedication of many acres of intact habitat,

93 Keiter, 91 U. Colo. L. Rev. at 95.

94 Michael Mazur & Patrick Hnilicka, A *Partnership Older than the U.S. Fish and Wildlife Service*, ArcGIS Storymaps (Sept. 9, 2021), https://storymaps.arcgis.com/stories/4bedb05104ac4f4ea6fc4a5a532b7ff9.

95 Jason Baldes, Native Memory Project, "Native Fire Management" (last accessed Oct. 16, 2024), https://nativememoryproject.org/voice/native-fire-management/.

and perhaps the traditional use of proscribed fires to encourage the growth of native grasses that bison prefer. These steps, in turn, will benefit the pronghorn, a species that according to Traditional Ecological Knowledge of these Tribes, benefits from the presence of bison. Restoring species like pronghorn and bison can repair lost cultural connections to wildlife, including those that predate the reservation era. In Baldes's opinion, it is important to continue to increase the presence of bison on the reservation, and "build[] the buffalo programs. That's very important for the ecological role of this keystone species being restored to the landscape that increases plant and animal biodiversity. It's important in carbon storage and climate resiliency. For the people here, though, it's very important culturally and spiritually."[96]

[96] Transcript: Jason Baldes on Buffalo and Land Rematriation, For the Wild Podcast (Oct. 4, 2023), available at https://forthewild.world/podcast-transcripts/jason-baldes-on-buffalo-and-land-rematriation-350.

7

Grazing Law, Water Law, and the Pine Creek Ranch

The water … controls the land. Wherever there is any water, there is a ranch.[1]

7.1 PUBLIC LANDS COMMISSION REPORT

The Pine Creek Ranch in Nye County, Nevada is another famous property in the annals of natural resources law and policy, especially for the role it played in revealing the tension that the environmental movement of the 1970s caused for some western public lands ranches. The ranch is either 7,000 acres in total, or closer to 707,000, depending who you ask. According to the federal government, the ranch consists of 7,000 acres of fee land. Federal records reveal that these private lands have served as a base to support the ranch owners' grazing of domestic livestock on 762,000 acres of federal public lands managed by the US Forest Service and Bureau of Land Management (240,000 acres under Forest Service management and 512,000 under the management of the BLM).[2] According to the most famous owners of this ranch, the Hage family, the ranch is "approximately 760,000 acres," encompassing the lands they own in fee and the federal lands near the ranch, where they pasture their cattle.[3]

Pine Creek Ranch was homesteaded in 1865, at a time when the adjacent federal lands could be grazed free of charge, and only one year after Nevada's admission into the Union as the thirty-sixth state.[4] At that time, water rights were essential to raise cattle in this incredibly arid region, and in the words of Judge Loren Smith, who described this era in a 2008 published opinion,

1 Pub. Lands Commn., Report of the Public Land Commission Created by the Act of Mar. 3, 1879, Relating to Public Lands in the Western Portion of the United States and to the Operation of Existing Land Laws, 46 H.R. Exec. Doc. 46, at 14 (Feb. 25, 1880).

2 *Hage v. United States*, Corrected Brief for Plaintiffs-Cross-Appellants,2011 WL 2006567, at *7 (filed Apr. 22, 2011).

3 American Rancher Uncut Interview Pt. 1, Wayne Hage at Pine Creek 2005, at 6:23, available at https://vimeo.com/8520897.

4 *Hage v. United States*, 35 Fed. Cl. 137, 153 (Ct. Fed. Cl. 1996).

homesteaders in the West in the late 1800s "faced a harsh natural fact: lack of water. Land without water, assuming no useful minerals, was useless and hence worthless. But with the application of human effort and capital water could be made to flow to some of this land."[5] And for these reasons, the ranch's founders prioritized the acquisition of water rights on private land and nearby federal land, including the lands that are now part of the Toiyabe National Forest.[6] They built ditches to transport water for irrigation, stock watering, and domestic purposes, on their fee lands and across the adjacent federal lands, which brought water from federal lands onto their private fee lands throughout the year.

The ranch's founders began using the nearby federal public land and water during the height of the disposal era. This allowed them to secure permanent legal rights to the water under the law in effect at that time, including the Ditch Act, which was enacted in 1866.[7] They also freely grazed and used the nearby federal land under the policy of the grazing commons. Yet, as early as the beginning of the twentieth century, the federal government transitioned from the disposal policy toward a retention and management policy, and this affected the Pine Creek Ranch in several ways.[8] The first manifestation of this transition was the establishment of the Toiyabe National Forest in 1907.[9] Upon the establishment of the Forest as a federal reserve, the agency charged with managing it, the newly formed United States Forest Service, assumed authority delegated by Congress to oversee grazing in national forests. Under this authority, the agency issued a grazing permit to the ranch founders based on their historical use of the lands within the forest for grazing.[10] Each successor in interest received similar privileges, which allowed them to continue to use the national forest lands for grazing their livestock, and draw water from within the forest boundaries.[11]

The development of water law also affected the ranch, because Nevada began regulating the use of water under a doctrine adopted by the other western states – prior appropriation – within a short time following its admission.[12] Prior appropriation was adopted for its efficacy in spurring settler colonizers to permanently establish themselves in the same manner as the founders of Pine Creek Ranch. If they settled upon the land and used the water for ranching or farming, they could obtain permanent rights to use the water. In the words of a prominent

5 *Hage v. United States*, No. 1:1991cv01470, at *2 (June 6, 2008).
6 *Id.*
7 43 U.S.C. § 661 (2018).
8 Rasband, pp. 147–48 (discussing the shift from disposal to the retention and resulting impacts on the management of forest reserves).
9 *Hage v. United States*, 51 Fed. Cl. 570, 580 (2002).
10 *Hage v. United States*, 35 Fed. Cl. at 153.
11 *Id.*
12 Fred W. Welden, *Chief Deputy Research Director, Research Division, Legislative Counsel Bureau*, Background Paper 03-2, *History of Water Law in Nevada and the Western States*, p. 3 (Jan. 2003).

Natural Resources Law textbook, "water was too precious to be left in the stream."[13] This system was designed precisely for places like Nevada, characterized by extreme aridity and relatively scarce water supply.[14]

In Nevada, the adoption of prior appropriation in the late nineteenth century not only helped establish settler colonizers' legal rights to water in the state, but created a "run" on the resource. The Nevada state government quickly realized that it would be necessary to bring some order to the system of allocating water rights. Thus, in 1903, the legislature created the Office of the State Engineer, a state agency that would establish a process of recognizing water rights and organizing them according to priority under state law.[15] The organic act establishing the State Engineer's office also proclaimed that all natural water sources, including streams, lakes, and other surface waters not already put to a beneficial use, were open and available for appropriation. Rights to unclaimed water would be considered "appurtenant to" the land where the claimant put them to use, which was a legal means of attaching water to land that would last into the twenty-first century. The only limitation on private appropriation was the condition of "beneficial use," which was the "basis, the measure, and the limit of the right" under the law.[16] Under this condition, water that was not consistently put to a beneficial use could be forfeited and made available to others who might use the water for farming or ranching, mining, or household use, all of which were legally established as beneficial uses at the time.

The threat of forfeiture kept appropriators busy maintaining their rights, so as not to lose them. This meant that, if the water was withdrawn using a well, and the well ran dry, it would need to be deepened, to find more water to put to beneficial use and maintain the right. If the water right was based on diversion and use of surface flowing water and there was inadequate precipitation, measures would need to be taken to secure approval from authorities to use less than the full quantity, and this approval would need to be granted, to prevent the State from declaring the right forfeited or abandoned.[17] Essentially, under prior appropriation, homesteaders who needed water from public (or private) land had to continually alter the natural flow of water by digging, tunneling, damming, or otherwise engineering water to prevent it from engaging in its natural tendency to disperse, and soak into the ground. This is exactly what the homesteaders of Pine Creek did – they dug ditches to transport water off the nearby public lands that would become the Toiyabe National Forest and consequently obtained what is known as "ditch rights-of-way" under federal law, and water rights under state law.[18]

13 Rasband, p. 862.
14 *Id.*
15 Welden, p. 3.
16 *Id.*
17 *See* Nev. Rev. Stat. § 534.090(1) (2022).
18 *Hage v. United States*, No. 1:1991cv01470, at *2 (June 6, 2008).

The post-Dust Bowl years saw Congress stepping in to protect the grassland regions of the western United States, as Chapter 5 discussed in some detail. Through the Taylor Grazing Act and its partner statute for the Forest Service, the Granger-Thye Act of 1950,[19] Congress sought to better organize and regulate public lands agriculture, hoping that some stability would flow from these efforts. Although each contains conservation-aligned goals, these laws and the management regimes and authority they established, did not result in sustainable grazing and healthy grasslands across the federal public domain. In some areas, grasslands were badly depleted by overgrazing, and they remained so well into the era of the Hages' arrival at Pine Creek. As mentioned earlier in Chapter 5, and as will be discussed further in this chapter, one of the successes of these statutes was their solidification of a power structure established by European American farmers and ranchers in the late nineteenth and early twentieth centuries, which would have included the founders of Pine Creek. But this success also came at a cost.

The Hages and their story illustrate well the relative costs and benefits of these statutes. In 1978, the Hages purchased the 7,000 acres of patented fee land constituting the "base property" of the Pine Creek Ranch. Base property is a term of art in public lands and natural resources law, describing the private land that supports grazing on nearby public lands. Base property is a qualification requirement to apply for and hold a federal grazing permit or lease.[20] Because the Hages held fee title to this base property, they could apply for and hold grazing privileges allowing them to run their livestock on nearby areas of federal public land, referred to as "allotments."[21] According to Wayne Hage, Sr., the economic prosperity of the combined private and public lands used to form the ranching operation was what initially attracted his interest in this particular ranch: It had a reputation of being "probably the best ranch in the State of Nevada, economically."[22]

Given that the story of Pine Creek involves some closer examination of some technical aspects of federal grazing law, some background on modern grazing law and policy and a brief explanation of some of the key terms of art can be a useful starting point. In the United States, the total footprint of private lands used for agricultural purposes is over one billion acres, which constitutes roughly 52 percent of the entire land base of the nation.[23] Federal public lands allocated for agricultural

[19] The Granger-Thye Act was passed to accomplish the same goals as the Taylor Grazing Act, but on national forests and national grasslands under the jurisdiction of the Department of Agriculture and the United States Forest Service. 16 U.S.C.A. § 580l.

[20] Hillary M. Hoffmann, *A Changing of the Cattle Guard: BLM's New Approach to Grazing Qualifications*, 24 J. ENVTL. L. & LITIG. 243, 245 (2009).

[21] *Id.*

[22] American Rancher Uncut Interview Pt. 1, Wayne Hage at Pine Creek 2005, https://vimeo.com/8520897.

[23] Daniel P. Bigelow & Alison Borchers, Major Uses of Land in the United States, 2012, U.S. Department of Agriculture Economic Research Service, Economic Information Bulletin No. 178 (Aug. 2017), www.ers.usda.gov/webdocs/publications/84880/eib-178.pdf?v=9793.6.

purposes can add another 330 million acres to this total, even by conservative estimates.[24] The western states hold additional lands in trust or in fee for the benefit of farmers and ranchers, adding millions more to this staggering calculus.[25] Tribes also allocate their lands to agricultural uses, and more than 8 percent of the current Tribal land base is under agricultural use,[26] tacking an additional forty-six million acres onto the total land base dedicated to growing crops and raising livestock. Ninety-eight percent of public lands were once Tribal lands, some of which are subject to outstanding Tribal treaty claims like those of the Blackfeet and the Ute.[27] The management framework for these lands is complex, primarily because Congress has created multiple agencies to manage federal public lands and the activity of agriculture as a whole, using different statutory mechanisms that approach agricultural use in different ways, as have the states.[28] In total, the federal government owns roughly 640 million acres of land,[29] most of which is managed by four federal agencies: the Department of Interior's Bureau of Land Management (BLM), United States Fish and Wildlife Service (FWS), the National Park Service (NPS), and the Department of Agriculture's US Forest Service.[30]

BLM manages a total of 245.7 million acres of public lands, primarily in the western states, including Alaska.[31] Subtracting the 90 million acres of land under BLM management in Alaska results in a total of 166 million acres across the West. Of these, approximately 160 million acres are authorized for livestock grazing, although the acreage actually grazed each year varies based on the availability of water and forage, and other conditions.[32] According to former Interior Solicitor John Leshy, As compared to other authorized uses of federal public lands, "grazing of domestic livestock is the most widespread extractive use of the federal lands," measured acre for acre.[33] Its footprint is an area of land that is roughly ten

24 Congressional Research Service, "Federal Land Ownership: Overview and Data," pp. 2, 4 (2020), https://crsreports.congress.gov/product/pdf/R/R42346/15.

25 Colorado State Land Board, *Agriculture*, visited June 7, 2023, available at https://slb.colorado.gov/lease/agriculture.

26 U.S. Govt. Accountability Office, *Indian Issues: Agricultural Credit Needs and Barriers to Lending on Tribal Lands*, p. 1 (May 2019), www.gao.gov/assets/700/699447.pdf.

27 Justin Farrell, *et al.*, *Effects of land dispossession and forced migration on Indigenous Peoples s in North America*, SCIENCE (Oct. 29, 2021).

28 Rasband, pp. 236–41.

29 Congressional Research Service, "Federal Land Ownership: Overview and Data," p. 2 (2020) https://crsreports.congress.gov/product/pdf/R/R42346/15.

30 *Id.* at 7.

31 *Id.*

32 U.S. Govt. Accountability Office, "Report to Congressional Requesters: Livestock Grazing; Federal Expenditures and Receipts Vary, Depending on the Agency and the Purpose of the Fee Charged," p. 14 (2005), www.gao.gov/assets/gao-05-869.pdf; Western Watersheds Project, "Renew or Review: How the FLPMA 402(c) Loophole has Limited Public Engagement and Enabled Environmental Degradation on Western Public Lands" (2022), https://storymaps.arcgis.com/stories/45ea3ebe6ef54bd0840bb41e63a79174.

33 JOHN D. LESHY, *et al.*, FEDERAL PUBLIC LAND AND RESOURCES LAW, p. 791 (Foundation Press 2022).

times that of Pennsylvania. Moreover, grazing takes more from public lands, acre for acre, than mining, whether for uranium, lithium, and other rare-earth minerals, or for coal, oil, or natural gas.[34]

The US Forest Service also manages federal public land for grazing. Roughly seventy-five million acres of Forest Service-managed lands are authorized for livestock use, whether reserved as national forests or as national grasslands,[35] and 90 percent of those lands are located west of the Mississippi River.[36] By contrast with the BLM-managed lands, livestock grazing is not the most widespread extractive use of Forest Service lands, although it is close. Roughly ninety-five million acres of Forest Service lands are authorized for timber harvesting, an activity that is mandated in the statutes Congress passed directing the use and allocation of resources on these lands, while ninety-three million acres are authorized for livestock grazing.[37]

The cumulative footprint of lands managed by federal agencies for animal agricultural purposes is 235 million acres, across all land categories and agencies, exclusive of Alaska.[38] As the above statistics demonstrate, the burden of this activity falls on public lands and other resources, like water, and mostly in the West. Because the western lands are generally more arid, western livestock operators need more land and depend on a combination of public and private land to graze cattle due to the need to rotate animals onto and off of seasonal pastures.[39] It may make sense to some, from a policy and resource perspective, that the relatively less populous western states, with more public lands available for livestock grazing, could be used for agricultural purposes because of their potential to provide food at a relatively low cost, using land that historically was deemed to be of little to no value by the federal government and many of the states. This allocation of resources would also seemingly benefit the economies of the western states, which are largely rural. Yet, despite the vast land base allocated for this use, the

34 An analysis of acres managed by BLM concluded that thirty-six million acres were dedicated to oil and gas use. Mason Cummings, "Open for business (and not much else); Analysis shows oil and gas leasing out of whack on BLM lands," www.wilderness.org/articles/article/open-business-and-not-much-else-analysis-shows-oil-and-gas-leasing-out-whack-blm-lands.

35 U.S. Govt. Accountability Office, "Report to Congressional Requesters: Livestock Grazing; Federal Expenditures and Receipts Vary, Depending on the Agency and the Purpose of the Fee Charged," p. 14 (2005), www.gao.gov/assets/gao-05-869.pdf.

36 *Id.* at 15.

37 Congressional Research Service, Report 45688, "Timber Harvesting on Federal Land," pp. 3–4 (2022), available at https://sgp.fas.org/crs/misc/R45688.pdf.

38 U.S. Govt. Accountability Office, "Report to Congressional Requesters: Livestock Grazing; Federal Expenditures and Receipts Vary, Depending on the Agency and the Purpose of the Fee Charged," p. 5 (2005), www.gao.gov/assets/gao-05-869.pdf. In Alaska, BLM issues grazing permits, but only for reindeer, under a program that was designed to benefit Alaska Native food sovereignty.

39 *Id.* at 10 (However, in some regions of the intermountain West, there is year-round grazing on federal lands, with little to no use of the base property except in cases of emergency.).

food produced from grazing on the federal public lands is a only a small fraction of the national meat production market, estimated at roughly 2 percent.[40] Most of the livestock raised for human consumption comes from private lands, including feedlots, in the midwestern and southeastern states.[41]

The figures in the preceding paragraphs reveal that a disproportionately large amount of the American public's land, roughly 235 million acres, is dedicated to a use that produces 2 percent of the nation's meat supply. The agencies primarily responsible for this allocation are the US Forest Service and the BLM, which, together administer the greatest number of grazing permits on federal land in the western states.[42] As of 2020, the agencies issued a combined total of 23,492 permits, with the BLM numbers dwarfing those of the Forest Service by a margin of nearly 4:1.[43] Like most of these permittees, Wayne Hage obtained his permits through purchasing the base property that had previously served as a base property for certain federal allotments. When Hage and his wife purchased this base property in 1978, after relocating to Nevada from California, they acquired not only the 7,000 acres of fee land but also what federal law refers to as a "preference," which is another term of art in federal grazing law, referring to a sort of "right of first refusal," placing the holder first in line to receive any associated federal grazing permits or leases for the allotment previously grazed using that base property.[44] More specifically, because Hage's predecessors had used Pine Creek's fee lands as base property for nearby allotments, consisting of 512,000 acres managed by the Bureau of Land Management and 240,000 acres of the Toiyabe National Forest, managed by the United States Forest Service, the Hages would be first in line to receive those same permits. Under federal law, each grazing allotment is associated with a single grazing preference, and the preference holder will always have priority in receiving a new permit once the previous permit expires, assuming no permit violations or other unlawful conduct.

The terms of art discussed thus far, including base property, preference, and grazing allotment, originated in Congress's 1934 grazing reform statute, the Taylor Grazing Act, and its implementing regulations.[45] In the statute's pream-

40 Leshy, p. 791 (noting that this figure could vary by up to 60 percent, depending on methodology used to calculate it and any seasonal or annual variations in stock turned out to graze or sold to market).

41 U.S. Dep't of Agriculture, "Meat Animals Production, Disposition, and Income," pp. 9–20 (2023), available at https://downloads.usda.library.cornell.edu/usda-esmis/files/02870v85d/kk91h129k/8s45rq36g/meatan23.pdf. Animal feedlot operations are more effective in terms of acreage put to agricultural use (and acreage saved from agricultural use), than so-called "free range" livestock operations, which may result in higher quality meat, but impact a much larger physical and ecological footprint.

42 Bradley J. Gentner & John A. Tanaka, Classifying Federal Public Land Grazing Permittees, 55 J. Range Mgmt. 55, 2–11 (Jan. 2002) (Gentner & Tanaka).

43 Gentner & Tanaka, p. 3.

44 *Id.*; *Est. of Hage v. United States*, 687 F.3d 1281, 1283 (Fed. Cir. 2012).

45 Taylor Grazing Act, ch. 865, 48 Stat. 1269 (1934), 43 U.S.C. §§ 315–315r (2018).

ble, Congress stated that the purpose of the Act was to "[t]o stop injury to the public grazing lands by preventing overgrazing and soil deterioration, to provide for their orderly use, improvement, and development, to stabilize the livestock industry dependent upon the public range, and for other purposes."[46] The second rationale, regarding organized and "orderly" use, was necessitated by the range wars that had broken out between sheep and cattle ranchers, and between those owning base property and those who lacked it. Usually, the base property owners were cattle ranchers, and the nomadic ranchers were sheep operations, as discussed in Chapter 5. This was largely due to the difference in grazing practices between cattle and sheep ranchers: the former typically being more likely based in one location and the latter being more nomadic. However, there was also a notable racial divide between cattle and sheep operations. Cattle ranchers were almost always white, as were the cowboys they hired, but sheep ranchers frequently hired Mexican, Mexican American, Indigenous, or Basque sheepherders to roam with their herds.[47]

Congress's attempt to resolve the historical disputes over access to public grazing land between cattlemen and sheepmen was the Taylor Act, and the mechanism that was used was discussed earlier in Chapter 5. The Act included further mandates, such as authorization for the Secretary of the Interior to establish grazing districts, develop a permitting system, and issue permits to graze designated tracts of land within each district.[48] Eventually, these tracts would be labeled "allotments," in the implementing regulations. Section 315b of the Act authorized the Secretary to issue permits to "such bona fide settlers, residents, and other stock owners as under his rules and regulations are entitled to participate in the use of the range."[49] It required permittees to have begun the naturalization process or prove US citizenship, and included provisions allowing for groups, associations, or corporations to apply. Finally, and perhaps most critically for the purposes of this analysis, section 315b requires the Secretary of the Interior to give "preference" to applicants "within or near a district who are landowners engaged in the livestock business, bona fide occupants or settlers, or owners of water or water rights, as may be necessary to permit the proper use of lands, water or water rights owned, occupied, or leased by them."[50]

46 48 Stat. at 1269. Once the statute was passed, President Roosevelt withdrew all lands in the public domain from disposition except for mineral exploration and development purposes.

47 Adam M. Sowards, "Why Sheep Started So Many Wars in the American West," What it Means to Be American: A National Conversation Hosted by the Smithsonian and Arizona State University (Oct. 5, 2017), available at www.whatitmeanstobeamerican.org/identities/why-sheep-started-so-many-wars-in-the-american-west/.

48 Hoffmann, 24 J. Envtl. L. & Litig. at 251.

49 43 U.S.C. § 315b.

50 *Id.*

The meaning of this language governing preferences has generated extensive debates over the years, with some arguing that it suggests a priority order for issuing permits, but gives the Secretary broad discretion to define the term, and others arguing that it creates a property right in federal grazing permits, which cannot be altered by the Secretary without the permittee's consent.[51] While the Act acknowledges Congressional intent to give "preference" to those engaged in the livestock business, owners of water rights, and others, it does not instruct the Secretary of Interior to ignore other applicants who meet the other mandatory requirements of residency and stock ownership. There are also multiple references to the Secretary's authority to promulgate regulations to further define and refine the broad statutory guidance, giving the impression that Congress intended the Secretary to determine precisely how the statute would apply on the ground.[52]

The Secretary promulgated several iterations of grazing regulations following the initial passage of the Act. As discussed in Chapter 5, the earliest regulations were informed by Ferry Carpenter's visit to the Boston Commons and his historical research regarding how to organize and regulate a public grazing commons. Using his experience homesteading Oak Point, and grazing his cattle on nearby public lands, in addition to his experience navigating the sheep wars, Carpenter sought to divide the western public grazing commons into grazing districts, the management of which would be guided by advisory boards that included permittees. It was also clear early on that some of the terms of the art of public commons grazing, including those in the Taylor Act, needed further regulatory definition. The base property definition was one of those in need of some further clarification. Under the statute, Congress clearly contemplated that preference should be given to certain categories of applicants, including those who owned land, those who had settled (read: homesteaded), and those who held water rights, because these attributes would assist the permittees in making "proper use" of the federal lands they grazed.[53] In the initial grazing regulations, the homesteaded lands and water rights were defined as "base property," and ownership of such base property was adopted as a qualification requirement. Over time, these initial regulatory definitions were further refined until the BLM had formed almost a caste system of federal permittees, with different "classes" of base property, prioritizing the applicants whose private lands and water rights were either located in or near the public allotments.[54]

These early grazing regulations would elevate operators like the Pine Creek Ranch founders, and Ferry Carpenter, as well as others who were similarly situated,

[51] *Pub. Lands Council v. Babbitt*, 529 U.S. 728, 741 (2000); Frank J. Falen & Karen Budd-Falen, *The Right to Graze Livestock on the Federal Lands: The Historical Development of Western Grazing Rights*, 30 IDAHO L. REV. 505, 514 (1994).

[52] Hoffmann, 24 J. Envtl. L. & Litig. at 251.

[53] 43 U.S.C. § 315b.

[54] Hoffmann, 24 J. Envtl. L. & Litig. at 258–59.

to a privileged class above sheep ranchers, who typically did not own land near the public lands they grazed because they moved their livestock across such great distances every year. Also, these early grazing regulations would elevate cattle and sheep ranchers, who tended to be white, above ranchers of color who did not own land, such as the land grant beneficiaries in Chapter 1, or the Indigenous ranchers who were confined to reservations during this time and unable to own their land in fee.

Even more controversial, and more consequential, are the regulatory changes to the term "preference" over time. The initial regulatory definition of a grazing preference was roughly described as the amount of land, defined in animal unit months, that the permittee had grazed during the so-called "priority period," which was the ten years leading up to the passage of the Taylor Act. So, if the owners of Pine Creek Ranch had grazed 500 cow–calf pairs on the allotment bordering their fee lands from 1924 to 1934, their preference right would equate to 500 animal unit months (AUMs) on that allotment. This would mean that when their permit expired after ten years, they would possess a preference to receive the next permit for that allotment, giving them priority over any other applicants. This regulatory framework and the caste system it created ran roughshod over the federal public domain until the late 1970s, when Congress took note of the general and pervasive deterioration of the public range yet again. As Congress later determined, the Taylor Act had organized grazing, but it had not accomplished Congress's 1934 goal of preventing overgrazing and soil deterioration.

In two congressional responses, the Federal Lands Policy and Management Act and the Public Rangelands Improvement Act, Congress called for better management of the public lands allocated for grazing in recognition of their ecological value and a growing public interest in protecting public lands and public resources like air and water.[55] In response, the BLM amended the grazing regulations, although the changes were relatively minor in light of what was to come, mostly ensuring that grazing use would be evaluated during the now-mandatory public-facing planning process that FLPMA required the BLM to undertake periodically on every acre of land under the agency's management. But the changes that FLPMA and its national forest counterpart, the National Forest Management Act, brought, were more substantial.

The overlay of planning and sustainability in FLPMA and NFMA increased the role of federal agencies and somewhat loosened the grip of permittees like the Hages on their grazing privileges. When combined with the provisions of the Taylor Grazing Act and its implementing regulations, federal agencies had the authority to modify, suspend, or cancel grazing permits under various circumstances. First, if a permittee grazed above the maximum limits allowed by the permit, lost base property in a foreclosure action or otherwise failed to use the permit without permission, or otherwise violated federal grazing

[55] Hoffmann, 24 J. Envtl. L. & Litig. at 277.

laws, the agency could cancel the permit.[56] Permit cancellation, in turn, would cancel the preference. Second, under the Taylor Act and FLPMA, agencies could reclassify or withdraw land from grazing use and redesignate it to a different use.[57] If forage had disappeared or was so reduced as to threaten the ecological health of an allotment, the agencies could reduce the amount of grazing allowed on that land, by suspending AUMs of grazing privileges "in whole or in part," and "for such time as necessary."[58]

According to the most comprehensive study of BLM and Forest Service grazing permittees, by economists Bradley Gentner and John Tanaka, public lands ranching operations are not homogenous, although they do share many characteristics.[59] For one, they generate a low-to-negative rate of return, which is estimated to be, on average, anywhere "from negative to 1–2 percent."[60] Market value of base properties, or the private land that legally corresponds to the public grazing allotments, was "well above" the market value calculated based on this low rate of return.[61] These relatively low rates of return and relatively elevated property values track across the other western states.[62]

Other shared characteristics reflected in the Gentner and Tanaka study are values associated with a family tradition of ranching, a desire to maintain the ranching "culture," the belief that a ranch is a good place to raise a family, and a sense of community.[63] Survey respondents also indicated that they shared a value of ranching as a means of being a good steward of land and the environment.[64] The distribution of these characteristics allowed Gentner and Tanaka to separate the respondents into two groups: hobbyists and professional ranchers. The hobbyists were those who did not derive their primary income from the ranching operation, as the category label implies, and included the following subcategory clusters: (1) small hobbyist, (2) retired hobbyist, (3) working hobbyist, and (4) trophy rancher. Conversely, among the "professional ranchers," or those whose

56 *Public Lands Council*, 529 U.S. at 735.

57 43 U.S.C. §§ 315f & 1712.

58 *Public Lands Council*, 529 U.S. at 735–36 (noting that under this authority, the Department of Interior had "so often reduced individual permit AUM allocations" that by 1964, the regulations included a distinction between "active" AUMs (the amount being grazed after any suspension) and "authorized" AUMs (the amount originally authorized to be grazed at permit issuance)).

59 Gentner & Tanaka, p. 3. The Gentner and Tanaka study is illustrative, but also not comprehensive, with only slightly more than 50 percent of the representative sample of 2,000 permittees responding. Also, the authors acknowledge the difficulty in gathering information about public lands operations in their report, because no entity, government or private, tracks comprehensive data on permittees holding privileges to graze cattle or other livestock on public lands, nor does any organization or government entity track the output of these operations. Permittees are not required to report to the agencies regarding the productivity of their herds, and as discussed in more detail in earlier chapters, the permits are in many ways self-enforced, leaving these and similar questions open and unanswered.

60 *Id.*

61 *Id.*

62 *Id.*

63 *Id.* at 4.

64 *Id.*

purpose for engaging in the ranching activity using public lands was to make a living, support a family, and who did not have significant other sources of income, the following subcategory clusters were identified using the multifactor questions described earlier: (1) diversified family rancher, (2) dependent family rancher, (3) corporate rancher, and (4) sheep rancher.[65] Across both types, and all subcategories, all ranked "consumptive objectives above profit maximizing objectives."[66] All groups ranked passing the business down to their children as the "first or second most important objective," while the profit objective was uniformly listed as only being of a medium priority level.[67]

Several of the conclusions regarding the individual subcategories of the hobbyist and professional ranchers are useful in understanding ranches like Pine Creek. First, 50.5 percent of the respondents were hobbyists and 49.5 percent were professionals. This figure is probably skewed more toward the hobbyists two decades after this study was conducted due to the large influx of private investment in ranches in the West, led by none other than Ted Turner himself. Many areas of the West have seen significant population growth in the first decades of the twenty-first century, particularly in locations close to regional airports, ski areas, and most acutely in the years of the Covid-19 pandemic, which saw a tidal wave of urban abandonment and a sea change from in-office to remote work.[68] But even in 2002, well before the pandemic, the hobbyists outnumbered the professionals, which debunks one of the many common narratives that surround public lands ranchers – that they rely on public lands to make a living.[69]

Gentner and Tanaka's research drew some valuable conclusions unique to each of the subcategories, as well. The small hobbyists, for instance, constitute 11.1 percent of the respondents and have the least reliance upon ranching and other "on-ranch sources of income" of any other subcategory.[70] Most of their income comes from off-ranch sources, and they are the most educated subcategory across the professional and hobbyist categories, with most possessing a graduate degree. They also own the least amount of private lands, have the smallest herd size, and rank profit as

65 *Id.* at 4.
66 *Id.* at 7.
67 *Id.*
68 Amanda L. Bentley Brymer, David T. Taylor, J. D. Wulfhorst, L. Allen Torell, Neil R. Rimbey, & John A. Tanaka, *Economic and Social Impact Assessment of Ranching on Public Lands: A Guide to Concepts, Methods, and Applications*, 4 J. Rangeland Applications, 7 (2018) (Brymer, *et al.*).
69 "Federal grazing lands have heavy implications for economy," Ag Daily (Nov. 29, 2022), available at www.agdaily.com/news/federal-grazing-lands-have-heavy-implications-for-economy/; Paul A. Lewin, J. D. Wulfhorst, Neil R. Rimbey, & K. Scott Jensen, *Implications of Declining Grazing Permits on Public Land: An Integrated Social and Economic Impact Analysis*, 17 J. of Western Ag. Economics Assn. 1, 86–87 (Spring 2019).
70 Gentner & Tanaka, p. 8.

the least motivating factor related to their use of public lands to support their private ranching operation.[71]

The "retired hobbyists," or those who are ranching as a hobby during their retirement, after working in a ranching or non-ranching related field for the duration of their careers, constituted 18 percent of the respondents.[72] This group was "the most dependent on ranching and agriculture for income compared to the other 2 groups." The factor that renders them "retired hobbyists" (as opposed to hobbyists) is solely their age – an average of sixty-four. This aspect of the study is somewhat confusing because the average tenure in ranching for this group is 29.23 years, suggesting that those in this group might be ranchers over the age of retirement, who have perhaps downsized their operations and begun to substitute "retirement income, investment income, and off-ranch jobs" for the ranch-based income, although there are no data to support that conclusion.[73] The members of this group also have the highest average age of all groups studied.

The working hobbyist group had a self-identified financial dependence on income from the ranching operation, as well as off-ranch job income, and constituted 15.4 percent of the respondents.[74] This group has a relatively small herd size compared to the other hobbyist and professional categories, owning an average of 1,563 acres of private land.[75] The family tenure variable, or the degree to which this group is motivated to continue ranching due to its perception of the sociohistorical importance of ranching, outranked all other motivating factors. According to the study authors, "[t]his suggests that individuals in this group ranch[] to continue a business started by their family because they appreciate the consumptive value of ranching, not because they are supporting their family with the income."[76]

The trophy rancher subcategory represented 6 percent of the respondent group and contained the largest percentage of four-year college degrees and the second highest percentage of graduate degrees.[77] This group might be best described as the "Ted Turner group," given these and other attributes, like the fact that this group has the highest income, but it is generated by off-ranch sources, and in particular, "investment income."[78] This group had the largest average herd size, at 466.7 cattle and 28.6 horses, and employed by far the largest percentage of ranch hands and other hired labor of the trophy group, likely to assist with managing the large herd size and because these are not traditional family operations.

71 *Id.*
72 *Id.*
73 *Id.* at 7–8.
74 *Id.* at 8.
75 *Id.*
76 *Id.*
77 *Id.*
78 *Id.*; *see also* Vickery Eckhoff, "Forbes Billionaires Top U.S. Welfare Ranchers List," The Daily Pitchfork (Mar. 25, 2015), available at http://dailypitchfork.org/?p=698.

The conclusions drawn by Gentner and Tanaka are that this group was likely "independently wealthy and owns very large ranches for purposes other than generating income," and that "the value of owning just any ranch is less to them than owning a very large, extensive, publicly visible ranch."[79]

Collectively, the factors that distinguish the hobbyist group are their higher average income, their lower dependency on public lands for forage (during any season), their relatively lower deeded (private) acreage, and the diversity of their herds (encompassing sheep, cow-calf operations, cow-calf-yearling operations, horses, and other species, such as llamas or bison).[80] They were also more educated, with 25 percent of the individuals in all subcategories reporting they held graduate degrees. The rise of hobbyist, or "amenity" ranchers, marks a transition in the West that has not yet reached its apex.[81] The landscapes of the Rocky Mountain region, depicted so captivatingly in "Yellowstone," provide an array of "non-commodity benefits" to landowners, including sociological, cultural, and viewscape values, which the hobbyist and amenity ranchers value more than property income potential.[82] While professional ranchers were historically motivated by consumptive and productive goals,[83] amenity landowners have less interest in personally overseeing or interacting with their ranches and usually delegate day-to-day responsibilities of running the property to ranch managers, lease their pastures to other operations for grazing, or even eliminate the "working" aspects of their ranches altogether.[84] The population movement that brought these ranch owners into the rural West for sociological, cultural, or other "lifestyle" reasons is predicted to grow as professional ranchers continue to subdivide their lands.[85] This rise in hobbyist, or amenity, ranchers can be described as a shift toward landowners living "on the land, but not off the land."[86]

In the professionals group, by contrast, most described themselves as living off the land. This group, which might have encompassed the Hages, had they participated in the study, also contains subcategories: the dependent family rancher, the diversified family rancher, the corporate rancher, and the sheep ranchers.[87] The dependent family rancher group was marked by their relatively strong reliance on on-ranch derived income, which was the highest of the professional group, and the least dependence on, or involvement with, off-ranch income sources.[88]

79 Gentner & Tanaka, p. 8.
80 *Id.* at 7.
81 Buckley Biggs, p. 1186.
82 *Id.*
83 *Id.* (citing Smith and Martin 1972).
84 *Id.* (citing Gosnell and Abrams 2011; Lubell et al. 2013).
85 *Id.* (citing Gosnell and Abrams 2011; Lubell et al. 2013; Walker and Fortmann 2003; Plieninger et al. 2012).
86 *Id.*
87 Gentner & Tanaka, pp. 8–9.
88 *Id.* at 8.

This group ranked the following objectives the highest of any subcategory: ranching for the sake of maintaining a family tradition, ranching to leave a ranch to children or other family members, living on a ranch to be closer to friends and family, choosing ranching over other types of work because skills learned on the ranch would not translate into any other employment arena, ranching to earn a living, and living on a ranch because it is a good place to raise a family.[89] Earning a living was ranked fifth across the group, suggesting that the other socioeconomic and sociohistorical reasons were the primary drivers of this group, combined with a perceived or actual sense of being "trapped" in ranching due to having a specific skill set and a relative lack of formal education.[90] The corporate form preferred by this group is pass-through, either sole proprietorship or partnership, and the group as a whole had the highest debt load, although it self-reported the least amount of financial stress. This group is also the least willing to engage in conservation practices and represents 18.6 percent of the total responses, making it the largest subcategory across both respondent types.[91]

The "diversified" subcategory of professional ranchers constituted 13.5 percent of respondents, possessed the smallest herd size of any of the professionals, and was marked by a dependence on family members to provide labor to support ranching operations.[92] This group had the lowest reported annual income across all groups, but the income was highly diversified. The diversified ranchers reported income derived from the production of agricultural commodities, forestry, and other off-ranch employment.[93] This group owned, on average, 4,765 acres of private lands to support ranching operations and reported a high interest in profit maximization from ranching, an interest in ranching to be closer to friends and family, and an interest in maintaining a family tradition of ranching. By contrast to the dependent subcategory, this group was much less interested in passing down the ranching operation to children or other family members.

The corporate subcategory constituted 13.1 percent of survey respondents and was marked by a high dependence on ranching for income, relatively large herd sizes, and the largest swaths of privately owned lands. This group also reported a heavy reliance on hired labor, a high degree of financial stress, and contained a relatively large number of operations. As the name indicates, the corporate subcategory was marked by their use of various corporate forms to conduct ranch business, from c-corporations to s-corporations to the quasi-corporate LLC structure.[94]

89 *Id.*
90 *Id.* at 9.
91 *Id.*
92 *Id.*
93 *Id.*
94 *Id.* at 6, 9.

Sheep ranchers are the last subcategory of survey respondents, at 4.3 percent of the overall sample.[95] This group had a large herd size and the highest overall average of private "deeded" acres. As the name indicates, sheep were the primary or sole stock involved in the operation, as compared to cattle, horses, or exotics, and this group had the greatest overall labor need, reporting that they hired the greatest number of external laborers. This group had a relatively large percentage of bachelor's degree holders and reported being "highly dependent" on on-ranch income, while also reporting the greatest interest in participating in conservation activities.[96] This group reported the greatest overall reliance on public lands to support grazing across all seasons.

The Hages share many of the values reflected across the groups in the Gentner and Tanaka study – the sense of identity that comes with being a rancher, the sense of community that comes from living among ranchers, including working with the land, and building a family legacy. They no doubt share these views with the thousands of survey respondents in that study. It is not clear whether they are in the ranching business to make money or if they have outside investments or other sources of income to offset any ranch losses.[97] If one had to draw a line between the Hages and other public lands ranchers, it would probably lie somewhere in the outer extremes of several categories. Similarly, although their legacy in the Monitor Valley only began in the 1970s, they seem to see this legacy as *the only* family legacy worthy of protecting in this Valley. Additionally, the Hages seem to value ranching in the Monitor Valley, but not as *a* valid use, rather, as *the* valid use of this land.

Congress most definitely does not share the Hages' views, having enacted statutes like FLPMA and NFMA, which require the Departments of Interior and Agriculture to engage in land use planning that balances a series of multiple uses of the federal public lands.[98] Included among these uses are some that might seem foreign to the authors of the Taylor Act and the Granger-Thye Act, like recreation and ecological values. The changes that these statutes imposed upon the public lands, including the grazing allotments that Wayne Hage and his wife were no doubt eyeing when they purchased Pine Creek in 1978, were felt nearly immediately by the Hages. They applied for and received their first grazing permit allowing them to graze livestock on six allotments in the Toiyabe National Forest, in late October 1978. This permit, like every other, contained a statement that

95 Gentner & Tanaka, p. 9.

96 *Id.*

97 In testimony before the Nevada State Legislature in 2015, Wayne Hage's daughter, Ramona Hage Morrison, testified that she serves as a "consultant and expert witness to ranchers regarding property title and vested water rights." www.leg.state.nv.us/App/NELIS/REL/78th2015/ExhibitDocument/OpenExhibitDocument?exhibitId=10578&fileDownloadName=SJR1RamonaMorrisontestimony.pdf.

98 Hillary M. Hoffmann, *Climate Change and the Decline of the Federal Range: Is Adaptive Management the Solution?*, 15 VT. J. ENVTL. L. 36, 281 (2014).

the permit could be "revoked or suspended, in whole or in part" if the permittee failed to comply with any of the permit terms, any regulations issued by the Forest Service, or any instructions of the Forest Service officers.[99] (Similar language was included in the BLM permits.) And over time, the Forest Service and BLM would take management actions on the allotments for which the Hages held grazing privileges that would result in no less than eleven judicial opinions, in which the Hages battled their neighbors and the government over water rights, grazing privileges, access to public grazing allotments, and wildlife management.[100]

At the core of these lawsuits were claims by the Hages that government management of federal public lands interfered with their private property rights in violation of the US Constitution and Nevada state law. They challenged every federal agency action in federal court, and at times they seemed to love litigation as much as they loved their ranch. Their first legal objection involved elk, released in 1979 into an area that included portions of one allotment for which the Hages held a grazing permit. Over the next nine years, the Forest Service tried to manage the Hage's cattle and the released elk on this allotment, but at times, the elk needed to feed free from interference by cattle, so the agency adjusted the permit terms and annual authorizations, requiring the Hages to remove their cattle periodically throughout the year. The Hages refused, and the agency began to take steps to enforce their management decisions, including through impounding the Hages' cattle and suspending some of their permits.[101] From the perspective of the Hages, these actions were the result of propaganda, fueled by "environmental groups," who were issuing "dictates" to agencies like the Forest Service and the BLM, which these agencies were blindly following.[102]

The courts largely disagreed with the Hages' assessment of the federal agency actions and the family was largely unsuccessful in terms of their substantive challenges to the authority of the federal agency to manage their grazing use by lowering their permitted AUMs and requiring them to remove stock from portions of allotments during certain seasons to allocate forage for the elk and other species

[99] *Hage v. United States*, 35 Fed. Cl. 147, 153 (1996).

[100] *Hage v. United States* (*Hage I*), 35 Fed. Cl. 147 (1996); *Hage v. United States* (*Hage II*), 35 Fed. Cl. 737 (1996); *Hage v. United States* (*Hage III*), 42 Fed. Cl. 249 (1998); *Hage v. United States* (*Hage IV*), 51 Fed. Cl. 570 (2002); *Estate of Hage v. United States* (*Hage V*), 82 Fed. Cl. 202 (2008); *Estate of Hage v. United States* (*Hage VI*), 90 Fed. Cl. 388 (2009); *Estate of Hage v. United States* (*Hage VII*), 93 Fed. Cl. 709 (2010); *Estate of Hage v. United States* (*Hage VIII*), 687 F.3d 1281 (Fed. Cir. 2012); *Estate of Hage v. United States* (*Hage IX*), 113 Fed Cl. 277 (2013); *United States v. Est. of Hage*, No. 2:07-CV-01154-RCJ, 2013 WL 2295696, at *1 (D. Nev. May 24, 2013), vacated in part, 810 F.3d 712 (9th Cir. 2016), and rev'd in part, 632 F. App'x 338 (9th Cir. 2016), and vacated sub nom. United States v. Hage, No. 207CV01154GMNVCF, 2017 WL 752832 (D. Nev. Feb. 27, 2017); United States v. Est. of Hage, 810 F.3d 712 (9th Cir. 2016).

[101] *Hage v. United States*, 35 Fed. Cl. 147, 155 (1996).

[102] American Rancher Uncut Interview Pt. 1, Wayne Hage at Pine Creek 2005, at 12:17, available at https://vimeo.com/8520897.

dependent on the forest grasses and forbs.[103] But they did notch some victories on their claims that the Forest Service and BLM had overreached when enforcing the permit and regulatory violations against the Hages, particularly as related to their water rights and fences and other grazing "improvements" they had constructed on their allotments. In Wayne Hage's perspective, the heart of the litigation was a dispute over water, and it may not have even kicked off in the first place if the agencies had not come in and "laid a claim to all of [the Hages'] water rights."[104] Courts viewed their claims through a more particular lens, though, separating the water and private property rights claims relating to fences and stock ponds from the claims to public grasses ("forage") and land ("allotments").

The law regarding the latter resources is clear. The Taylor Grazing Act explicitly states that grazing permits "shall not create any right, title, interest, or estate in or to" federal lands.[105] Grasses and other "forage" that domestic livestock consume are public property, and a grazing permit confers no legal right, title, interest, or estate in to these resources either. Conversely, water on federal lands can be converted into a private property right through beneficial use, and the Hages *did* hold these rights, including rights to the ditches that the original homesteaders had constructed to divert water from the national forest onto their private land. In the third *Hage* decision, a Federal Court of Claims judge decided to bootstrap forage rights onto the Hages' ditch rights-of-way, holding that the grass growing along the ditches was the property of the Hages because it was necessary to feed their cattle as they moved along the banks of the ditch, drinking the water.[106] The court delineated a fifty-foot forage zone on either side of the ditch and declared this an "appurtenant" right to the ditch.

The Hages lost their last grazing permit in 1990, despite their attempts to defend against the agencies' claims that they had violated the terms of the permits and various federal laws and regulations. Between 1990 and 2008, the Hages continued to graze their cattle on the allotments, but without permits. This choice carried consequences under the federal grazing laws, which characterize this type of activity as a trespass against the United States.[107] The Department of Justice filed an

[103] *Hage v. United States*, 35 Fed. Cl. 147, 167 (1996).

[104] American Rancher Uncut Interview Pt. 1, Wayne Hage at Pine Creek 2005, at 8:35 & 8:50, available at https://vimeo.com/8520897.

[105] 43 U.S.C. § 315b.

[106] *Hage v. United States*, 42 Fed. Cl. 249, 251 (1998), *decision rescinded in part*, 51 Fed. Cl. 570 (2002). ("The court holds that the extent of the right to forage around an Act of 1866 ditch is contiguous with the scope of the ditch right-of-way: the ground occupied by the water and fifty feet on each side of the marginal limits of the ditch.").

[107] *Camfield v. United States*, 167 U.S. 518, 524 (1897) ("the government has, with respect to its own lands, the rights of an ordinary proprietor, to maintain its possession and to prosecute trespassers"). It probably did not ease tensions any that the Clinton Administration in the 1990s undertook grazing reform, which focused in large part on the definition of grazing preference. The 1995 Department of Interior amendments to the grazing regulations signaled a shift toward "restoration" of public lands used for

enforcement action against the Hages in federal court, seeking all available remedies, including monetary fines. The district court judge held largely in favor of the Hages, finding that they held easements along their ditch rights-of-way that were one-half mile on either side of the ditch centerline, despite the earlier ruling by the Court of Claims confining the ditch and forage rights of way to fifty feet on either side of the centerline.[108]

On appeal, the Ninth Circuit Court of Appeals reversed the decision of the federal district court, invalidating the half-mile easement by necessity, finding that the Hages had violated federal and state trespass laws by grazing their livestock on federal lands without a permit and chastising the district court judge for his obvious bias against the federal parties in the case. Noting that the government had proven that the Hages had "openly trespassed on federal lands" for many years, the Ninth Circuit opined that the district court should have limited its inquiry to one involving the facts, such as "when and where the cattle grazed illegally."[109] Instead, the district court invented a new rule of law (the one-mile easement by necessity for grazing along ditch rights), which plainly "contravened" existing federal law.[110] The Ninth Circuit quoted extensively from the transcript of the trial court proceedings, in which the district court judge freely opined that the federal government had a history in Nevada of impairing "substantiated rights of landowners," including grazing "rights," which he characterized as property rights. These statements, of course, directly contradicted the plain text of a federal statute – the Taylor Grazing Act – and several binding judicial opinions, including from the United States Supreme Court.

The seeming diatribes against the federal government by Judge Jones in the Hage district court case in Nevada, and public statements that Hage and his son have made over the years in interviews, have similar themes, which are not anomalous in Nevada, or indeed throughout the West. These themes have combined under a label for a movement that began in Nevada in the 1970s, in response to the federal government's pivot toward sustainability, improvement

grazing, to ensure that lands authorized for grazing use would be managed in a way that was "more compatible with ecosystem management," and to increase grazing fees such that the public would be more fairly compensated for the private use of these lands. Significantly, the 1995 regulations also changed the definition of "grazing preference," from a quantifiable right (based on AUMs and past usage) to the following: "a superior or priority position against others for the purpose of receiving a grazing permit or lease," attached to "base property owned or controlled by the permittee or lessee." In essence, this new definition removed a seemingly guaranteed right to graze a certain number of livestock on a given allotment and replaced it with an unquantified right of first refusal associated with a given allotment. The response from the livestock industry was predictable and rapid. Litigation ensued, and it reached the Supreme Court, which ruled in favor of the Department of Interior. *Public Lands Council*, 529 U.S. at 735.

108 *United States v. Est. of Hage*, 810 F.3d 712, 715 (9th Cir. 2016).

109 *Id.* at 722.

110 *Id.*

of public health, and environmental protection in statutes like NFMA, the National Environmental Policy Act (NEPA), the Clean Air Act, and the Clean Water Act. This movement is referred to as "the Sagebrush Rebellion," and one of its early leaders was Wayne Hage, Sr., the John Dutton-esque patriarch of the Pine Creek Ranch.

The primary historical driver of the Sagebrush Rebellion arose due to a consequence of the intermittent pace of settler colonialism west of the Mississippi River, which came in waves and targeted certain areas of the West that would be conducive to ranching, railroads, and mining. These targeted areas tended to be near water sources and in regions that experienced enough precipitation to make agricultural endeavors possible. Areas that lacked adequate water or contained soils that could not be irrigated remained sparsely populated by settler colonizers and this caused disproportionate land tenure patterns in and among western states. The pattern that resulted was a relatively larger percentage of federal land in the drier, more alkaline, and less agriculturally hospitable western states, which left these states at somewhat of a disadvantage in terms of levying property taxes to support public schools, general welfare programs, and other public institutions and assistance (due to the relatively small percentage of private lands that could be assessed and taxed). Thus, states like Nevada and Utah often were burdened (in the Sagebrush Rebels' view) with more federal land inside their borders than eastern states and they complained heartily of this perceived injustice. The disparate treatment, in their view, rendered them poorer as far as enticements they could offer to their residents, and, in turn, made them less appealing places for settler colonizers to move into and make a life for themselves.

One way to rectify this historical injustice, according to Sagebrush Rebels, was to convert federal land into state land, or better yet, private land. As noted earlier, almost immediately after the Hages acquired the grazing permits for the allotments surrounding Pine Creek Ranch, problems began. In judicial opinions that resulted from these disputes, they were characterized as disagreements over the "nature and scope" of the Hages' water rights and grazing permits.[111] In court proceedings, the Hages filed streams of objections to the federal agencies' management of what they considered to be "their" grazing allotments, despite the clear terms of the permits, which conveyed no "right, title, or interest" in the public lands to the holder of the permit. Below the surface, though, in the words of Wayne Hage, these complaints represented more than just property or water rights disputes – they stemmed from a belief that the federal government's ownership of any public land in the State of Nevada was unconstitutional. In Hage's view, holding the grazing privileges associated with grazing permit and possessing water rights located on the federal

[111] *Id.* at 1284.

allotment created a legal right to graze, which was protected by the US and Nevada Constitutions. Following this chain of logic, the federal government's purported ownership of the lands and its corresponding management actions constituted a "cloud" on the title of the permittee rancher, reducing its value and marketability.[112]

So, although the dispute involving the Pine Creek Ranch manifested as Hage's objections to the Forest Service's decision to release elk onto one of the allotments, which affected the quantity of forage and water available to Hage's cattle,[113] the real dispute was much deeper, and based on a fringe, ultra-conservative reading of the Constitution that continues to ripple through ranching communities well into the twenty-first century. For lawyers, it can be easy to dismiss the arguments of Sagebrush Rebels because they so plainly contravene existing federal law, dating back to the late 1700s. For over 200 years, it has been a rule of law that the federal government has the authority to establish ownership of the federal property through purchase or conquest (*Johnson v. M'Intosh*), and once the title is established, the federal government has authority to hold, use, manage, or sell it. This makes it challenging to give any credence to arguments that the federal government lacks authority over public lands, in the way that Hage and other Sagebrush Rebels so often do. Yet, in the opinion of former Interior Secretary Bruce Babbitt, it is a "mistake to dismiss the Rebellion as a regional curiosity," because "behind the simple proposal of the sagebrush rebels lie complex intergovernmental issues relating to ownership and management of the West's natural resources."[114] In Babbitt's view, "[w]hile the rebels' motives are suspect, the movement has been fueled by genuine uneasiness and increasing conflict between states and the federal government over management of the public domain."[115] In the chapters that follow, a deeper exploration of the motive and arguments of the Sagebrush Rebellion will unfold, revealing the extent to which the influence of this movement shapes federal land management and land use in the West well into the twenty-first century.

112 Jeffrey J. Wechsler, *This Land Is Our Land: Ranchers Seek Private Rights in the Public Rangelands*, 21 J. Land Resources & Envtl. L. 461, 462 (2001).

113 *Id.*

114 Bruce Babbitt, *Federalism and the Environment: An Intergovernmental Perspective of the Sagebrush Rebellion*, 12 Envtl. L. 847, 848 (1982).

115 *Id.*

8

Sage-Grouse Conservation and the West Lake Ranch

Reach for the stars, so if you fall, you land on a cloud.

Kanye West.[1]

In 2019, Kanye West made national headlines when he purchased a ranch near Cody, Wyoming, as part of his vision to create a modern western homestead for his family, a community for his friends, and a place of worship for his spiritual followers. The Monster Lake Ranch was 3,885 acres of windswept high desert sagebrush steppe with hardly a tree in sight, and had been listed in 2019 for $14 million.[2] The property had undergone somewhat of an identity struggle in the years prior to West purchasing it, having been owned and sold by a succession of wealthy individuals and families who sought to maximize the property's revenue generating potential as a destination hunting and fishing property within an easy half-day's drive of Yellowstone National Park. Previous owners had included Tim Blixseth, who was best known for having developed the Hollywood-celebrity and ultra-wealthy destination Yellowstone Club resort and ski area near Big Sky, Montana. When Blixseth lost most of his assets in a divorce, he was forced to sell Monster Lake, and an investor from Montana, Dan Eddleman, bought it with hopes of turning it into a dude ranch and destination resort for sport hunting and fishing.[3] At one point, Eddleman employed sixty-nine people at the Ranch, secured a commercial liquor license, and advertised flat water fly fishing, bird hunting, and lodging choices from cabin rentals to tipi camping.[4] This concept concept did not pan out either, though, and by 2019, Eddleman had listed the property for sale.

1 Kanye West, "Homecoming" (2007).

2 Zac Taylor and Leo Wolfson, *Opinion: Goodbye, Kanye West. Wyoming Hardly Knew Ye*, The Washington Post (Oct. 27, 2021), available at www.washingtonpost.com/opinions/2021/10/27/goodbye-kanye-west-wyoming-hardly-knew-ye/.

3 Mark Heinz, *Monster Lake to be Revived*, Cody Enterprise (July 3, 2013), available at www.codyenterprise.com/news/local/article_fb2bb5b2-e41b-11e2-b522-001a4bcf887a.html; McCoy's Farm & Ranch Family: the Eddleman Family, Texas High School Rodeo Ass'n (last visited Mar. 14, 2024), available at www.thsra.org/single-post/2019/06/06/mccoys-farm-ranch-family-the-eddleman-family.

4 www.datanyze.com/companies/monster-lake-ranch/447295907.

The property is dry, rugged and rocky, which is not ideal for ranching, but perfect for dystopian-themed music videos, which was perfectly alright with West.[5] In a music video shot on the property shortly after he purchased it, West's famous family, including his then-wife Kim Kardashian and their four children, are seen strolling together and sleeping among the rocky buttes and buttresses. The single featured in this video, "Closed on Sunday," focuses on the need to disconnect from technology and the pressures of modern city life, to spend time with loved ones enjoying nature and fresh air. Rather than eating Chick-Fil-A or scrolling on Instagram, West raps, families should spend Sundays together, in worship or simply just in each other's company, away from it all.[6] The calm family scenes are interspersed with film of a line of tank-like all-terrain vehicles, mostly manufactured by the Ukrainian company SHERP, driving across an area filled with sagebrush. At one point, the most expensive of these vehicles, a $500,000 Ripsaw mini tank with butterfly doors, enters the scene and speeds across the sagebrush toward the line of SHERPs, stopping and veering hard to avoid colliding with them. When the mini-tank comes to a stop, West and his then-mother-in-law, Kris Jenner, emerge.

Shortly after he filmed "Closed on Sunday," West began the first of a series of construction projects on the ranch. In interviews, he discussed plans to turn the property into "Yeezy Campus," where his friends, followers, and family could live in dome dwellings and practice their faith amid the stark beauty of the sagebrush.[7] He moved a lot of earth, including enough to partially complete a berm that would block passersby from seeing the construction and other activity on the ranch property. But by Election Day in 2020, West's time at the ranch, and in Wyoming, seemed to have suddenly ended. He cast his ballot at the Cody recreation center and disappeared, never to be seen around town again.[8] West Lake Ranch was placed on the multiple listing service for Wyoming in the fall of 2021, with an asking price of $11 million.[9]

There was a lot of speculation about why West left the ranch and stopped work on the property, ranging from theories about the well-documented demise of his marriage to Kim Kardashian, a changed artistic direction for his work, and county residents' theories that the harsh Wyoming winters were too long and too cold for the transplant from southern California. West had also declared his candidacy for President in the summer of 2020 on a Republican ticket that included a local Cody resident, but received

5 *Id.*

6 Chris Lambert, *Analyzing and Explaining Kanye West's "Closed on Sunday" Music Video*, FORBES (Nov. 28, 2019). In a famous clip from the video, Kanye's eldest daughter, North West, can be seen at the end of the song, standing on a rocky buttress and screaming "Chick-Fil-A!"

7 Anna L. Caplan, *Kanye West Reportedly Takes $11M "Yeezy Campus" Wyoming Ranch off the Market*, PEOPLE (Sept. 1, 2022), available at https://people.com/home/kanye-west-wyoming-ranch-yeezy-campus-for-sale/.

8 Taylor & Wolfson.

9 Emma Reynolds, *Kanye West Is Selling His Wyoming Ranch for $11 Million*, FORBES (Oct. 13, 2021), available at www.forbes.com/sites/emmareynolds/2021/10/13/kanye-west-is-selling-his-wyoming-ranch-for-11-million/?sh=6701310aae6a.

a lukewarm reaction, from the press and his family alike. Many suspected that the move away from Wyoming was somewhat of a reset of everything that Wyoming had entailed for West, including the Yeezy Campus, but also his family and his Presidential campaign, which failed to ever really launch. But there may have been something else that alienated Kanye – a small bird that has interrupted a lot of development plans in Wyoming and throughout the West, and one that is known well to the residents of Cody and Park Counties. This bird, the greater sage-grouse, is known to scientists as *Centrocercus urophasianus*, and to many westerners as the "prairie chicken."[10]

Sage-grouse were once ubiquitous in the West. Ferry Carpenter noted their prolificacy in the hills around Oak Point in his autobiography, *Confessions of a Maverick*, and the species was described as "blacken[ing] the sky" when Lewis and Clark began their reconnaissance of the Missouri River.[11] There may have once been as many as eleven million sage-grouse when Teddy Roosevelt took a hunting trip to the Badlands in 1883.[12] The adult greater sage-grouse is about the size of a large chicken, with a charismatic mating display occurring annually in communal mating areas called leks. Sage-grouse are committed to these mating rituals, as they are to their leks, returning year after year to the same area, where the males perform their signature strutting routines with puffed chests and spiked tails spread, hoping to attract a mate. The males are attracted to the lek areas due to their relatively sparse vegetation cover, which allows females to easily see the full mating display, and the females are attracted to the lek due to the presence of the males.[13] The grouse, and especially their needs specific to these mating locations, have caused innumerable headaches for those seeking to develop lek areas for oil and gas, livestock grazing, or construction projects like Yeezy Campus.[14]

The reason that sage-grouse have been problematic for early twenty-first century development is that their habitat is one of the last bastions of open land in the West. Historically, the more verdant lands along riparian corridors or higher elevation lands with greater annual precipitation were more attractive to immigrants arriving in the West, but as those lands were snapped up, the remaining open and available land is the drier, less verdant home of the sagebrush. And where there is sagebrush, historically there have been sage-grouse; the two species having evolved in a symbiotic relationship of mutual dependency over a very long time. Their relationship is so important that sage-grouse are referred to by biologists as an umbrella species,

10 Gov. Mark Gordon, State of Wyoming Executive Department, Executive Order 2019-3: Greater Sage-grouse Core Area Protection (Aug. 21, 2019).

11 Laird J. Lucas & Sarah Stellberg, *Can Sage-Grouse Save the West?*, NAT. RESOURCES & ENV'T 57 (Summer 2021).

12 *Id.*; Brad Fitzpatrick, *The Hunt that Changed America*, OUTDOOR AMERICA (Issue 4, 2013), available at www.iwla.org/docs/default-source/Outdoor-America-articles/the-hunt-that-changed-america.pdf?sfvrsn=2.

13 Wyo. Game & Fish Dept., "Sage-Grouse Lek Viewing Guide" (last visited Mar. 20, 2024), available at https://wgfd.wyo.gov/Habitat/Sage-Grouse-Management/Sage-Grouse-Lek-Viewing-Guide.

14 Peter O. Daniels, *Defending Science & Collaborative Conservation: Sage-Grouse & Western Watersheds Project v. Schneider (D. Idaho 2019)*, 44 HARV. ENVTL. L. REV. 591, 593 (2020).

meaning that they serve as "barometers" for the overall health of the sagebrush ecosystem, which is home to so many other plants, birds, and wildlife, including elk, pronghorn, mule deer, rabbits, eagles, and songbirds.[15]

But development, grazing, and other alterations of the sagebrush steppe have caused severe population declines in sage-grouse populations, such that perhaps that only 7 percent of the historic population remains. In the 2010s and 2020s, the species' decline has become precipitous, with studies showing that sage-grouse populations have declined across all states by an average of 44 percent from 2015 to 2019 alone.[16] The causes of these population declines are varied, but include oil and gas development and other mineral extraction activities, residential home-building and surface-disturbing development, invasive species consuming sagebrush steppe ecosystems, and ranching.[17] Activities that disturb leks are particularly harmful to the birds, whether through noise and other forms of intangible disturbance, as well as those that physically alter or destroy the lek area itself, because reproduction is so tied to these locations. Biologists have documented some leks that have been used continuously for over eighty years and because sage grouse have such a large range, returning to the same location for their annual mating rituals organizes the species well for propagation, ensuring that genetic diversity is maintained.[18] Livestock grazing has been described as one of "the main causes of sagebrush habitat degradation," and thus, is one of the main contributors to sage-grouse population decline.[19]

The federal government has been aware of sage-grouse population decline since at least 1954, although concrete efforts to do something about it did not start until the 1990s. In the meantime, Congress had passed a significant law that would impact the trajectory of the species, although not in ways that one might necessarily have expected. This law, the Endangered Species Act (ESA), has been called the "most powerful federal wildlife law, and perhaps the most powerful law in the whole field of natural resource management."[20] It has also been labeled by scholars as a legal "pit bull," because unlike other laws that have only procedural requirements, the ESA has "real teeth that can bite hard," stymying development of all kinds to protect endangered and threatened species and their habitat in the decades since its passage in 1973.[21] In the House Committee Report leading to the Act's passage, the loss of biological species was listed as a threat to the nation's "genetic heritage," the value of which was, in Congress's estimation "quite literally, incalculable."[22]

15 Working Lands for Wildlife, "Sage Grouse," last visited Mar. 9, 2023, available at www.wlfw.org/wildlife/sage-grouse/.

16 Daniels, 44 Harv. Envtl. L. Rev. at 593.

17 *Id.* n. 17.

18 *Id.* at 594.

19 Pl.'s Mot. for Summary J. & Mem. In Support, W. *Watersheds Proj. v. Bernhardt*, 2019 WL 5684330, p. 13 (filed Sept. 19, 2019).

20 Rasband, p. 395.

21 *Id.*

22 *Id.*

The ESA is complex, but its structure can be broken down into roughly five essential parts: (1) listing, (2) designation of "critical habitat," (3) consultation and avoidance of jeopardy, (4) prohibition on "takes," and (5) delisting. The listing process is the reason that this statute is so well known, as it culminates in the US Fish and Wildlife Service formally and publicly placing a given species on the famous "list" of those protected under the Act. Once a species is on this list, which is a process that can take months or even years, depending on the political and other pressures facing the agency surrounding the listing, the agency is charged with designating areas of critical habitat, which are discrete habitat locations within the species' larger habitat that are necessary to protect to ensure the species can feed, shelter and propagate.[23] Under section 5 of the ESA, upon listing a species, the agency is required to designate critical habitat locations within one year.[24] However, subsequent judicial opinions interpreting this section of the statute have clarified that this is not as mandatory as the statutory language of this provision alone might suggest – there is discretion not to list critical habitat if the listing would not be prudent because it would cause undue economic impact, among other considerations the statute allows the agency to consider.[25] The agency's current regulations allow it to decline a critical habitat designation if: (1) the species is under threat by human activity and the designation of critical habitat would further imperil the species (because people might affirmatively target the habitat once they know of the designation); or (2) the designation would "not be beneficial to the species" otherwise.[26] Even without a critical habitat designation, though, the agency is required to protect the species once it is listed.

The third and fourth parts – consultation and avoidance of jeopardy and the prohibition on takes – fall under sections 7 and 9, of the statute, respectively. The former imposes an "affirmative duty" on agencies to prevent violations of section 9, which prohibits a "take" of any listed species.[27] This requires consultation between federal agencies whenever the federal government is engaging in an action that could result in jeopardy to the species, and prohibits actions that result in jeopardy or a "take," as defined under section 9.[28] Section 9, in turn, prohibits anyone or any entity from effecting a "take," which the statute defines expansively to include actions like harassment, harm, pursuit, hunting, shooting, wounding, killing, trapping, capturing, collecting, or attempting to do any of these prohibited acts.[29] In the context of a species like the sage-grouse, this provision would require a federal agency engaged in permitting oil and gas development, such as the BLM, to consult with the agency that

[23] *Id.* at 413.

[24] *Sierra Club v.* U.S. *Fish & Wildlife Serv.*, 245 F.3d 434, 436 (5th Cir. 2001) (16 U.S.C.A. § 1533(a)(3)).

[25] *Id.* at 438–39.

[26] *Id.* at 438.

[27] *Arizona Cattle Growers' Ass'n v. U.S. Fish & Wildlife, Bureau of Land Mgmt.*, 273 F.3d 1229, 1237 (9th Cir. 2001).

[28] *Id.* at 1239.

[29] 16 U.S.C. §§ 1538(a)(1)(B); 1532(19).

oversees the listed species, which is the US Fish and Wildlife Service, to ensure that any development authorized by the BLM will not result in jeopardy to the sage-grouse's habitat or any harm to the individual grouse themselves.

Section 9 is probably the most controversial provision of the ESA because its scope is so broad. It impacts companies, individuals, federal agencies, state and local governments, and private landowners, protecting listed species from jeopardy posed by development and direct or indirect takes of the species. The expansive scope is intentional and based on scientific studies demonstrating that, at the time the ESA was passed, more than 50 percent of all endangered and threatened species had over 80 percent of their habitat on private lands.[30] Scientists estimated that somewhere between one-third and half of endangered and threatened species did not have any habitat on federal lands.[31] These facts would make it somewhat illogical to pass a statute that only protected species on federal lands, or habitat on federal lands, if the goal of the statute was to protect biodiversity. Thus, Congress chose the broader route – protecting the species and its habitat wherever they are found.

It is possible to violate section 9 directly or indirectly, which also sparks fear in the minds of developers and other private and public entities undertaking construction and other surface-disturbing projects and activities. In the context of sage-grouse, a direct take would include acts like an intentional shooting or harming of one or more birds, in a scenario in which the actor means to inflict harm or kill the bird(s). An indirect take is contemplated by the broad definition of the term "take" in the statute and the regulations, which authorize penalties for actions that "harm" or "harass" listed species.[32] In the context of the sage-grouse, these might be actions like digging a hole in the middle of a lek area to install a septic system, which would inhibit mating and thereby cause "harm" to the species, even though the acts are not motivated by an intent to harm the lek or the grouse.

The final major part of the ESA is surprising to many, given the highly protective and proactive bent of the first four. This portion of the statute requires delisting of a species once it has met certain population thresholds and other requirements established by the agencies with jurisdiction over the species – the US Fish and Wildlife Service (for terrestrial species) or the National Marine Fisheries Service (for marine species).[33] The delisting action releases any previously existing protections for a species' habitat, rendering it available once again for hunting, trapping, and other subsistence purposes and uses. The idea is that a species will not be delisted until its population has reached a healthy level that would thrive despite hunting, habitat modification, and other potentially harmful or adverse effects. So,

30 Rasband, at 441 (quoting Karin P. Sheldon, *Habitat Conservation Planning: Addressing the Achilles Heel of the Endangered Species Act*, 6 N.Y.U. Envtl. L. J. 279, 286 (1998)).

31 *Id.*

32 *Id.* at 444.

33 *Id.* at 400–01, n. 6.

for sage-grouse, this might include species numbers reaching certain population thresholds throughout the areas of the western states that form part of the species' traditional range, as well as certain guarantees from federal agencies regarding limiting mineral development authorizations and other activities that would harm or destroy habitat.

There is a problem with using the sage-grouse to illustrate the operation of the various sections of the ESA discussed previously, though. The sage-grouse has never been listed and, therefore, it is not protected under any of the various parts of the ESA. The US Fish & Wildlife Service's evaluation of this species for potential listing under the ESA was complex and fraught, with conservation organizations strongly advocating in favor of listing and states and private landowners advocating against it. The arguments in favor of listing were simple – the species required listing to avoid further precipitous drops in population, particularly in the face of intense national interest in developing the vast oil and gas reserves located under prime sage-grouse habitat.[34] Ranching and livestock grazing activity has been found to harm sage-grouse in direct and indirect ways, from destruction of protective biological soil crusts necessary to keep soils in place, causing erosion and allowing invasive species like cheatgrass to take root and spread, to alteration of the composition and distribution of key endemic plant communities, which also allows invasive plant species to overtake native species that have co-evolved with sagebrush.[35] The cascading impacts of overgrazing and soil degradation are far-reaching and often lead to increased wildfire outbreaks and increased severity of existing wildfires, due to the flammability of invasives like cheatgrass.[36] Ranchers also contributed to the decline of the grouse through the use of mechanized farm equipment.[37] Because of this correlation, livestock grazing is often identified as a "promoter" of larger and more frequent wildfire episodes. Fire, in turn, harms sage-grouse by destroying or heavily damaging the sagebrush plants in the path of the flames, given that sagebrush do not regenerate after they have been burned.[38]

More directly, ranch-related construction on outbuildings, corrals, fencing, and irrigation infrastructure damage and destroy sage-grouse habitat by encouraging invasive plant species to take root, posing collision hazards for the birds, creating optimal perches for sage-grouse predator species like eagles and other raptors, and causing sage-grouse to flee the area that has been cleared to find shelter and protection from predators.[39] This would include structures that would be labeled "environmentally

[34] Daniels, at 598.

[35] Pl.'s Opening Br. in Support of Mot. for Summary J., *Western Watersheds Project v. U.S. Department of the Interior, et al.*, 2015 WL 13590237 (filed Aug. 15, 2015).

[36] Young & Allen, p. 530.

[37] *Id.* at 531.

[38] *Id.*

[39] Peter M. Lacy, *The (Legal) Plight of the Greater Sage-Grouse*, FED. LAW, June/July 2018, at 32, 35.

friendly," like wind turbines and solar panels. But even low-profile infrastructure, like fencing, causes significant harm to the birds because they often fly quite low and fast through their sagebrush habitats. Sage-grouse fence strikes have been extensively documented throughout the West.[40]

This is not to say that *all* livestock grazing operations and ranches pose a threat to sage-grouse, and this is precisely what the anti-listing crowd argued. They raised concerns that regulatory impacts would harm ranching, energy development, and other private interests[41] (think Yeezy Campus), and they had some compelling arguments. At the time the US Fish & Wildlife Service was considering listing the sage-grouse, its historic range totaled roughly 173 million acres, 45 percent of which were private. Thus, ranching would have been immediately and potentially dramatically impacted by a listing decision.[42] These arguments found enough support at the national level that in 2014, Congress passed an appropriations rider that prohibited the US Fish & Wildlife Service from[43] expending any money to write a rule to list the sage-grouse under the ESA, which President Barack Obama signed into law. This was an effective prohibition on using the ESA to protect the grouse.

With its hand forced by Congress, the US Fish & Wildlife Service issued a decision in 2015, declining the petition to list sage-grouse. Among the agency's findings included one that listing was "not warranted" because federal agency plans adopted by the BLM and Forest Service "include[d] substantial provisions for addressing activities that occur in sage-grouse habitats and affect the species, including those threats identified [earlier] as having inadequate regulatory measures."[44] In plain English, the agency's assessment was that the growing public–private partnership movement seeking to avoid a listing decision had made enough progress on legal and other protections for sage-grouse and their habitat that an ESA listing would be superfluous. This criterion – the loophole through which the agency avoided listing the birds – is known as the "adequate regulatory mechanisms" provision.[45]

The plans that these federal agencies had developed, which involved significant buy-in from state agencies, local governments, and private landowners, resulted in significant restrictions on development in areas of sage-grouse habitat, like West Lake Ranch. There, the relevant authority that governed West's plans to build out

[40] *Oregon Nat. Desert Ass'n v. Bureau of Land Mgmt.*, No. 2:10-CV-01331-SU, 2014 WL 4832218, at *23 (D. Or. Sept. 29, 2014).

[41] Daniels, at 599.

[42] Sandra B. Zellmer et. al., *Species Conservation & Recovery through Adequate Regulatory Mechanisms*, 44 Harv. Envtl. L. Rev. 367, 396 (2020).

[43] Bret Birdsong, *The Grid and the Grouse: Cooperative Federal-State Conservation Planning in the Ages of Obama and Trump*, 13 FIU L. Rev. 103, 126, n. 116 (2018).

[44] *Finding on a Petition to List Greater Sage-Grouse (Centrocercus urophasianus) as an Endangered or Threatened Species*, 80 Fed. Reg. 59,857, 59,887 (Oct. 2, 2015).

[45] Zellmer, at 396.

Yeezy Campus was a 2019 Executive Order of Wyoming Governor Mark Gordon establishing "core areas" of sage-grouse habitat that must be protected under state law.[46] Included among the other clauses explicating the Governor's rationale behind the Executive Order was the specter of the ESA, clearly indicating that avoiding listing (under the ESA) was one of the Governor's primary motivations in signing the Order. Noting everything from the feared "significant, adverse effect on land and natural resource management, and the economy of the State of Wyoming," to the "adverse effect" of listing on the "custom and culture of the State of Wyoming," the Governor made a compelling case for the substituted state-level protections as an effective alternative.

Meanwhile, even before Gov. Gordon's Executive Order, West's plans for a "meditation center" on his ranch property, with a significant "underground" component, had required a zoning variance because the structure could not be approved under existing planning and zoning codes.[47] The zoning variance request had been submitted by an attorney for West's corporate entity involved in the Ranch development plans – Psalm 2019 – before Gov. Gordon's 2019 Executive Order was issued. Once the Executive Order took effect, it imposed a superseding state-level review of the portions of West's property where the meditation center and other buildings would be sited, to ensure that they avoided sage-grouse habitats and populations inside "Core Population Areas, Connectivity Areas, and Winter Concentration Areas."[48] After the Executive Order's publication, West and his corporate affiliate withdrew the variance request, stating publicly that the Governor's order "ought to be concerning to everybody with the impact that it has to potential development in Park County and any county in Wyoming."[49]

The Executive Order also required all new construction projects to be at least 0.6 miles from lek areas and limited surface-disturbing activity to the period from July 1 to March 14 to avoid lek activity (usually occurring in March and April) and nesting.[50] According to news reports at the time, it appeared that West had already engaged in some work prior to the Executive Order being issued and without securing a variance, which violated both county ordinances and eventually, state laws. But in short order, Donald J. Trump was elected President and a shift in the national dialogue around protecting wildlife and other public resources occurred, as well as significant shifts in federal policies regarding wildlife. After applying for and initially being denied a variance in the winter of 2019, West's zoning applications were

[46] Gov. Mark Gordon, State of Wyoming Executive Department, Executive Order 2019-3: Greater Sage-Grouse Core Area Protection (Aug. 21, 2019).

[47] Leo Wolfson, *West Ranch Structure Delayed By Governor Order*, CODY ENTERPRISE (Dec. 18, 2019), available at www.codyenterprise.com/news/local/article_e11a5e96-21d9-11ea-aa41-b34acef39623.html.

[48] *Id.* at 2.

[49] *Id.*

[50] "Sage Grouse Habitat Requirements," University of Nevada-Reno College of Ag., Biotech. & Natural Res. (last visited Mar. 14, 2014), available at https://extension.unr.edu/publication.aspx?PubID=3211.

granted in the spring of 2020, and he received approval to expand his ranch footprint, even within the core areas of sage-grouse habitat. According to the permits issued by Park County, West received approval to add a two-bedroom lake house, two underground, 10,000-square-foot parking garages, and a ten-bedroom, 52,000-square-foot residence, the latter of which is approximately the size of the White House.[51]

These local approvals came at a time when the Trump Administration was signaling to states that they did not need to maintain their existing "regulatory mechanisms" because sage-grouse were not actually under threat and White House staff had conveyed this policy decision to the US Fish and Wildlife Service. The Administration's actions sent the message that states and local governments, like that of Park County, could loosen their restrictions on development that impacted sage-grouse habitat or the birds themselves, without fear of federal reprisal.[52] President Trump's first Interior Secretary, former Montana Congressman Ryan Zinke, began his tenure in Washington with a directive that a "Sage-Grouse Review Team" be convened to review previous Administration's sage-grouse plans and "enhance State involvement," to "align" federal agencies' actions with state plans.[53] The Team was assembled and got to work, eventually issuing a report that recommended a number of modifications to the previous plans. Following the release of the report, federal agencies that managed sage-grouse habitat, like the BLM, began revising their management plans to align with the new policy direction of the Administration and the report of the Sage-Grouse Review Team.[54] These plans were far less protective of sage-grouse and their habitat than previous plans had been, revealing another attribute of the overall shift in federal policy toward sage-grouse (and other wildlife species).

The BLM's final planning changes in 2019 triggered litigation by wildlife conservation organizations, including the Western Watersheds Project, Wildearth Guardians, the Center for Biological Diversity, and others, because they weakened or rescinded numerous science-based conservation strategies incorporated into the agency's earlier plans.[55] These measures appeared to be closely aligned with the Trump "energy dominance" agenda, which elevated fossil fuel development over other public lands and natural resources priorities, including protection of sage-grouse habitat. In short, according to Bobby McEnaney, then senior deputy director for the Western Renewable Energy Project at NRDC, the Trump administration's "blueprint" for sage-grouse conservation was "basically a wish list for industry," with "no biology

[51] Jackie F. Mogensen, *Donald Trump, Kanye West, and a Weird Western Bird are all Somehow Involved in a Major Conservation Battle*, Mother Jones (Aug. 17, 2020), available at www.motherjones.com/environment/2020/08/trump-kanye-west-sage-grouse-conservation-wyoming/.

[52] Mogensen.

[53] *W. Watersheds Project v. Schneider*, 417 F. Supp. 3d 1319, 1327 (D. Idaho 2019).

[54] *Id.*

[55] Pl.'s Opening Br. In Support of Mot. for Prelim. Inj., *W. Watersheds Project v. Schneider*, 2019 WL 1772836 (D. Idaho 2019) (filed Apr. 19, 2019).

or science to support it."[56] As it turned out, this was not just a catchy quote – there was an *actual* wish list from industry, in the form of a July 19, 2017 letter from the Western Energy Alliance to the Review Team, requesting input on habitat designations, reducing lek buffers, and identifiying other protective measures that industry deemed to be "overly broad."[57]

There also appeared to be a wish list from the livestock grazing industry, as the 2019 BLM plan amendments weakened what the plaintiff conservation groups labeled "already inadequate protections" from previous plans, "in numerous ways."[58] These included requests to eliminate or weaken BLM's requirement (imposed upon itself in the earlier plans) to assess terms and conditions for achieving sage-grouse "habitat objectives" in the agency's periodic review of grazing permit terms and conditions; allowing BLM to avoid public notice and comment whenever it needed to "adjust" habitat objectives through a plan; and watering down the agency's prior commitment to incorporate certain scientifically-recommended objectives, such as a seven-inch grass height requirement on grazing allotments.[59] BLM also reduced or simply eliminated its previous commitment to evaluating the impacts of fences, stock tanks, and other so-called "range improvements" to determine whether they would need to be modified to account for sage-grouse habitat, nesting, feeding, or breeding needs.[60] Upon making these changes pursuant to the new policy edicts of the Trump Administration, BLM began implementing them almost immediately.

Conservation groups filed a lawsuit against the Trump plan amendments, seeking a preliminary injunction due to the pressing need to protect sage-grouse from the immediate impacts of BLM's implementation-level decisions across the western states. The immediacy stemmed from the agency's statements that threatened to green-light a number of problematic proposals, including large oil and gas leasing and development projects, coal, gold, and phosphate mining projects, 14,000 acres of off-highway vehicle use areas, hundreds of rights-of-way applications for infrastructure like power lines and pipelines, and hundreds of livestock grazing permits awaiting renewal.[61] Although the initial court proceedings involved only the plaintiffs' request for a preliminary injunction to stop the agency's implementation of the 2019 Trump-era sage-grouse plans, rather than a substantive analysis of the merits, the district court found that the plaintiffs had demonstrated evidence that the BLM had failed to consider scientific evidence supporting or opposing their intended plans, which likely violated the ESA and

[56] Mogenson.
[57] Pl.'s Opening Br. In Support of Mot. for Prelim. Inj., W. *Watersheds Project v. Schneider*, 2019 WL 1772836 (D. Idaho 2019) (filed Apr. 19, 2019).
[58] *Id.*
[59] *Id.*
[60] *Id.*
[61] *Id.*

the National Environmental Policy Act (NEPA). Both statutes require agencies to consider impacts to wildlife and bird species like sage-grouse prior to making a final determination on any course of action, including in a resource management plan.

The court did not need to find that the agency had violated those statutes, though, because the standard for issuing a preliminary injunction is less onerous, requiring a judge to determine only that it would be "likely" that the plaintiffs would prevail at trial. Ultimately, that is exactly what the court found. Specifically, the court determined that the agency's 2019 sage-grouse plans aligned with State sage-grouse plans but did not mention sage-grouse protections, which rendered the federal plans vulnerable to the plaintiffs' claims that the agency had violated NEPA and the ESA while developing them. The court also found that the agency failed to take a "hard look" at the consequences of its revised management actions encompassed in the 2019 plans, which was required due to the extensive scientific record created by the BLM itself (supported by input from other agencies, like US Fish & Wildlife and the Environmental Protection Agency) indicating that sage-grouse populations were under threat of further precipitous decline due to habitat loss associated with various types of development in sagebrush ecosystems.[62]

This case, *Western Watersheds Project v. Schneider*, also included findings that the plaintiffs would suffer irreparable harm in their efforts to conserve sage-grouse and their habitat if the court did not issue a preliminary injunction. Under the "weakened protections" of the 2019 plans, the agency would be approving "oil and gas leases; drilling permits; rights-of-way for roads, pipelines, and powerlines; coal and phosphate mining approvals; and livestock grazing permit renewals," and it was "likely that these actions [would] cause further declines of the sage grouse under the weakened protections of the 2019 Plan Amendments."[63] Finally, in its analysis of the "balance of hardships and public interest" element, the court held that the sage-grouse would suffer more hardship from the 2019 plans than the agency would suffer from having to return to the 2015 plan framework. The court concluded by recognizing the "well-established public interest in preserving nature and avoiding irreparable environmental injury" and found that this interest was present in the plaintiffs' case.[64]

After the district court issued this ruling in 2019, BLM appealed to the Ninth Circuit Court of Appeals, but the federal defendants ultimately petitioned the court to dismiss the appeal, which was unopposed by the conservation organizations. The Ninth Circuit ultimately dismissed the appeal in March of 2020, which rendered the district court's opinion as the judicial "last word" on the Trump-era plans. Yet,

62 *W. Watersheds Project v. Schneider*, 417 F. Supp. 3d 1319, 1332 (D. Idaho 2019).
63 *Id.* at 1334.
64 *Id.*

despite the ruling in the *Western Watersheds* case enjoining the 2019 plans in every state in which they would have taken effect, BLM continued to use these plans to justify implementation-level approvals that would result in harm to sage-grouse and destruction of their habitat. This forced environmental groups to file suit again, arguing that these individual approvals violated the rule of law established by the court in *Western Watersheds*.

In a 2022 opinion from a federal district court in Oregon, considering a complaint filed by the Oregon Natural Desert Association against the Oregon State BLM Director, the plaintiffs argued that a series of decisions eliminating protective designations for habitat areas mandated by the 2015 plans effectively left these areas open to livestock grazing. According to the plaintiffs, livestock grazing activity in these areas would threaten the continuing viability of key sage-grouse populations within the state and the agency had made a binding commitment to close these areas to grazing to protect the grouse in the 2015 plans. In a ruling on the plaintiffs' pretrial motion for summary judgment, the court agreed with the plaintiffs and ordered the thirteen special protection areas closed to grazing immediately. The agency defendants initially appealed this decision to the Ninth Circuit Court of Appeals also, but like the *Western Watersheds* opinion from the Idaho district court, the appeal was later dismissed.[65]

The ultimate question of whether ranching is "good" or "bad" for sage-grouse conservation may depend on whom you ask, and what type of ranching activity is contemplated. Yeezy Campus' futuristic dome-like structures and the activities associated with the filming of "Closed on Sunday" and other music videos might drive grouse away from the lek on West Lake Ranch. If the construction destroys the lek site, that will obviously also have an adverse impact on the grouse. Traditional cattle ranching operations' adverse impacts on sage-grouse habitat, as well as the birds themselves, have been well-documented dating back to the early 1990s when US Fish and Wildlife first began considering a listing decision for the sage-grouse. However, some cattle ranching activity might not be incompatible with sage-grouse protection, especially if the ranch owner is amenable to seasonal closures, grouse-friendly fencing, and other modified ranching techniques.

In 2022, Kanye West took Monster Lake Ranch off the market. A tabloid news publication, The Sun, obtained aerial photographs of the property showing a building (the former fishing lodge) that had been torn down, circular areas where dirt, topsoil, and vegetation had been removed, a vast "mud hole" partially filled with water, and several partially completed futuristic looking dome structures near the fishing lake.[66] According to earlier reporting in Forbes, the dome structures were

65 *Oregon Nat. Desert Ass'n v. Bureau of Land Mgmt.*, No. 23-35101, 2023 WL 5012123, at *1 (9th Cir. June 5, 2023).

66 Kasey Broekema, *Bad Buy? Kanye West's Monster Lake Ranch almost Desolate with Mud Holes after Rapper Failed to sell $11M Property*, THE U.S. SUN (Oct. 8, 2023), available at

"inspired by the rounded huts on Luke Skywalker's home planet of Tatooine," made famous by the original Star Wars film.[67] Speculation was rife that there were no serious buyers and activity at the ranch had seemingly come to a complete halt, with reporters labeling the ranch as "abandoned," save for a lone security guard occasionally patrolling to guard against for curious onlookers.

Ironically, aside from the mudhole and the dome dwellings, the "abandoned" West Lake Ranch of 2024 provides a potential semi-desirable habitat for sage-grouse, at least relative to the active construction period on the ranch two years prior. Although it is not clear what Kanye West plans to do with this property, the grouse would benefit from it remaining "abandoned," so long as they can return to their lek in the spring. If things remain quiet, the grouse are definitely better off at West Lake Ranch than they are on nearby ranches actively running cattle. They are also probably better off than they would be on nearby federal or state public lands, which have relatively "weaker" protections for sage-grouse in Wyoming than in other states, according to attorney Sarah Stellberg, who litigated the *Western Watersheds Project v. Schneider* case and authored an article about sage-grouse conservation for Natural Resources and Environment magazine in 2021. Stellberg and her co-author titled the article "Can Sage-Grouse Save the West?" and when asked in 2024 to revisit whether her answer to that question was still "yes," given the fraught history of sage-grouse and ranching, the pro-agricultural bias of federal and state agencies, and the damage done under the Trump Administration, her answer was not a definitive "yes" or "no," but instead seemed to be a rather hesitant "maybe." She explained that impediments to sage-grouse habitat protection remain, and in some ways they have increased under the Administration of President Joseph R. Biden. The long-awaited revisions to the sage-grouse plans enjoined by the *Schneider* decision came out in March 2024 and disappointed many sage-grouse advocates, including Stellberg and other advocates at nonprofit organizations whose missions center on the preservation of wildlife. These plans were demonstrably weaker than the original Obama-era plans, which offered more concrete measures to conserve the species' habitat. The long and the short of the relationship between sage-grouse and ranching is that the present state of things likely will result in further species decline, unless something changes about ranching. As Stellberg reflected, "there are too many cattle for sage-grouse conservation to be done effectively right now."[68]

www.the-sun.com/entertainment/9279287/kanye-west-wyoming-ranch-monster-lake-abandoned-photos/#:~:text=Kanye's%20Wyoming%20property%20appears%20to,2021%2C%20asking%20for%20%2411million.

[67] Zack O'Malley Greenburg, *Kanye's Second Coming: Inside the Billion-Dollar Yeezy Empire*, FORBES (Jul. 9, 2019), available at www.forbes.com/sites/zackomalleygreenburg/2019/07/09/kanyes-second-coming-inside-the-billion-dollar-yeezy-empire/?sh=133047b45ec3.

[68] Interview with Sarah Stellberg, Staff Attorney, Advocates for the West (Mar. 19, 2024) (on file with author).

9

National Wildlife Refuges and the "War on Rangelands"

The firing of these lethal rounds was part of the pre-planned operation.

– Jeanette Finicum[1]

On January 26, 2016, along a remote stretch of Oregon's Highway 395, about nineteen miles north of the small town of Burns, the Oregon State Police and the Federal Bureau of Investigation set up something called a "deadman's roadblock." This police technique is known for the element of surprise, typically involving a physical barrier placed across a lane of travel that is not visible to a driver being pursued by police until immediately prior to encountering it. The reason for the roadblock is the subject of litigation, but it is an extreme measure (given the likelihood that a suspect operating a vehicle at high speed and encountering the roadblock will likely suffer serious injury or death) and in this case followed an equally extreme act – the twenty-four-day occupation of the Malheur Wildlife Refuge by a group calling itself the Citizens for Constitutional Freedom, who were protesting the federal government's management of grazing permits on portions of the Refuge.[2] The grazing permits were held by the Hammond family, but the protest was organized by their friends, members of the Bundy family, who were famous (or infamous, depending on one's perspective) for protesting federal agency management of federal grazing activity on public lands in Nevada. The first vehicle to encounter the roadblock that cold January day was driven by Robert "Lavoy" Finicum, a part-time rancher, activist, and author of an end-times novel depicting a western family's struggle to survive when the government falls apart. Finicum had stood out during the Malheur occupation, often appearing on the porch of the refuge's main building, maintaining a solitary vigil on behalf of his comrades inside, and appearing as the protestors' de facto spokesperson. He even gave the occasional interview to local news outlets portraying the Citizens for Constitutional Freedom as the victims of a government plot.[3]

1 *Finicum, et al., v. Bur. of Land Mgmt., et al.*, Pls.' Third Amended Compl, ¶ 246, 2021 WL 9595813 (filed Oct. 15, 2021).

2 *Id.* ¶ 26.

3 Amelia Templeton & Conrad Wilson, *Deceased Militant LaVoy Finicum: Rancher, Patriarch, Bundy Believer*, Oregon Publ. Broadcasting (Jan. 27, 2016), available at www.opb.org/news/series/burns-oregon-standoff-bundy-militia-news-updates/robert-lavoy-finicum-dead-rancher-bundy-burns-oregon/.

Within minutes of encountering the roadblock and veering off the road into a snowbank, Finicum would be dead, shot by a state police officer a few feet outside his vehicle, as he reached into his pocket. Apparently, his dying words were – "go ahead and shoot me."[4] The facts that led to Finicum's death are the same facts that shape many of the stories in Chapters 5–7. Finicum is a rancher, and he was in Oregon to express his solidarity with the Bundy family. The Bundy family is one of the best-known public lands ranching families in the nation, having battled the Bureau of Land Management for decades in Nevada over their use (or misuse, in BLM's opinion) of the Bunkerville Allotment, which President Obama established as the Gold Butte National Monument during his second term. Finicum had attended a 2014 protest at the Bundy ranch following the BLM's attempt to impound Bundy's cattle pursuant to a court order finding that he had failed to pay his permit and trespass fees. In Finicum's opinion, which was shared by the Bundy family, the BLM and the FBI had "targeted" the Bundys due to their political views, which centered on what they saw as an unlawful occupation of land in Nevada and other western states in violation of the US Constitution.[5]

The Bunkerville situation looked slightly different from the perspective of the federal government, though. According to the Bureau of Land Management, its law enforcement division had attempted to carry out several federal court orders authorizing the agency to impound Bundy's cattle because he refused to remove them from a federal allotment near the ranch, where they were unlawfully grazing after Bundy's permit had been revoked.[6] Under federal law, this situation constitutes a trespass against the public lands and BLM has the statutory and regulatory authority to take enforcement actions to protect public lands and resources, at several levels, culminating in cattle seizure and impoundment. As soon as the BLM began its impoundment efforts near the Bundy Ranch in Bunkerville, hundreds of protestors, "including many openly carrying firearms, converged on the impoundment site demanding that the BLM personnel leave the site immediately and release the impounded cattle."[7] Local BLM leadership became so concerned about the safety of the law enforcement division that they paused the impoundment, then released Bundy's cattle. The tense situation during the standoff was captured by national and social media, and heavily armed protestors could be seen aiming their automatic weapons at BLM law enforcement from various positions around the impounded cattle.

Cliven Bundy, the family patriarch, along with his sons Ammon and Ryan, were indicted for taking part in the confrontation, but the charges against them were ultimately dismissed due to prosecutorial errors committed during the lead-up to the trial.

4 Sandra B. Zellmer, *Mitigating Malheur's Misfortunes: The Public Interest in the Public's Public Lands*, 31 GEO. ENVTL. L. REV. 509, 514 (2019).

5 *Finicum, et al., v. Bur. of Land Mgmt., et al.*, Pls.' Third Amended Compl, ¶ 55.

6 *United States v. Ehmer*, 87 F.4th 1073, 1085–88 (9th Cir. 2023).

7 *Id.*

Following the Bunkerville standoff, Ammon Bundy found himself with a national platform and a rapt audience, which devoured his pontifications on land rights, unconstitutional overreach by the federal government, and that specific form of populism known only in the West, rooted in the Sagebrush Rebellion. He pitched his family's saga with the BLM and the Bunkerville Allotment as the ultimate David and Goliath story, and by 2015, his email distribution list had reached approximately 28,000 people.[8] His legal arguments were arcane, including one that the Federal Government lacked authority to control or regulate any land located within a state except through the Enclave Clause of the US Constitution, which authorizes Congress "[t]o exercise exclusive Legislation in all Cases whatsoever, … over all Places purchased by the Consent of the Legislature of the State in which the Same shall be, for the Erection of Forts, Magazines, Arsenals, dock-Yards, and other needful Buildings."[9]

The Supreme Court holds a different view of the Enclave Clause, though, having ruled many times that State consent is not required for Congress to act with respect to federal public lands, even in a manner that is contrary to state law.[10] Moreover, even when a State "retains jurisdiction over federal lands within its territory," the Constitution's Property Clause gives Congress the power to enact legislation "respecting those lands," which "necessarily overrides conflicting state laws under the Supremacy Clause."[11] It was this Clause that seemed to draw the ire of the Hammonds, Bundys, and Finicum, and their irritation echoes the complaints of the Hages and so many others, including Indigenous Peoples whose lands were taken and converted to federal property subject to the Property Clause (using the Doctrine of Discovery). The roots of what happened in Oregon were deep, and reached back to the text of the Constitution itself.

Ammon Bundy, the most visible of Cliven Bundy's fourteen children, learned of the federal prosecution of Dwight and Steven Hammond sometime in 2015. Prosecutors had charged the Hammonds with violating a federal law that prohibits damaging or destroying federal property using fire, based on their repeated and unpermitted burning of areas of federal land where they grazed livestock.[12] The Hammonds characterized these as controlled burns, which western ranchers frequently light to clear undesirable brush from pastures, but witnesses at the Hammonds' trial testified to a different motive. One teenage relative stated under oath that Steven Hammond handed out matches to several individuals with instructions to strike and drop them on the ground, so they could "light up the whole country on fire."[13] The ensuing flames were eight to ten feet tall and spread quickly, sending the teenager running to a nearby creek for protection. This fire,

8 *Id.*

9 *See* U.S. CONST. art. I, § 8, cl. 17 (emphasis added).

10 *Kleppe v. New Mexico*, 426 U.S. 529, 541 (1976).

11 U.S. CONST. art. IV, § 3, cl. 2; *Kleppe*, 426 U.S. at 543.

12 *United States v. Hammond*, 742 F.3d 880, 881 (9th Cir. 2014).

13 *Id.*

set in 2001, burned 139 acres of federal land, and it was not the first time that the Hammonds had caused damage to federal land using fire. The first incident occurred in 1999, when they set a fire on their private property that crossed over onto and burned approximately ninety acres of nearby federal land.[14]

The Hammond family owns a ranching corporation, Hammond Ranches, Inc., which holds private property in eastern Oregon, near Burns. But this chapter is not about their ranch. This chapter focuses on the Malheur National Wildlife Refuge, which the Hammonds were treating as if it were their ranch, despite the law, policy, and public interest in this land and its wildlife as an area designated for protection, above all other uses. The Hammonds' tie to the Refuge stems from their historical possession of the grazing preference and grazing permits for federal allotments located partially within the Refuge. Some of the area burned because of the fires they set also fell within the boundaries of this Refuge, a 187,000-acre preserve established in 1908 by President Theodore Roosevelt to protect the breeding grounds of several species of migratory birds.[15]

But as was the case with so many other conservation designations, to create the Refuge, the federal government needed first to remove the people who were living there. These people, the Paiute and Bannock, were somewhat of a mystery to the United States government, and even to the early settler colonizers who first arrived in eastern Oregon in the 1800s. It was not until 1860 that much was written down in English about the "Snake" and "Piute" Indians in the southeastern portion of the State, except that they were "a nomadic, nonvillage type of Indian," in the words of one government report.[16] They moved throughout the area that is now eastern Oregon, southwest Idaho, northern California, and northern Nevada, hunting and following game species as they migrated from lower lying winter grounds to higher elevation summer grazing areas.[17] The precise boundaries of their ancestral homelands were not known to the US government, which nevertheless pursued treaty negotiations to attempt to put limits around the areas they occupied, as settler colonizers began arriving in eastern Oregon. In this arid region of the state, access to water was incredibly important, especially for homesteaders who wanted to raise crops and livestock, and Malheur Lake offered people, animals, and birds alike an oasis amid the vast desert east of the Cascade Mountain range.

According to the historical records kept by the settler colonizers and the federal government, the so-called Snake and Piute Indians were "hostile to the whites,"

14 Brief for the United States in Opposition to Petition for Certiorari, *Hammond v. United States*, 2015 WL 512898, at *2 (filed Feb. 9, 2015).

15 U.S. Fish & Wildlife Service, *Malheur National Wildlife Refuge* (last visited Mar. 21, 2024), available at www.fws.gov/refuge/malheur/about-us#:~:text=Today%2C%20Malheur%20consists%20of%20more,of%20birds%20and%20other%20wildlife.

16 *Snake or Piute Indians of Former Malheur Rsrv. in Or. v. United States*, 112 F. Supp. 543, 553 (Ct. Cl. 1953).

17 Idaho State Hist. Soc'y, "The Snake War: 1864–1868," No. 236 (1966), available at https://history.idaho.gov/wp-content/uploads/0236.pdf.

especially as the numbers of white people moving through the Boise Basin in Idaho increased rapidly in the early 1860s.[18] The Tribes organized raids on the settler camps and the miners and merchants of the Boise region requested assistance from the War Department, which at that time, handled relations between the United States and Tribal Nations.[19] The United States Army entered the picture in 1864 and initiated what ended up being a four-year war against the Tribes, only ending when the winter of 1868 proved too much for the dwindling Indigenous resistance and over two-thirds of the Tribal population had died or been killed.[20] Tribal leaders reluctantly agreed to a treaty council to discuss a formal agreement to confine themselves to a defined territory in hopes that the agreement would save some land for their people. A treaty of so-called "peace and friendship" was negotiated under the direction of the Department of Interior's Indian Affairs Superintendent for Oregon, J.W. Perit Huntington, and signed by seven Tribal leaders – We-You-We-Wa, Gsha-Nee, E-He-Gant, Po-Nee, Chow-Wat-Na-Nee, Ow-Itz, and Tash-E-Go on December 10, 1868.[21]

According to the terms of the treaty, Tribal leaders agreed that they would confine their "terrified," "destitute and defeated" members to a reservation in eastern Oregon, just northeast of Malheur Lake, and the United States would "guarantee to protect their persons and property while they were upon such reservation."[22] The United States also promised that "future provisions would be made by the Government for the permanent location of the Snakes," and to support "their education, government, food, clothing, and allotment of lands in severalty when their advancement warranted it."[23] By its express terms, this 1868 treaty was only a preview of "a more complete treaty to be made at a later date," and that may have been why it was never even submitted for congressional ratification.[24] In the end, the parties never signed another treaty and by 1882, President Chester Arthur issued an Executive Order abolishing the Malheur Reservation.

Dwight Hammond's grandfather was born in 1866, halfway through the Snake Wars. His father was born in 1906, during the end of the allotment era, and Dwight was born in 1942, eight years after the Taylor Grazing Act was passed. Dwight's son Steven, his co-defendant in the criminal prosecutions, was born in 1969, in what many ranchers believe to be the waning glory days of unregulated ranching under the Taylor Act. These were the days before NEPA, FLPMA and the Public Rangeland Improvement Act, which kicked off a new era of valuing public lands for their

18 *Snake or Piute Indians*, 112 F. Supp. at 545.

19 Idaho St. Hist. Soc'y, *The Snake War, 1864–1868*, No. 236, p. 1 (1966), available at https://history.idaho.gov/wp-content/uploads/0236.pdf.

20 *Snake or Piute Indians*, 112 F. Supp. at 557.

21 *Id.* at 545.

22 *Id.* at 554, 557, 558.

23 *Id.*

24 *Id.* at 553.

ecological characteristics, and not just as pastureland for roaming cattle, sheep, and horses. By the early 2000s, the Hammonds were grazing cattle in eastern Oregon and becoming known to local BLM range managers for their proclivity to set fires affecting public lands.[25] By 2004, they held four permits to graze limited AUMs on allotments managed by the Burns District of the BLM, near the Malheur Refuge.[26]

It was their actions on these allotments that resulted in the federal criminal terrorism charges, for which the Hammonds were initially convicted and sentenced to three months (Dwight Hammond) and twelve months (Steven Hammond) in prison. The Government appealed these sentences, though, on the grounds that the district court was required to impose sentences of at least five years for both, according to the mandatory minimums required by the federal sentencing guidelines. The court of appeals agreed with the government and remanded the case for resentencing, holding that the "district court illegally sentenced the Hammonds to terms of imprisonment less than the statutory minimum."[27] Ultimately, the Hammonds were resentenced to five years in prison by Chief Judge Ann Aiken of the United States District Court in Eugene, Oregon, on October 7, 2015, ending the federal government's decade-long battle to bring them to justice.[28]

The resentencing set off a fire of its own, though, among the Bundys, Lavoy Finicum, and other Sagebrush Rebels. Ammon Bundy was particularly affected by what he saw as a targeted federal campaign against the Hammonds "for burning grass," and he began making public statements that "what was happening to them [the Hammonds] was very similar" to "what happened to [his] family" in Nevada.[29] He began rallying support for the Hammonds, traveled to meet them in Oregon, added their case to his email distribution lists, and spoke of their cause on the internet, in print, and on the radio. He also met with the Sheriff of Harney County, Oregon, to express his decision to take a "stand for the Hammonds."[30] In December 2015, he sent a "Redress of Grievance" letter to Oregon Governor Kate Brown and other elected officials, requesting an investigation of the federal government's actions directed at the Hammonds. When he did not receive any response, he decided to take "a harder stand," with court records indicating that he made statements like the following: "we should go into the [Malheur] refuge and occupy the refuge, and that would wake them up."[31] Later that same month, Bundy organized a meeting in Burns, during which he presented a plan to occupy the Malheur

[25] Pl.'s Mot. for Summary J. & Mem. In Support, W. *Watersheds Proj. v. Bernhardt*, 2019 WL 5684330, p. 13 (filed Sept. 19, 2019).

[26] *Id.*

[27] *Hammond*, 742 F.3d at 884.

[28] U.S. Attorney's Office, District of Oregon, Press Release: "Eastern Oregon Ranchers Convicted of Arson Resentenced to Five Years in Prison" (Oct. 7, 2015), available at www.justice.gov/usao-or/pr/eastern-oregon-ranchers-convicted-arson-resentenced-five-years-prison.

[29] *Ehmer*, 87 F.4th at 1086.

[30] *Id.*

[31] *Id.*

Wildlife Refuge. According to one of the meeting attendees, who testified for the Government during the Hammonds' trial, Bundy's plan was to take over the refuge "while armed with weapons," and if the occupiers "encountered employees as [they] went in there, [they] were told to ask them to leave politely."[32]

These federal refuge staff were charged with administering the laws Congress passed to direct the management of the National Wildlife Refuge System, which contains the only lands in the country that have been set aside by the federal government for the primary purpose of protecting wildlife and their habitat. Other statutes, such as those guiding the management of National Parks, National Monuments, and other protected public lands, may have the indirect effect of protecting wildlife and habitat, but the National Wildlife Refuge system is the only national system that was created for this purpose and remains dedicated to it today.[33] According to the enabling act that established the management guidelines for national wildlife refuge lands and resources, the purpose of this system is to create "a national network of lands and waters for the conservation, management, and where appropriate, restoration of … fish, wildlife, and plant resources and their habitats."[34] The National Wildlife Refuge System Administration Act also authorized the US Fish and Wildlife Service to administer refuges for "public recreation," and other purposes, "including, but not limited to hunting, fishing, … and accommodations," as long as the "uses are *compatible* with the major purposes" for which the refuges were created.[35] In the late 1990s, Congress passed a subsequent statute designed to replace the initial enabling act, which tightened the management framework for US Fish and Wildlife and required the agency to ensure that wildlife conservation was elevated above the other uses, including grazing, which had crept into many refuges in the thirty years since the original administration act was passed. This more recent statute, the National Wildlife Refuge System Improvement Act (NWRSIA), has governed the management of wildlife refuges ever since.[36]

Under NWRSIA, the agency must prioritize "the biological integrity, diversity, and environmental health" of national wildlife refuges, elevating species conservation above other uses, while still allowing other uses, if compatible with the primary goal of conservation. NWRSIA ensures that the agency follows these priorities set by Congress through a tiered framework of refuge lands and resources, which can be separated into three basic categories. The first category, and paramount purpose of refuge lands, is the conservation and restoration of "the fish, wildlife, and plant resources and their habitats" according to the original statute or executive order that created the refuge.[37] The second category consists of uses of land and resources

[32] *Id.*
[33] Rasband, at 737.
[34] Nat'l Wildlife Refuge System Admin. Act, 16 U.S.C. §§ 668dd(a)(2).
[35] *Id.* §§ 668dd & 668ee.
[36] *Id.*
[37] *Id.* §§ 668dd(2)-(3).

that are "wildlife-dependent," such as "hunting, fishing, wildlife observation and photography, and environmental education."[38] The lowest priority uses are the non-wildlife-dependent uses, including some that would surprise those unfamiliar with refuge management, such as oil and gas development, electric transmission lines, mineral development, logging, harvesting hay and stock feed, and grazing of domestic livestock.[39]

The NWRSIA directs US Fish and Wildlife to organize human activity within refuges according to this tiered priority framework, using a mechanism that is by now familiar – comprehensive planning. NWRSIA requires planning at two primary scales, national (system wide) and refuge specific (unit level). The refuge-specific plan typically includes an analysis of land and resources within the refuge, the current uses allowed, management zones designated for certain uses, development opportunities, and an analysis of environmental consequences of actions taken to alter any of the above resources, designations, or uses due to the interplay of NWRSIA with the NEPA.[40] Under the refuge statute, plans must be updated every fifteen years, or sooner if conditions change significantly in a way that renders the original analysis in the existing plan obsolete. Plans must also incorporate the so-called "compatibility criterion," which provides that the agency "shall not initiate or permit a new use of a refuge or expand, renew, or extend an existing use of a refuge," unless the agency has made a written determination that the use is "compatible" with "the major purposes for which" the refuge was established.[41] Once the plan is in place, the agency is required to follow statutes, any relevant regulations, national, system-wide plans, and the unit plan governing the individual refuge. These legal mandates require the agency to step in if an existing permitted use, such as livestock grazing, changes in a way that raises compatibility concerns, triggering the requirement for a new compatibility analysis.

Judicial precedent interpreting the interplay of the Taylor Grazing Act and NWRSIA's predecessor statute has clarified that once the refuge system laws were passed, all grazing activity in wildlife refuges is subject to and governed by these laws.[42] Thus, the establishment of a wildlife refuge signifies that the preference and permitting system established by the Taylor Act no longer applies to the lands within its borders, in the same way they had previously. In a famous challenge to the first refuge statute by a group of Montana ranchers who had grazed their livestock on the 823,456-acre Charles M. Russell National Wildlife Refuge in northeastern Montana, *Schwenke v. Secretary of the Interior*, the plaintiffs sought a declaratory

[38] *Id.* §§ 668dd(a)(3)(c); Rasband at 739.

[39] Robert L. Fischman, *The National Wildlife Refuge System and the Hallmarks of Modern Organic Legislation*, 29 ECOLOGY L.Q. 457, 530, 536 (2002).

[40] *Id.* at 540.

[41] 16 U.S.C. §§ 668dd(d)(3)(A) & 668dd(d)(1)(A).

[42] *Schwenke v. Sec'y of the Interior*, 720 F.2d 571, 577 (9th Cir. 1983).

judgment from the federal district court in Helena establishing as a matter of law that the Taylor Act, rather than NWRSAA, governed their grazing activity. They further argued that the Secretary of the Interior, by way of the US Fish and Wildlife Service, had "unlawfully subordinated" their livestock grazing use to the goal of wildlife protection.[43] Resolving the issue these arguments raised required the federal courts involved to examine the text of the NWRSAA to glean congressional intent regarding the extent to which this law should overlap with, supplant, or supplement the Taylor Act.

Ultimately, the Ninth Circuit Court of Appeals ruled that although the language of NWRSAA did not expressly change the administration of wildlife refuges from the Taylor Act's framework to NWRSAA's, the legislative history clarified that this was what Congress intended when passing NWRSAA. This history revealed that Congress deliberated over the extent to which existing grazing activity in national wildlife refuges would be impacted by the passage of the wildlife refuge statutes and noted that the intent was not to eliminate grazing in refuges across the board. Rather, "the Service will continue to honor valid existing grazing permits that were issued by BLM under the Taylor Grazing Act," and when the existing permits expire, "the Service will then reexamine them to determine if continued grazing is compatible with wildlife needs."[44] Moreover, it was Congress's intent that "[g]razing [would] be permitted to the extent compatible" with the Service's system-wide purposes and those of the individual refuge.[45] Upon examining this legislative history, the Ninth Circuit concluded that, while NWRSAA "did not change the relative priorities of wildlife and livestock" in national wildlife refuges, it did change the statute under which grazing activity in refuges should be managed, "from the Taylor Grazing Act to the National Wildlife Refuge System Administration Act."[46]

A rally had been scheduled in Burns, Oregon for Saturday, January 2, 2016, in support of the Hammonds, two days before they were set to report to prison to begin their new longer sentences. After one supporter expressed concern to Ammon Bundy on December 31 that the upcoming rally was being portrayed as a "Bundy Ranch style call to action," he responded in a private Facebook message that "It is much more than a protest."[47] As the rally proceeded, it seemed peaceful, with no reports of threats or violence. But as the event wrapped up, three vehicles headed out of town, bound southwest toward the Malheur Wildlife Refuge. When the vehicles arrived at the Refuge entrance, their occupants got out and went through the federal buildings, checking to ensure no staff were present. These occupants were armed, including with automatic assault weapons, and at this point, even though the buildings were

[43] *Id.* at 572.
[44] *Id.* at 577 (citing 112 Cong. Rec. 2294 (1976)).
[45] *Id.* at 577.
[46] *Id.*
[47] *Ehmer*, 87 F.4th at 1086.

empty, the Refuge was technically open to the public. A witness who testified at a later trial noted that a group of about twelve men seemed to be "securing a perimeter" at the refuge, and later, setting up a "watch" at the fire tower near the front gate.[48]

Ammon Bundy arrived in the second group of vehicles with some of the Burns protestors, followed by additional supporters over the ensuing days. They continued to trickle in for two weeks following the initial group's arrival on January 2. Many came bearing arms, including automatic, assault-style weapons, and the occupiers continually patrolled the entrance. The same witness who observed the initial patrols of the perimeter and establishment of the tower watch, a neighboring rancher, monitored events at the refuge and later testified that the tower guards were always armed, exchanged shifts "like clockwork," and "looked like a sniper team."[49]

The occupiers did not hide their activities, making a written schedule of guard posts and shifts, and posting on social media about their duties and roles. They documented their "consensus" decision to stop any federal employees or law enforcement officers who tried to enter the refuge gates, presumably with weapons if necessary. Throughout the weeks that followed, the occupants used the federal buildings as their living quarters and borrowed the vehicles and other equipment they found on the premises. They also posted notices throughout the refuge that the buildings were "CLOSED PERMANENTLY."[50] Later, Ammon Bundy testified at trial that this siege was initiated "to challenge federal ownership of the Malheur [National Wildlife Refuge]" by "perfecting title through adverse possession," which is a cause of action by which squatters can obtain title to property by occupying it in opposition to the lawful owner's title if they maintain their presence for a given length of time.[51] According to their statements in interviews, brothers Ammon and Ryan Bundy were not only protesting in solidarity with the sentences imposed upon the Hammonds, which they deemed to be excessive, but also "federal landownership and land-management policies in general."[52]

Federal law and policy in effect at the time allowed grazing activity to occur on most types of public lands, even protected public lands like national wildlife refuges, if the agency charged with managing the grazing activity found that it was not inconsistent

48 *Id.* at 1086–87.

49 *Id.* at 1087.

50 *Id.* (noting that "at some point during the occupation, Patrick was filmed cutting through one of the refuge's wire fences, while it was announced that the land was being restored for 'beneficial use,'" a term of art in western water law that equates to "finder's keepers").

51 *Id.* Adverse possession is not possible against the federal government on public lands absent the express consent of Congress, which has been firmly established by the United States Supreme Court in several cases dating back to 1875. *See, e.g.*, *Oaksmith's Lessee v. Johnston*, 92 U.S. 343, 347 (1875) (holding that "mere possession" of public land owned by the United States, even if "through open, exclusive, and uninterrupted" occupancy for twenty years, creates no cause of action for adverse possession against the United States).

52 *Ehmer*, 87 F.4th at 1087.

with the primary purpose for which the area was designated. Grazing is often authorized in national wildlife refuges in the West, and in some cases, is encouraged as a method of controlling invasive species and promoting habitat for species like sage-grouse.[53] In the Klamath Basin of southwestern Oregon, the US Fish and Wildlife Service has authorized livestock grazing in several wildlife refuges since the 1870s, including in the Clear Lake Refuge, which was established by President Taft in 1911 as a preserve for endemic bird species like sage-grouse.[54] The agency was so enthusiastic about the use of grazing to improve habitat for the resident bird species that it decided to increase grazing on the Clear Lake Refuge in its 2017 Comprehensive Conservation Plan, for the reasons noted above, but also (ostensibly) to help restore bird habitat that had been damaged by a large wildfire in 2001.[55]

One week after the agency adopted the Comprehensive Conservation Plan for the Clear Lake Refuge in 2017, a group of wildlife conservation organizations sued in federal court, arguing that the agency's decisions to continue to allow grazing activity and the specific decision to increase grazing in Clear Lake Refuge violated federal law. The decision, *Audubon Society of Portland v. Haaland*, depicts well the discretion that federal agencies like US Fish and Wildlife Service have when implementing public lands statutes such as NWRSIA and NEPA.[56] Dismissing the plaintiff conservation organizations' complaint, the court held that as long as the agency conducts a reasonable assessment of the impacts to refuge resources, including birds and their habitat, from the grazing activity, and finds that the grazing activity will not conflict with other Refuge goals, or "materially interfere with" the purposes for which the refuge was established, it is within the agency's discretion to continue the grazing activity and even to allow the activity to increase.[57] Interestingly, the court also noted that portions of the plan allowing grazing-associated activities, such as clearing of trees and invasive grasses, were consistent with NWRSIA and other federal laws. The plan at issue in the *Audubon Society case* had included significant detail regarding the potential interaction between grazing and sage-grouse, concluding that grazing and related activities are "beneficial to sage-grouse habitat."[58] According to the plan, grazing gives endemic plant species "a competitive advantage" against invasives, assists with habitat restoration, reduces the load of fine fuels, which decreases "the frequency, intensity, and spread of wildfires" and enhances "the growth and survival of shrubs, such as sagebrush."[59] Restoration of sage-grouse habitat, in turn, benefits "obligate species, such as sage grouse, that prefer habitats composed of forbs, moderate-height grasses, and larger diameter sagebrush."[60]

53 *Audubon Soc'y of Portland v. Haaland*, 40 F.4th 967, 977 (9th Cir. 2022).
54 *Id.*
55 *Id.* at 977–78.
56 *Id.*
57 *Id.* at 989–90.
58 *Id.* 992.
59 *Id.*
60 *Id.*

Over several weeks in January 2016, while the Hammonds sat in prison, the Malheur National Wildlife protestors were in contact with the Harney County Sheriff, who encouraged them to peacefully leave the refuge. Nevertheless, his entreaties fell on deaf ears. Local residents' reactions to the protest ranged from neutral agnosticism to public statements of criticism, with the latter including several members of the Burns Paiute Tribe, whose lands had been taken to create the National Wildlife Refuge. The occupiers' claims of ownership did not sit well at all with the descendants of those Paiute and Shoshone Tribal members who had been forced to live on the Malheur Reservation in the late 1860s. The Burns Paiute Tribal Council issued a formal statement denouncing the occupation of the Malheur Refuge, with Tribal Council members noting that the occupants were causing damage to the sacred ancestral property of the Tribe and that they needed to leave. The Chairwoman of the Tribal Council gave an interview in which she noted the painful irony of the occupants' statements regarding the rightful owners of this land, which in her view, include the citizens of her Tribe. She guessed aloud in a press conference that this was not the group to which Ammon Bundy and Lavoy Finicum intended to "return" the refuge.[61] Moreover, another council member, Jarvis Kennedy, asked a reporter rhetorically – "What if it was a bunch of natives that went out there and overtook that?"[62]

A reporter posed the Tribal leaders' questions to Ammon Bundy at a press conference during the occupation. Bundy responded – "That is interesting," and conceded "[t]hey have rights as well. I would like to see them be free from the federal government as well. They're controlled and regulated by the federal government very tightly and I think they have a right to be free like everybody else."[63] Yet, it seemed that the Tribal Council preferred to work with the US Fish and Wildlife Service, which in their view had served as a "protector" of important cultural sites within the refuge, including cultural artifacts.[64] These sites and the land and other resources within the refuge, are part of the heritage of the 420 enrolled members of the Burns Paiute Tribe, half of whom live on the 1,000 acre Burns Paiute Reservation. According to the Tribal Chairperson, Refuge land is not the Hammonds', nor even necessarily the federal government's. According to her, "[t]his is still our land, no matter who is living on it."[65]

The FBI, which was monitoring communications among the occupiers and their supporters outside, as well as the occupiers' communications with local law enforcement, learned that some of the Citizens defending Constitutional

[61] Amanda Peacher, *Tribe Denounces Malheur Refuge Occupation*, Oregon Public Broadcasting (Jan. 6, 2016), available at www.opb.org/news/series/burns-oregon-standoff-bundy-militia-news-updates/tribe-denounces-malheur-refuge-occupation-/.

[62] *Id.*

[63] *Id.*

[64] *Id.*

[65] *Id.*

Freedom planned to leave the refuge on January 26, to travel to an event in John Day, Oregon, a small town about ninety miles north. After the group departed, local law enforcement and the FBI pursued them, and at the deadman's roadblock on Highway 395, Lavoy Finicum was shot. After the shooting, Ammon Bundy and his sons, along with the other occupants of the convoy vehicles, were arrested, and the FBI immediately sent word of the arrests "to all the individuals whose telephone numbers [it] had on the refuge to try and persuade them to leave the refuge immediately."[66] The FBI also relayed that it intended to set up roadblocks around the refuge and that "if the [protestors] wanted to leave the refuge, now was the time to go."[67]

Although the remaining Citizens at the refuge held a gathering that night in which some expressed an interest in staying, to "defend the Constitution," the events of the day appear to have influenced many, and they soon began to leave. As they drove out of the refuge, they were arrested and charged with various crimes, including conspiracy to impede officers of the United States by "force, intimidation, and threats," possession of firearms in a federal facility with intent to commit another crime, using and carrying a firearm during and in relation to a crime of violence and for those who had damaged land, vehicles, or buildings, depredation of Government property.[68] The last of the Citizens defending Constitutional Freedom left the Malheur Wildlife Refuge on February 11, 2016.

Under NWRSIA, and precedent like *Audubon Society*, the Hammonds could still be grazing their cattle lawfully within the refuge, partnering with US Fish and Wildlife scientists and management staff to clear brush, and perhaps even using controlled burns. That would have required some communication between ranchers and the agency, to allow this activity to continue. Yet, something happened in the Hammond-BLM-Malheur situation that resulted in a very different ending. The Hammonds lost their grazing permits and saw their preferences cancelled, then went to prison. Lavoy Finicum died. Over two dozen individual occupants were charged with various crimes by federal prosecutors, although they failed to secure guilty verdicts against some of the higher profile participants, like Ammon Bundy.

The Bundy brothers, including Ammon and Ryan, and Lavoy Finicum, were seen by outsiders as the "leaders" of the Malheur occupation, but internally, the Citizens were somewhat "leaderless," which made it very difficult for federal prosecutors to prove their conspiracy charges. In addition, the FBI had planted nine informants inside the refuge to help monitor developments, which made it even more difficult to prove the conspiracy charges and seemed to sway at least one juror. The jury pool for the Bundy prosecution was drawn from across the

66 *Ehmer*, 87 F.4th at 1087.
67 *Id.*
68 *Id.* at 1088.

state, not just the area immediately around the courthouse in Portland, and thus included some who were sympathetic to the Bundys' plight. There was a theory circulating in eastern Oregon at the time that the Bundys and Finicum had been targeted by the FBI and local law enforcement due to their political views, rather than their criminal conduct.[69] Ultimately, the Bundys were acquitted on October 27, 2016.

It took some time for eastern Oregon to recover from the Hammond–Bundy–Malheur occupation. But one bright spot has begun to really shine in the wake of the the Malheur occupation, in the form of the High Desert Partnership – a collaborative that represents the opposite of the Malheur refuge standoff as a strategy to effect change in federal land management and wildlife habitat conservation. If the results produced by the 2016 occupation are any indication, the Bundy–Finicum model is an ineffective way to go about managing the refuge and the relationships between the federal agency staff and neighboring ranchers. The High Desert Partnership, by contrast, offers a very different approach.

The idea for the High Desert Partnership emerged in 1999, when assistant Malheur Refuge manager Chad Karges met local rancher Gary Marshall. As the two got to know each other, they began sharing their ideas for how to resolve the tension that had stymied refuge management under a succession of leaders dating back to 1971. Local ranchers heard about Karges and Marshall's talks and showed an interest in participating, and a small group started to form. They looked around the West for models to follow and found the Blackfoot Challenge in Montana, the Quivira Coalition in New Mexico, and the Malpai Borderlands Group in Arizona. As they researched, they discovered a commonality among the successful collaboratives, which was that participation from interested stakeholders increased the likelihood of success for any plan to manage federal lands, especially when livestock grazing activity and conservation were involved.[70] Fast forward to 2016, and the High Desert Partnership was a fully formed 501(c)(3) nonprofit, with a Board of Directors, funding, and a published mission. The group had demonstrated the value of the organization through facilitating the amendments to the Malheur Wildlife Refuge's Comprehensive Conservation Plan in 2013 and fostered several other initiatives to address wildfires, habitat preservation for migratory birds and other wildlife species in the refuge, and responsible livestock grazing. By the time the Citizens for Constitutional Freedom took over the refuge, the organization did not view the ensuing standoff or even the violence as a threat, but more of a "test," according to founder Gary Marshall. In Marshall's view, that was just "another thing that came

69 *Finicum, et al., v. Bur. of Land Mgmt., et al.*, Pls.' Third Amended Compl, ¶ 246, 2021 WL 9595813 (filed Oct. 15, 2021).

70 Tay Wiles, *After Malheur, Side Effects of the Bundys' Extremism Linger*, High Country News (June 14, 2018), available at www.hcn.org/issues/50-12/ammon-bundy-after-malheur-side-effects-of-the-bundys-extremism-linger/.

along that showed that it's worthwhile do things this way. I'm 100 percent convinced that the High Desert Partnership was a big part of the reason this community came through the occupation the way it did."[71] In other words, according to another local rancher, the High Desert Partnerships' model was "what inoculated us from the Bundy disease."[72] It also provided one concrete model for communities in the West looking for a different future.

[71] Lauren Brown, *How It All Began*, HIGH DESERT PARTNERSHIP (last visited Mar 25, 2024), available at https://highdesertpartnership.org/about/our-story.html.

[72] Wiles.

10

The Reckoning

Law and Policy Reform and the Path Forward

At the far end of the Trail of Tears was a promise.

– Justice Neil Gorsuch[1]

The preceding chapters demonstrate the legacy of several laws and policies that have influenced the present landscape of agriculture in the West, especially with respect to lands and resources that are commonly owned or used. First, communal agriculture has thrived in this region, as demonstrated by the Ancestral Puebloan and Spanish Land Grant models in the southwest. It has also failed, and dramatically so in some instances, such as during the public grassland commons-Dust Bowl era that Ferry Carpenter tried to resolve by way of the Taylor Grazing Act. Second, the national values around grass and other plant species that wildlife and domestic livestock consume, and which form habitat for species like pronghorn antelope, bison, and sage-grouse, especially on public lands, have shifted from the utilitarian, extractive model of the 1700s and 1800s to one based on sustainability and greater resilience in the 1900s and 2000s, even if there has been disagreement about how to implement those values. Third, grass is still a modern form of gold in the West, in the sense that loss of it, or loss of access to it, evokes feelings that are strong enough in some to die for, as evidenced by the situation involving the Bundys and Lavoy Finicum at Malheur National Wildlife Refuge.

Earlier chapters touched on federal attempts at legal reform in the areas of property law, Constitutional law, and natural resource law to address the shift in national values towards sustainability and balancing extraction with conservation. Some of these were driven by popular concern for charismatic wildlife species like polar bears, grizzly bears, and bison, and a desire to protect irreplaceable national landmarks, like the Grand Canyon, Yellowstone, and Yosemite. But they were also motivated by the public's concerns over serious health threats posed by the externalities associated with the nation's rapid pace of post-war industrialization, including

[1] Camfield v. United States, 167 U.S. 518, 521 (1897).

pollution from industrial agriculture, factories, and refineries. The American public of the 1970s and 1980s was horrified to learn that rivers were bearing loads of phosphates, toxic chemicals, and sediment that rendered them undrinkable, and in at least one case, susceptible to catching fire.[2] Air pollution from factories, power plants, and the transportation sector was rendering cities like Los Angeles nearly unlivable during parts of the year and causing smog to descend upon places that had seemed untouchable by the hand of industrialization, like the Grand Canyon.[3] Childhood asthma rates were on the rise, and lead poisoning posed hazards to children in public housing and urban public schools. When Congress acted, the field of environmental law was born, and the hazards of some of the worst pollution and toxins were abated.

In the West, the statutes Congress passed to address the myriad pollution and other environmental concerns of the second half of the twentieth century did not really impact ranching activity. Agricultural lobbies ensured that agricultural land uses were exempt from statutes like the Clean Water Act and Clean Air Act, while age-old statutes like the General Mining Law and Taylor Grazing Act (and their grazing friendly or pro-grazing language) remained in effect. Tribal Nations could adopt their own versions of the Clean Water Act and the Clean Air Act, but very few elected to, leaving the environmental health of Indian Country largely subject to the regulatory discretion of the Environmental Protection Agency and federal laws that exempted agricultural activity. At the same time, unintended consequences of some environmental laws, like the Resource Conservation and Recovery Act, turned Tribal reservations into dumping grounds for solid waste, which compounded health issues for Tribal members. Meanwhile, the multiple-use statutes of the 1970s required public land managers to authorize timber harvesting and mineral development on public lands, and as the demands for timber, natural gas, and oil increased, the resources of the public lands were used to meet them. The externalities associated with these activities included erosion, stormwater runoff, methane gas plumes, contaminated water, and radioactive soils.[4] Invasive species that farmers and ranchers had introduced in earlier decades suddenly exploded at an unprecedented rate in the second half of the twentieth century.[5] Some, like the prolific cheatgrass, quickly established themselves as the dominant grass species within a matter of decades.[6] These invasives may have stayed somewhat contained (cheatgrass notwithstanding) except for another phenomenon

[2] Jonathan H. Adler, *Fables of the Cuyahoga: Reconstructing a History of Environmental Protection*, 14 FORDHAM ENVTL. L. J. 89, 90 (2002).

[3] Steven H. Bergman, *To See or Not to See: The Viability of Visibility at the Grand Canyon*, 13 UCLA J. ENVTL. L. & POL'Y 127, 143 (1995).

[4] Tim Vanderpool, *New Mexico Has a Methane Cloud Visible by Satellite. It also Has Bold Climate Plans*, NRDC.ORG (Oct. 2, 2019).

[5] United States Dep't of Ag., Natural Resources Conservation Service, *Regional Interpretation: Great Plains*, available at www.nrcs.usda.gov/Internet/FSE_DOCUMENTS/stelprdb1255057.pdf.

[6] U.S. Fish & Wildlife Service, *Cheatgrass Origin* (2000), available at www.fws.gov/invasives/volunteerstrainingmodule/nwrsystem/cheatgrassorigin.html.

that has ripped through prairie grasslands with increasing frequency: wildfires.[7] None of these issues were addressed, nor abated in any meaningful way, by the slate of environmental statutes passed in the second half of the twentieth century.

Because of the land tenure patterns that earlier laws established, and the locations of many reservations in drought and fire-prone grassland and former grassland regions, Indigenous farmers and ranchers were particularly impacted by the ecological changes wrought by invasive grass species, drought, and wildfires.[8] Some Tribal Nations have used economic development incentives like the Indian Gaming Regulatory Act or the Indian Mineral Leasing Act to spur land and resource conservation initiatives and develop wildland fire-fighting squads, but others rejected gaming or extractive uses of their land and resources and sometimes struggle to fund agricultural reform. Agricultural reform is also a tricky platform for Tribal political leaders because of the need for food security and food sovereignty in Indian Country. Finally, the ranchers who are not descendants of the original permittees under the Taylor Grazing Act, who are largely non-white, cannot benefit from the subsidized public lands permitting system to add valuable public grasslands to their private ranchlands unless they are able to find a willing seller and have the money to purchase a base property and the preference. This is often cost-prohibitive.

While the following is not by any means proposing a comprehensive overhaul of the laws and policies that resulted in the vast discrepancies in access and control of land and water discussed in the earlier chapters, this chapter will pose some ideas for legal reform that could result in a more just allocation of public resources, like land, water, and grass, for farmers and ranchers in the West, including those operating on Tribal lands. These reforms may also have ancillary benefits to grassland regions, which, in many places, have been almost decimated by centuries of relentless livestock grazing activity.

7 FABIAN MENALLED, *et al.*, CHEATGRASS: IDENTIFICATION, BIOLOGY AND INTEGRATED MANAGEMENT (Montana State University 2008), available at http://msuinvasiveplants.org/documents/mt_noxious_weeds/Cheatgrass_MT200811AG.pdf. Cheatgrass, or *Bromus tectorum*, originated in Europe and Asia but made the transatlantic crossing as a contaminant in seed and straw imported into the United States in the 1800s. Together with other related species of *bromus*, this invader has become the dominant grass species of the Western United States. Had cheatgrass landed in a region that retained some of its natural defenses to invasives, the story might have had a different ending. Instead, though, it arrived on the virtual cusp of the Great Depression and the Dust Bowl, a time when most ranchers and farmers were struggling to eke out a living even in regions with abundant water and resources. In the West, with its lack of consistent precipitation, and relative lack of forage for grazing livestock, ranchers were hard-pressed to sustain their herds. Unsustainable and damaging grazing practices followed, with cattle and sheep being turned out onto lands without adequate forage, denuding them of what remained and giving cheat a prime opportunity to take over once it arrived.

8 DIANE AUSTIN & BARBARA WOLF, FIRE IN INDIAN COUNTRY: TWO CASE STUDIES IN THE SOUTHWESTERN UNITED STATES, Climate Assessment for the Southwest (University of Arizona 2000), available at https://climas.arizona.edu/sites/default/files/pdfcl1-01.pdf.

10.1 THE DOCTRINE OF DISCOVERY

The reality of the current circumstances of federal, state, and Tribal property and natural resources laws is that they are all progeny of the Doctrine of Discovery. This Doctrine created a system of allocating rights to land that is now 200 years old. Given the passage of time and the investment of money into land rights in the United States, the Doctrine is unlikely to be completely erased from the annals of American law – it is simply too fundamental to the original organization of property rights, including chains of title, for most land in the United States. While even a first-year law student could identify the fallacious reasoning of the Supreme Court in the opinion that established the Doctrine as a component of American law, *Johnson v. M'Intosh*, completely unwinding the damage done by this rule of law throughout the entire nation for the past 200 years may take some time. A comprehensive and immediate overhaul could destabilize real estate markets, affect private property values, and likely cause significant economic upheaval.

But some incremental change could go a long way toward undoing the harms of this Doctrine. For one, the Supreme Court could discard the Doctrine of Discovery as a basis for congressional power in legislation involving Tribal Nations, and as a valid source of authority in cases involving disputes over land and property rights, sovereign immunity, and other matters that can be resolved on other grounds. The Court can cite the Catholic Church in support of any changes to its interpretation of the Doctrine, given Pope Francis's 2023 directive repudiating it. If a sixteenth-century papal bull was the genesis of the Supreme Court's doctrine, a twenty-first-century condemnation of that papal bull by a Presiding Pope can serve as an equally valid rationale for rejecting it. At the very least, this step would send a message that the highest Court no longer recognizes the Doctrine of Discovery as a valid basis for resolving disputes between Tribal Nations and the United States, states, or private corporations.

In addition, Congress could eliminate the naked fee title of the United States in trust lands, allotments, and reservations, which would effectively give Tribes and allottees their land back, *without* eliminating the federal trust responsibility or infringing Tribal sovereignty over these categories of land. This would accomplish many ends, including answering the twenty-first-century call for the land back from Tribal Nations, while preserving the legal responsibility of the United States to provide healthcare and other services that derive from the federal trust by severing the United States' property interest in Tribal land from its obligations owed to Tribal Nations in treaties and by virtue of its history of conquest. There is legislative precedent for this in the form of the Indian Land Claims Acts passed by Congress to resolve disputes between Tribal Nations and States over treaty lands and other unceded areas.

These changes would also move the United States one step further from the colonial model of the Doctrine of Discovery and one step closer to compliance with the mandates of the United Nations Declaration on the Rights of Indigenous Peoples (UNDRIP), which is widely recognized by Indigenous scholars and Tribal leaders and allies as the best path forward for undoing the harms of the past and realizing a legal framework that is respectful of the human rights of Indigenous Peoples, including their rights to land, self-determination, and sovereignty.[9] The United States has thus far refused to ratify UNDRIP and remains far from compliance with its principles, due in no small part to its refusal to reject colonial rules of law like the Doctrine of Discovery. According to renowned Pawnee scholar Walter Echo-Hawk, who poses a blueprint for adopting UNDRIP into domestic law in his 2010 book, *In the Courts of the Conqueror: the 10 Worst Indian Law Cases Ever Decided*, the campaign to achieve the goals of UNDRIP "should be conducted on several levels" including internationally, within Tribal Nations of the United States, in federal and state courts, and in social and political advocacy campaigns similar to that which "brought Jim Crow to its knees."[10] Echo-Hawk's call is great, but eroding the *Johnson v. M'Intosh* opinion through the Supreme Court or Congress is achievable and would mark an important step for the US in recognizing the rights protected by UNDRIP. Taking action along these lines would also provide a more meaningful response to the recent calls for truer respect for Tribal sovereignty and land back by advocates throughout Indian Country.[11]

10.2 ALLOTMENT ACTS

As discussed in earlier chapters, allotment acts were an effective method of accomplishing Manifest Destiny and injecting the fledgling American economy with seed money that it would need to springboard to an early success before everything came crashing down in the Great Depression. But in the twenty-first century, they have come to symbolize the nadir of the American collective conscience involving the United States' and its states' relationship with Tribal Nations. Even conservative Supreme Court justices have criticized these laws and federal policies for their barely veiled dictatorial attributes and their devastating effects on Tribal Nations and Indigenous Peoples. They have also now demonstrated themselves as terrifically bad ideas given the federal government's decision to shift federal policy away from disposal and toward retention and conservation in the early twentieth century. Picture trying to conserve sage-grouse habitat on the checkerboard described in Chapter 8, using only alternating squares on the board, and you will begin to have an idea of the complexity involved in wildlife conservation due to the lasting impact of the allotment acts.

As with the preceding discussion about the Doctrine of Discovery, there is a blueprint for reversing some of the harm done by these acts, involving two incremental

[9] Walter R. Echo-Hawk, In the Courts of the Conqueror: The 10 Worst Indian Law Cases Ever Decided, p. 428–29 (Fulcrum 2010).

[10] *Id.* at 428.

[11] Kalen Goodluck, *The Land Back Movement Unravels Manifest Destiny*, SIERRA MAGAZINE (Sept. 11, 2023), available at www.sierraclub.org/sierra/2023-3-fall/feature/land-back-movement-unravels-manifest-destiny.

steps. First, like the legal reform proposed for the Doctrine of Discovery, Congress can pass a statute that divests the federal government of its partial ownership stake in allotted lands. It would be necessary to secure the support of members of Congress representing the states with reservations that contain allotted lands, or allotted lands located outside the boundaries of reservations, but signing on might not be as big a political risk as they might first imagine, given what is at stake if the federal government retains the ownership interest in these lands but cannot ever properly act as a fiduciary with respect to the federal trust attributes of that ownership status. The risk of doing nothing involves the potential for further lawsuits like the one waged by Eloise Cobell against the federal government, discussed in Chapter 3. There are also significant administrative costs associated with managing allotments, royalties, and distributions, especially for fractionated allotments, and alleviating the federal government of that administrative burden may prove enticing for legislators, especially those who favor a smaller federal government and less federal regulation. This dysfunctional system, which has been criticized by leading Indigenous lawyers and scholars, seems perpetually designed to render the United States vulnerable to claims of breach of trust, breach of fiduciary duty, and fraud, given the seeming inability of the Bureau of Indian Affairs to carry out its legal duties as trustee.[12]

In addition, the federal government can offer to settle past claims of mismanagement of allotted lands and monies derived from the leasing or use of these lands with individual Tribal Nations. This would require the Department of Interior to identify the total number of allottees with an interest in allotment revenue and estimate the losses to date, then propose a settlement package to each Tribal Nation. Although, as the *Cobell* litigation demonstrated, it is likely not possible to account for every dollar of lost revenue to Indigenous allottees over time, but it is possible for accountants to calculate estimates of total losses and produce a number from which to start negotiations. The *Cobell* settlement of $3.4 billion in 2009 produced $1.5 billion for individual allottees and $1.9 billion for Tribes, enabling affected Tribal Nations to buy back fractionated interests in allotments on their reservations and return them to Tribal ownership.[13] According to a government report produced at the end of the *Cobell* buy-back period, nearly three million acres in fifteen states were restored to fifty Tribal governments.[14] Combining these two legal reform efforts, of the Doctrine

[12] Echo-Hawk, at 445.

[13] T. Rees Shapiro, *Eloise Cobell, American Indian Who Led Suit against U.S. Government, Dead at 65*, The Washington Post (Oct. 17, 2011), available at www.washingtonpost.com/local/obituaries/elouise-cobell-american-indian-who-championed-class-action-lawsuit-against-us-government-dies-at-65/2011/09/02/gIQAVQwBrL_story.html.

[14] U.S. Dep't of the Interior, "Three Million Acres of Land Returned to Tribes Through Interior Department's Land Buy-Back Program for Tribal Nations" (Dec. 4, 2023), available at www.doi.gov/pressreleases/three-million-acres-land-returned-tribes-through-interior-departments-land-buy-back. Although the numbers might seem daunting, especially if they again surpass the $1 billion mark, it is worth noting that the United States Congress has spent well over $75 million supplying aid and arms to Ukraine, to defend its sovereignty against the invasion by Russia, between 2022 and 2024.

of Discovery and the allotment acts, also would respond to Indigenous calls for land back as reparations for past human rights violations and unlawful land divestiture, and further shift the United States closer to the goals of UNDRIP.

10.3 AIARMA

Similar to the recommendations above for legal reforms to the Doctrine of Discovery and the allotment acts, AIARMA is in need of incremental amendments to align this statute with the goals of UNDRIP and alleviate certain burdens on Tribal governments imposed by the federal trust relationship as it has existed for the past two centuries – with the United States serving in the role of trustee/owner and Tribal governments serving in the role of governmental beneficiaries, overseeing individual beneficiaries (their members and descendants). As discussed in Chapter 3, AIARMA does not release the BIA's authority over individual allotments, nor releases it as trustee manager.[15] Reversing this dynamic and placing Tribal government in the role of the BIA, while not eliminating the federal trust obligations (especially for payment to resolve past mismanagement claims) owed to Tribes would loosen the overly intrusive and highly bureaucratic role of the BIA and allow Tribal Nations to design agricultural leasing frameworks that arise out of their own values, cultural norms, and laws. Similarly, the provisions of AIARMA that require agricultural lease agreements to be approved by the Secretary of the Interior, via the local Bureau of Indian Affairs office, could be amended to provide for Tribal governmental oversight rather than BIA oversight.[16] Moreover, AIARMA could be amended to position Tribal Nations as they see fit, whether as lessees or lessors, to account for, or provide for, other types of arrangements that would give them the flexibility to address the twenty-first century complexities of administering agricultural leases on heavily allotted reservations. As noted in Chapter 3, the leasing framework in AIARMA contains gaps that pose significant barriers to agricultural producers across Indian Country.[17] With these targeted reforms, Congress could relieve the Department of Interior of its paternalistic trustee role, rooted in colonization and Manifest Destiny, and replace it with a relationship that more truly recognizes the sovereign authority of Tribal Nations to manage their affairs, which is consistent with the modern values of the United States as a democratic nation that respects human rights and Indigenous sovereignty.

15 United States Senate, Committee on Indian Affairs, American Indian Agricultural Resource Management Act Report to Accompany H.R. 1425, the American Indian Agricultural Resource Management Act, p. 11 (Nov. 18, 1993).

16 *Id.*

17 Judith V. Royster, *Tribal Energy Development: Renewables and the Problem of the Current Statutory Structures*, 31 STAN. ENVTL. L. J. 91, 110–11 (2012) (citing Harvard Project on American Indian Economic Development, The State of the Native Nations: Conditions Under U.S. Policies of Self-Determination 167 (2008)).

10.4 TREATIES

Treaties between Indigenous Nations and the United States form the bedrock of Tribal sovereignty, securing many legal rights for Tribes, including the protection of natural resources like plants, fish, wildlife, land, water, and others. The federal government estimates that approximately 374 treaties were signed and ratified by the United States before Congress ended the practice of treaty making in 1871. Under the Supremacy Clause of the US Constitution, treaties are "the supreme law of the land" and only lose their legal power when Tribes disavow them, or the United States (through Congress) abrogates them.[18] Because of their power and effectiveness, treaties do not require any legal reform, even if their interpretation could be improved by more thorough historical investigations of the context surrounding their signing.

There are a few areas of law relating to treaties that should be reformed, though. For one, unratified treaties could be ratified by Congress, which would ensure that the United States held up its end of the bargain following the signing of a treaty. These claims could theoretically be enforceable by Tribes. This would allow Tribes to vindicate these rights in court, especially if the following change is made to legal precedent. This change is the elimination of what Professor Echo-Hawk calls "the dark side" of the plenary power doctrine – the legal rule that allows Congress to exercise plenary power over Tribal Nations and individual Tribal members, including the power to take away land, resources, and rights.[19] Eliminating this "sword" of plenary power – while keeping the beneficial side (the "shield") would rid American legal precedent of its Manifest Destiny-informed, racist, and paternalistic roots, while preserving elements of the federal trust and the general obligation to act in a way that benefits Tribal Nations, rather than harming them. The twenty-first century legal tides may bode well for change along these lines, given that the Supreme Court has largely discarded the "dark side" of plenary power in recent opinions.

Ratifying unratified treaties would probably raise some eyebrows among states and private landowners, but there is precedent for these changes to occur without divesting states or private landowners of their property rights. This precedent – the Supreme Court's 2020 opinion in *McGirt v. Oklahoma* – provided a case study of what happens when a previously ignored treaty is finally recognized by the federal government, and there is a wholesale transfer of governing authority from a state to a Tribal Nation. Despite some initial and vocal fearmongering and threats of Congressional repeal of the decision, nothing of real consequence occurred to diminish any rights of non-members when the Supreme Court ruled that the former Muskogee Creek Nation was unlawfully diminished, returning the area to its status as a reservation, and even the most vocal critics soon realized that the did not affect nonmembers or landowners to any great degree, given the rules of law that presumptively prohibit Tribal

[18] U.S. Const., Art. VI, cl. 2; *Herrera v. Wyoming*, 139 S. Ct. 1686, 1696 (2019).

[19] Echo-Hawk, at 31.

governments from directly regulating private land and nonmember conduct.[20] These rules, which were not touched by the *McGirt* ruling, remain in effect and are unlikely to be changed anytime soon, given the Supreme Court's longstanding concerns about subjecting noncitizens to Tribal governmental authority and jurisdiction.

As for the Supreme Court, incremental legal reform looks like shedding the "dark side" of the plenary power doctrine, which was a judicial tool of conquest, with a very tenuous connection to the Constitution. The doctrine, which holds that Congress possesses authority to pass legislation "with respect to" Indian Tribes and individual members of those Tribes, including the authority to unilaterally abrogate treaties, arose out of the Doctrine of Discovery and the Marshall Trilogy cases discussed in Chapter 2. The reasoning in these opinions, laden with racist, paternalistic, and anti-Democratic reasoning, has no proper place in twenty-first-century American jurisprudence. Similarly, Congressional legislation that takes from, rather than supports, Tribal sovereignty or the individual rights of Tribal members under the auspices of this rationale is an affront to Tribal self-determination and undermines the line of Supreme Court cases respecting Tribal sovereignty. As scholars have long argued, the dark side of congressional plenary power is anathema to the doctrine respecting Tribal sovereignty.[21] Thus, it is time to move on from this troubling rule of Federal Indian Law and policy.

10.5 WATER LAW

Water law reform is an equally tall order as federal Indian law and policy reform, and perhaps even taller, because like grass, water is also "gold" in the West. Access to water and the security of its use are necessary for nearly every human activity in this region, including agriculture. Water is so highly valued in the West that the law assigns only use rights to it, rather than rights of absolute ownership. This legal categorization is also a reflection of the nature of water, as a resource that is constantly in motion, changing form and appearing in cycles, not responsive to human efforts to keep it constantly in one form or in one place.[22] Even dammed water in the West will disappear, evaporating only to return to the earth as precipitation, but not necessarily in the same location from which it left. Water transported in pipelines and through canals will also find its way through cracks and leaks, depositing itself along the trajectory but not necessarily in the place that it was engineered to go. As noted water law scholar Joseph L. Sax so eloquently puts it,

20 Jacob Fischler, *Three Years after Landmark Ruling, Congress Silent on Tribal Jurisdiction in Oklahoma*, COLORADO NEWSLINE (Aug. 30, 2023), available at https://coloradonewsline.com/2023/08/30/three-years-after-landmark-ruling-congress-silent-on-tribal-jurisdiction-in-oklahoma/.

21 *See, e.g.*, Echo-Hawk, at 445; Hillary M. Hoffmann, *Congressional Plenary Power and Indigenous Environmental Stewardship: The Limits of Environmental Federalism*, 97 OR. L. REV. 353, 355 (2019).

22 Rasband at 820 (citing Joseph L. Sax, *Proceedings of the 2001 Symposium on Managing Hawai'i's Public Trust Doctrine*, 24 U. HAW. L. REV. 21, 24 (2001)).

"[t]he water we use today is not the same water we'll use tomorrow, and the water we use is routinely used again and again by someone else downstream or downgradient."[23]

In the West, water is legally a public resource, but states recognize use rights, which are a form of property rights, in surface and subsurface water.[24] As discussed briefly in Chapter 7, a western water right will endure under state law if it is used for permissible purposes, such as watering livestock. The seniority date of a water right under the typical Western state legal system is the date that the user, or appropriator, in water law parlance, first put the water to a beneficial use. In this way, many homesteaders acquired water rights for ranches that became some of the most senior water rights in a system. If there is plenty of water, senior and junior appropriators can share the bounty. If there is not enough water in the system to satisfy the rights of all users, the senior user takes their full allocation and does not have to reduce their use in proportion to the deficit.[25]

Water law reform has come very slowly to the West, and a thorough discussion of reforms needed is outside the scope of this book. However, as Chapter 7 demonstrated, there is a specific need to reform water law to the extent that it has become intertwined with grazing privileges on federal lands. The Taylor Grazing Act is clear that any permit or grazing use allowed by the Department of Interior does not convey any "right, title, or interest" in the public lands that are the subject of the permit or lease. In fact, according to the letter of this law, a grazing permit applicant must have base property to qualify for a permit, whether that is land or a water right. Under the existing canons of statutory construction, therefore, it is illogical to construe the Taylor Grazing Act permits (or leases) as implicit sources of water rights. Yet, that is precisely how the district court interpreted the Act under the circumstances of the Pine Creek Ranch and the Hage's grazing activity on public allotments nearby, as discussed in Chapter 7.

In addition, the *Hage* court found that because the Forest Service and BLM had revoked the Hages' grazing permits, due to their past noncompliance with the permit terms, this effected a taking of the Hages' *water rights* in violation of the Fifth Amendment to the US Constitution. In plainer terms, the court ruled that revoking the Hages' grazing permits unlawfully deprived them of their water, which meant that they were entitled to compensation from the federal government. In a separate case, the federal court of claims ruled that the Hages possessed property rights, akin to easements, in the lands along the ditches that their predecessors had constructed to carry water off the federal lands. These ditch rights then secured a right to use the land on fifty feet of either side of the ditch. Even though subsequent statutes gave

[23] Sax at 24.

[24] Reed D. Benson, *So Much Conflict, Yet so Much in Common: Considering the Similarities Between Western Water Law and the Endangered Species Act*, 44 Nat. Resources J. 29, 35–36 (2004).

[25] *Id.*

both agencies limited authority to provide "reasonable" access for private landowners and water rights holders to access these private property "inholdings" on public lands, the court of claims held that the government "cannot deny [the Hages] access to their vested water rights without providing a way for them to divert that water to another beneficial purpose if one exists … The [Hages] have a right to go onto the land and divert the water."[26]

The rule announced in the Hage cases cries out for repeal, chiefly because it undermines federal agencies of the authority Congress delegated to them regarding the management and stewardship of federal public lands. The grazing allotments in the Hage case are after all, public lands, owned by all citizens of the United States. The Taylor Grazing Act allows the agencies to permit grazing activity on these lands, but only if the grazing activity is lawful. If it crosses the line into unlawful grazing activity, which is what happened with the Hages, the agencies are required to enforce the law, including assessment of fines, reduction in use, or revocation of the permit. Allowing the Hages to violate the law and then sue the federal government and secure compensation for a taking of grazing-based property rights on federal lands is the exact opposite of the framework of borrowing land from the public that the Taylor Grazing Act and other federal laws envisioned.

Legal reform in this area could be politically fraught, but eventually, the public lands will need more water to ensure adequate habitat protections for terrestrial and aquatic species, among other uses, and the federal government will have to step into the power it possesses under the Constitution to regulate and protect its water, especially on federal lands and in interstate waterways. The *Hage* ruling easily could be overruled, which would effectively reverse the troublesome takings precedent and remove the problematic perverse incentive discussed above. This would likely be much easier than the alternative, an act of Congress clarifying the relationship between its disposal-era statutes and the water rights they established (including the Ditch Act, the General Mining Law, and the Homestead Acts) and the conservation-oriented statutes of the 1970s (including the Multiple-Use Sustained Yield Act, the National Forest Management Act, and FLPMA). This legislation would likely be opposed by many western legislators representing rural districts with a large percentage of public lands ranching operations, but stranger things have happened in the twenty-first century West thus far. The Colorado River allocation between various states in the West, which many have thought was essentially immune to reform despite its known shortcomings dating back to the signing of the Colorado River Compact, has been challenged in the 2020s by groups of states seeking to finally resolve shortfalls in river flow that are two decades old.[27] If the competing groups of states cannot come to an

[26] *Hage v. United States*, 51 Fed. Cl. 570, 584 (2002).

[27] Ella Nilsen, *With New Plans, Colorado River States Draw Battle Lines Over Who Should Bear the Brunt of Future Water Cuts*, CNN (Mar. 6, 2024), www.cnn.com/2024/03/06/us/colorado-river-water-crisis-west-climate/index.html.

agreement about how to divide the dwindling flow of the Colorado River, they will likely come knocking on Congress's door to ask for help. The ranchers of Nevada, Utah, Arizona, New Mexico, and other states may soon be in the same boat, opening the door to negotiations about private water rights on public lands and striking a balance that more equitably allocates this essential resource among humans, wildlife, and domestic livestock.[28]

10.6 THE HOMESTEAD ACTS

The Homestead Acts have been repealed and thus, they are not in need of reform.[29] But the legacy of these statutes should be addressed by the law at some point, in the process of undoing the systems these laws enabled, which bestowed privilege on white ranchers and ranching corporations and effectively denied the same privileges to ranchers of color. These legacy laws allowed the consolidation of power over public resources by an extra-privileged subset of white ranchers and ranching corporations (those who hold the preference for public allotments, either by virtue of inheritance or through purchase). The disposal-era statutes discussed in Chapters 4 and 5 seemingly allowed everyone the same opportunities, but that was not the reality of Indigenous Peoples and African Americans. Indigenous Peoples were not citizens of the United States until 1924 and therefore could not avail themselves of the homestead acts, and the laws that brought homesteading to their Tribal lands were not for them, but rather a form of settler colonialism in an ill-fitting disguise. Homesteading was available to African Americans after the Emancipation Proclamation was signed, but their experience was fraught and tenuous, and ultimately did not lead to the legacy of farming and ranching in the West that visionaries like O.T. Jackson strove for. One need only compare the experience of Ferry Carpenter and his descendants, who still own the Oak Point homestead, with that of O.T. Jackson's, who do not own any land at Dearfield, to understand how the homesteading experience was for most African Americans. Yet, creating a more just future for Black farmers and ranchers in the West is not an easy or quick path, due to the heavy influence of social factors like racism and implicit bias that remain embedded in law and policy, as well as social and economic frameworks, well into the twenty-first century.

While it is clear to the small group of scholars researching Black homesteading that "the law has played a powerful role in shaping the destiny of many black

[28] These measures might include recognition of in-stream flow rights to protect public wildlife and other natural resources, curtailment of new well-drilling and drawdowns of public water sources for private ranching operations, and more.

[29] Abigail M. Hunt & Robin M. Rotman, *Stewarding America's Federal Public Lands*, PRAC. REAL EST. LAW. 3, 4 (Nov. 2023); Rasband at 158.

landowners,"[30] it is not so clear how to pursue legal reform, nor even where to start. The prevailing theme in this area is loss – and the losses are daunting. According to census data from 1997, there were 16,560 Black farmers in the United States, who collectively owned 1,499,083 acres of land.[31] Comparing this with census data from 1910 revealed that "by the end of the twentieth century, Black farm operators as a group had lost more than 90 percent of the land that their predecessors had acquired," whether through purchase or by homesteading.[32] These numbers are similar to the land loss (measured by the total percentage lost, not the total acreage) that Tribal Nations suffered in the century leading up to and through the allotment era, but Tribal Nations had some protections for collective land rights by way of treaties, Executive orders establishing reservations, and legislation.

Black agricultural communities like Dearfield had none of these legal protections and were emerging relatively soon after Black Americans experienced one of the worst human rights atrocities in the nation's history – slavery. The field of epigenetics has been established to study the intergenerational consequences that flow from historical traumas targeting entire groups of a population, like slavery. Research has shown that "trauma can actually impact an individual's DNA, and the manifestations of the traumas experienced by prior generations can be passed along genetically to future offspring."[33] Given these data, it is not difficult to imagine that it had some adverse impacts on the homesteaders who landed in Dearfield.

Some Black communities have begun the process of healing from the intergenerational traumas of slavery and the Jim Crow era through restorative and transitional justice measures. While not traditional legal reform, these movements incorporate principles that undergird legal systems, like notice, public airing of harms, and justice. Restorative justice measures that have been utilized effectively include public fora in which dialogue about the past injustices and traumas is discussed openly and with a group sharing that experience, and through public commemorations of loss, including memorials to Black people who were enslaved, hanged, tortured, and beaten. Yet more communities have used film, and other forms of art to document the past and educate all age groups about the atrocities committed against African Americans during and after slavery.

30 Thomas W. Mitchell, *Destabilizing the Normalization of Rural Black Land Loss: A Critical Role for Legal Empiricism*, 2005 Wis. L. Rev. 557, 559 (2005).

31 *Id.* at 564.

32 *Id.* Black farmers claim that they "lost hundreds of thousands of acres in the past few decades as a direct result of the discriminatory practices of employees and agents of the USDA." The Civil Rights Action Team, appointed in 1996 by former Secretary of Agriculture Dan Glickman, concluded in its final report that the farmers' claims were well-founded: "[m]inority farmers have lost significant amounts of land and potential farm income as a result of [USDA] discrimination."

33 Camille L. Campbell, *Getting at the Root Instead of the Branch: Extinguishing the Stereotype of Black Intellectual Inferiority in American Education, A Long-Ignored Transitional Justice Project*, 38 Law & Ineq. 1, 16 (2020).

Restorative justice for African American homesteaders thus far is limited. There is a marked lack of data from which to begin to design a system of legal reform that would address the embedded racism and discrimination that caused so much Black land loss. Without this data, it is somewhat difficult to know where to start with more specific suggestions for reform. A leading legal scholar in this field, Professor Thomas W. Mitchell of DePaul University College of Law, has called out the legal academy for its seeming total lack of interest in researching rural Black land loss. In a 2005 law review article addressing this phenomenon, Mitchell observed that,

> In contrast to the AP investigative series on Black land loss (picked up by newspapers all across the country and often on the front page), and reports produced by some community-based organizations that have addressed legal proceedings of one kind or another that have been used to force sales of Black-owned property, few legal scholars have considered the "legal dispossession" of Black-owned property holdings to be an area worthy of independent study.[34]

In Mitchell's view, this "fits a general pattern" in legal academia of "a lack of mainstream interest" in "addressing the dispossession of property from people of color ... within the United States."[35] In the years since his article was published, there have been less than a handful of subsequent publications on the topic of Black land loss, and fewer still on the topic of Black homesteading. More research is clearly needed to begin to reform the law and policy of agriculture in the West in a way that would deliver justice to the descendants of O.T. Jackson and other Black homesteaders.

10.7 COMMUNAL GRAZING RIGHTS

The preceding chapters identified several commons-based grazing frameworks, three of which have a valid legal basis in the twenty-first century: the public grassland commons of federal land, the grassland commons of Tribal Nations like the Blackfeet, and the Land Grant rights to graze livestock held by descendants such as the Beaubien beneficiaries. This section will address the first and third of these categories. The second category – Tribal communal grazing lands – was addressed above in the discussions of federal Indian law and other reforms of statutes like AIARMA.

A. *Taylor Grazing Act*

Many legal scholars of natural resource law and a growing cadre of federal agency leadership and staff view the Taylor Grazing Act as a statute long past its prime,

34 2005 Wis. L. Rev. at 569.
35 *Id.*

which no longer serves the purposes for which it was passed, and which has been ineffective in maintaining any level of ecological sustainability on public lands. According to the BLM's own data, nearly 50 percent of allotments fail to meet ecological health standards developed by the agencies.[36] Cattle, sheep, horses, and other domestic livestock have a tremendous impact on wildlife that share their grazing allotments and use these lands as habitat, including as nesting, breeding, and feeding grounds. They also heavily impact public water resources, consuming, polluting, and depleting water reserves in some of the driest areas of the country.[37]

There have been several attempts to reform grazing on federal lands to curtail the overuse of "the range," and to address ecological harms caused by livestock, dating back to the Taylor Grazing Act itself. Subsequent efforts included Congress's passage of PRIA, FLPMA, and failed attempts to pass legislation to ensure that grazing fees, which have traditionally been well below market value, were increased to provide a fair return to the American taxpayers. There have also been attempts at reform coming from the Executive Branch, with the Clinton Administration's attempt at regulatory range reform emerging as the most prominent and successful. Although the latter effort was the most successful, it produced a Supreme Court opinion that many viewed as a victory for ranchers, rather than for the agency or the American public. Following that opinion, *Public Lands Council v. Babbitt*, which was issued in 2000, there have been some private grazing reform initiatives, including one that positioned environmental organizations to purchase base property and preferences from existing permittees and retire the grazing privileges. But these efforts have met their own unique challenges.

There are some unifying themes that emerge from each of these efforts, which may be of use to those who seek to do better by the public "range" in the future. For one, these efforts were often led by, or largely informed by, interest groups that are firmly entrenched in the power structures of Washington, DC, including ranchers (Taylor Act), traditional environmental organizations (Clinton regulatory reform and private grazing reform), and others with more than a passing interest in this issue. These efforts have never been very inclusive of those outside the circles of money, influence, and power in Washington, DC, or those in possession of the privileges associated with a grazing permit. They have traditionally failed to include Indigenous leaders, Indigenous scientists (and Indigenous science), and people of color more generally, and this exclusion has, in some ways, served to perpetuate enduring and problematic power structures of the past, while failing to change circumstances on the ground.

[36] Public Employees for Environmental Responsibility, "Rangeland Health and BLM Grazing Programs: Fact Sheet," https://peer.org/wp-content/uploads/2022/03/03-14-2022-Rangeland-Fact-Sheet.pdf.

[37] Rasband at 1023 (citing Robert H. Smith, *Livestock Production: The Unsustainable Environmental and Economic Effects of an Industry Out of Control*, 4 Buff. Envtl. L. Rev. 45, 48–73 (1996)).

One missing ingredient in regulatory reform efforts to date is the public. Not in the narrow sense in which agencies typically involve the public, with the hyper-specific and difficult-to-understand NEPA process, for example, but more broadly and in a way that is truly inclusive. There has been no national conversation about whether private agricultural use of so much public land and water still has a place of value in the collective public vision of twenty-first century America. While some of these conversations have started on a local level, it is not at all clear that urban and suburban residents living outside the West, understand the scale and scope of this private benefit that they continue to give to such a privileged few in the West.

On a more concrete level, there is one specific element of federal grazing law that the preceding chapters call to the forefront for attempts at reform, which is the grazing privilege. This is the element of the public lands grazing framework that gave the permittees in the Gentner and Tanaka study, along with the other public lands permittees discussed in Chapters 5–7, and Chapter 9, their foothold on public lands. As discussed there, this framework was created by, and therefore centers the values of, Euro-American settler colonizers and their descendants, and it has marginalized and continues to marginalize massive sectors of society, including most prominently, Black, Indigenous, and other people of color. The framework arises from the text of the Taylor Act, which provides that "grazing privileges recognized" by the Act "shall be adequately safeguarded" by the agency administering the statute.[38] The term "preference" is the fourth sentence of section 315b of the Act, which states: "Preference shall be given in the issuance of grazing permits to those within or near a district who are landowners engaged in the livestock business, bona fide occupants or settlers, or owners of water or water rights, as may be necessary to permit the proper use of lands, water or water rights owned, occupied, or leased by them."[39] This means that a permittee like Ferry Carpenter could apply for a permit in 1934, the year the Act was passed, and obtain it once he showed ownership of the Oak Point homestead and proof of the size of his herd. Further, the statute states that the term of the permit[40] is ten years, and there is a "preference right of the permittees to renewal in the discretion of the Secretary of the Interior."[41] This language has been interpreted as giving a permittee like Carpenter a legal preference to permit renewals, seemingly in perpetuity, so long as he and any successors in interest comply with the terms of the permit and other instructions from the administering agency. When FLPMA was passed in 1976, Congress further solidified the preference, adding language to the effect that "existing grazing" permit holders would retain a first priority for renewal so long as the land use plan continued to make land "available for livestock grazing."[42]

38 43 U.S.C. § 315b.
39 *Id.*
40 *Id.*
41 *Id.*
42 *Id.* § 1752(c).

The preference element is the low-hanging fruit in the Taylor Act and FLPMA framework. This is the element that gives the privileged class of livestock graziers their hold on public grazing and several options exist for reform of this aspect of the framework. For one, the Secretary of Interior has the authority under the Taylor Act and FLPMA to amend land use plans and cancel grazing on mismanaged and degraded allotments. This could be mandated across multiple states by the Secretary at a national level, or the Secretary could direct each state or district to conduct an analysis of the allotments that had failed to meet rangeland health standards during the most recent review and require the cancellation of grazing on those allotments. That would eliminate the preference because there would be no permit to renew. The Secretary could direct land managers to allow the allotments to rest and restore themselves to a condition where they would be capable of sustaining grazing again and could re-authorize them for grazing under the authority of the Taylor Act. At that point, anyone with private property or a water right could apply for a new permit and it would be more of an even playing field in terms of the analysis of the applicants, at least in theory.

This route would be easier than amending the Taylor Act and FLPMA, and the sister statutes of grazing on national forest lands, the MUSYA and NFMA, to create an open application process for grazing privileges and perhaps even a system that allows for shared use of allotments. Statutory reform could probably only follow the type of national dialogue envisioned earlier, in which the Executive Branch and Congress determine to educate the public and assess the national polity's appetite for allowing continued private use of public lands in the West for this purpose. In 2024, this seems far away, although climate change could spur this level of action more rapidly than one might anticipate.

B. *Land Grant Rights*

Another category of communal grazing supported by an enforceable legal framework is the Spanish- and Mexican-derived land grant rights of individuals like the Beaubien beneficiaries discussed in Chapter 1. Following the Colorado Supreme Court's decision in *Lobato v. Taylor*, which recognized rights to access the Cielo Vista Ranch for communal grazing and other purposes protected by the 1863 Beaubien document, land grant grazing rights were deemed to be easements under Colorado law.[43] This is incredibly important as precedent because easements are not use rights, and they do not lapse. They are vested property rights, and they exist in perpetuity, capable of being transferred, sold, or passed down through the laws of inheritance from one generation to the next. They are also rights vested in some of the poorest and most politically marginalized groups of people in the American Southwest – those of Spanish American and Mexican American descent.

[43] *Lobato v. Taylor*, 71 P.3d 938, 947 (Colo. 2002).

The reform in this area will flow from the adjudication of all descendant land grant rights throughout every portion of every state that was acquired pursuant to the Treaty of Guadalupe Hidalgo. This could have significant consequences for massive private ranches like Ted Turner's Vermejo Park, which traces its title to the Maxwell Land Grant, and many others. *Lobato* provides a precedent that other state courts can follow, and there could be additional ways to recognize beneficiaries' property rights outside of the traditional property law of easements. The spark was lit by the *Lobato* opinion, but the work of pursuing justice for land grant claimants has moved slowly, with state legislators seeming unmoved by the opinion and the reality of pursuing these rights becoming clearer to other descendants. This reality is that, while descendants may have a legal right on paper to access land, water, and grass on a ranch like Vermejo Park or Cielo Vista, converting that into a right that can be used on the ground may require money, time, and access to the justice system. Furthermore, since property rights are matters of state law, descendants will need to pursue their claims in state courts, which have often been hostile to land grant claims in the past. And finally, because the determination of the nature and scope of the right could vary among states, there could be differing rules of law that emerge from the states containing lands and waters subject to these land grants. Nevertheless, the work may be worth it, given the success of the Beaubien descendants in *Lobato*.

10.8 WILDLIFE AND BIODIVERSITY PROTECTION LAWS

From a definitional perspective, wildlife and biodiversity are not interchangeable, and the terms reflect a different value set. Wildlife laws have tended traditionally to protect animal, bird and fish species that human beings in this country have used, either for adornment on hats or clothing accessories, or consumed as a food source. The early wildlife laws protected migratory birds for their plumage and habitat for "game" species, like deer, for subsistence purposes. Later laws protected wildlife species that people cared about, known to natural resources scholars as the "charismatic" species that draw people in, such as grizzly bears, wolves, whales, and others that capture the national fascination. Traditionally, uncharismatic species like snails, slugs, bees, insects, and others have been deprioritized in this framework, although this is beginning to change in the twenty-first century as the American public comes to understand the role that some of these species play in an ecosystem and the benefits they bring for people who interact with those ecosystems.

This relationship between a species, and the species' relationship to the land, water, and plants they rely on for their survival, is the subject of the field of ecology. Biodiversity involves the number and diversity of species within an ecosystem, and the presence or lack of biodiversity can have a dramatic effect on an ecosystem. Thus, it is a matter of near consensus among legal scholars that the future of laws addressing wildlife will likely be oriented more toward ecology and biodiversity, rather than focusing on game species, species used for fashion, and those that invoke childhood memories of a Disney movie. If past is prologue, these future laws will also intersect with livestock grazing and other agricultural activities.

In the West, wildlife and biodiversity face so many challenges that stem from the fundamental truth of the legal framework that governs ecosystems and habitat in this region – it is designed for and around domestic livestock. Whether on federal or state public lands, Tribal lands, or private lands, livestock grazing interacts with and impacts wildlife and their habitat on many levels. Many wildlife species need adequate ground cover in the form of specific grass plants, shrubs, or trees, all of which are impacted by livestock grazing. Fish and aquatic species need oxygenated water, and domestic livestock herds passing through riparian areas often create sediment loads that water bodies cannot absorb, resulting in deoxygenation of the water and death of fish and other aquatic species. Dams, catchment basins, and stock tanks pose other types of threats to wildlife, inhibiting reproduction, causing death by drowning, and blocking key migration routes. Roads present still more hazards. Fences that keep cattle contained can directly or indirectly kill wildlife like sage-grouse and pronghorn antelope, and non-native plant species that ranchers brought to the West for their cattle and sheep have in some places taken over endemic vegetation species entirely. This transition has left many areas of the West vulnerable to erosion, drought, and severe wildfires.

Climate change has been a concern among scientists in the United States for nearly half a century, and policymakers at the state and federal levels have finally begun to address this challenge in the first decades of the twenty-first century. These conversations have taken on a particular urgency in the West due to the increasing rate and temperature of wildfires, which when combined with population growth into forested areas, have resulted in devastating losses of property and even human life. The traditional relationship between people, fire, and animals has been upset by many factors, many of which were discussed or alluded to in earlier chapters of this book. Traditional Indigenous Knowledge of fire and western ecosystems has been disrupted by allotment, removal, and the reservation policy; disruptions that were codified into law by the early years of the twentieth century. In their place came immigrants, with their own ideas about how to manage land, cultivate crops, and steward domestic livestock, some of which had catastrophic consequences for the West well into the twenty-first century. The immigration has never really stopped, either, as people seek privacy and sometimes, affordable housing, in increasingly rural areas, especially after the Covid-19 pandemic from 2020 to 2023. This has placed even more pressure on wildlife due to habitat encroachment from residential and commercial development.

Reforming the areas of law that created the present situation facing wildlife in the West will likely require public sentiment to shift toward the preservation of biodiversity as a national value, rather than the preservation of certain charismatic species of megafauna. But, law reform could redound to the benefit of biodiversity through climate-focused law and policy drivers. Climate-change drivers are, after all, the same drivers that lead to biodiversity loss.[44] Curbing these causes is not only more likely to effect favorable outcomes for wildlife, but more palatable to the American public, especially when their choice is framed as saving their property or saving a endangered snail or bee. And although the goals of biodiversity and a liveable climate have been separated by the law in the past, this does not necessarily spell doom for species dependent on both in the future.[45]

It is important to note that mitigating climate change does not mean that biodiversity will improve. It depends on the mechanisms used, and whether there is a sufficient analysis that adequately assesses adverse impacts to species and their habitat because of the changed policies or practices. For instance, increasing solar energy production on public lands reduces the need for carbon-emitting coal-fired power plants, but that is only if the solar energy generated is used, which means it must be affordable and there must be adequate infrastructure to ensure that it can be distributed. Moreover, the size and siting of the solar-generating infrastructure can cause catastrophic damage to sensitive ecosystems and regional biodiversity.

However, some climate mitigation and adaptation strategies seem like natural allies of biodiversity conservation. One of them materialized in January 2021, when the Biden-Harris Administration announced the national goal of conserving 30 percent of the nation's lands and waters by 2030, for the purpose of "tackling the climate crisis." Recognizing climate change as a matter of foreign policy and national security, the Administration instructed federal agencies to immediately start planning to meet this goal. This action was part of a global reaction to reports issued by the United Nations Intergovernmental Panel on Climate Change, which is considered the foremost international "think tank" addressing climate change across the globe, and the United Nations Convention on Biological Diversity. In the West, this initiative had significant popular support, with one 2020 poll showing that 70 percent of surveyed voters approved of the Administration's call to action.[46]

Roughly one-third of the nation's land is federal public land of one category or another, as of 2024. So, federal public lands are natural candidates for helping the United States achieve the goals of 30 × 30, especially in the West, where there are incredibly large and relatively intact tracts of public land. Maximizing this land base for carbon sequestration, watershed protection, healthy plant communities, and other ecosystem services, is part of the existing (discretionary) legal mandate governing these lands, all of which would benefit wildlife biodiversity more broadly.

[44] Jamie Pleune, *Creating a Transparent Methodology to Measure Success Within a Continuum of Conservation for the America the Beautiful Initiative*, 14 Geo. Wash. J. Energy & Envtl. L. 107, 108 (2023).

[45] Daniel A. Farber, *Separated at Birth? Addressing the Twin Crises of Biodiversity and Climate Change*, 42 Ecology L. Q. 841, 843 (2015).

[46] Pleune at 108.

The sage-grouse discussed in Chapter 8 is a great example. Landscape-level protection of sagebrush steppe ecosystems inures to the benefit of the grouse, and because they are such a foundational species in this ecosystem, more grouse will benefit the species up and down the food chain, as well as many that are outside of it.

Achieving wildlife or biodiversity protection using legal reform is a tricky subject, though, which is why the Biden-Harris Administration was smart to start the 30 × 30 effort as a policy change. Policy change is relatively easy, whereas law reform can be harder. But as this nation has shown so many times, policy change can lead to legal reform over time. In the meantime, there are some intriguing collaborative efforts involving nonprofit organizations, federal agencies, Tribes, and states, which have yielded positive initial results as they experiment with methods and new models. These models are often based on values of stewardship and shared mutual interests, rather than focusing on "rights" or exclusivity. One example was discussed in Chapter 9, the High Desert Partnership, but even as that group's founders acknowledge, they borrowed their model from others: the Blackfoot Challenge in Montana, the Quivira Coalition in New Mexico, the Malpai Borderlands Group in Arizona,[47] and the Clearwater Basin Collaborative in Idaho.[48] Starting from the foundation that these other collaboratives initiated, and with the understanding that a nongovernmental entity could foster the kind of change that the community sought, they got to work making their dream a reality, without any legal or policy reform at all. This inspires hope in some that even without it, change can occur. In the words of founder High Desert Partnership co-founder Chad Karges, partnerships provide "the community an alternative way of addressing important issues so they don't have to become a crisis in the future."[49] According to Karges, they're "looking specifically for people, not only with different skill sets but also looking at the world through different lenses."[50] Those lenses can serve as incubators for policy reform, and sometimes, legal reform, which can eventually change the arc of history.

47 Wiles.

48 Wyo. Outdoor Council, "Examples of Successful Land Management Collaboration in the West," (2017), www.wyoleg.gov/interimCommittee/2017/05-0508APPENDIXH.pdf.

49 Brown.

50 *Id.*

Conclusion

[C]olor is not used to describe natural landscapes, but instead is the framework to understand law's primary role in determining benefits, rewards, access, opportunity, penalties, and punishment depending upon where one sits in relation to an enforceable and durable color line of Whiteness and non-Whiteness.

– Tom I. Romero, II[1]

Monitor Valley, Nevada, is alluring by anyone's measure. It is captivatingly beautiful, with tall grasses blowing in the wind and the occasional raptor riding a thermal wave in the sky, framed by steep, snow-capped mountains. It looks like a movie set, the Nevada equivalent of the valley the Yellowstone Ranch calls home in the Paramount series. The cattle pictured grazing in the Valley in a Hage family promotional video, "The Last Cowboy at Pine Creek Ranch," look placid, well-fed, and happy, and gentle guitar music adds even more of a sense of peace to the overall setting.[2] Cowboys on horseback with ruddy cheeks, flannel shirts, and blue jeans amble near the grazing cattle, keeping a loose eye on the herd. In the video images, the valley looks serene, calm, and healthy, with abundant grasses.

Some of those grasses are Indian ricegrass, which is native to the Monitor Valley. The species is so important to Nevada ranchers that it was named the state grass of Nevada.[3] Ricegrass is almost perfectly adapted to the Monitor Valley – it prefers sandy soils and is adapted to arid ecosystems like those of central Nevada. As in southern Utah, Indian ricegrass was highly appealing to people, livestock,

[1] Tom I. Romero, II, *A Brown Buffalo's Observations on Color (Blindness), Legal History, and Racial Justice in the Rocky Mountain West*, 2022 Utah L. Rev. 751, 753 (2022).

[2] Wall St. Journal, *The Last Cowboy at Pine Creek Ranch* (Mar. 30, 2018), available at www.wsj.com/video/the-last-cowboy-at-pine-creek-ranch/448D091F-7C62-423D-99EF-DFE3DD784EB7.

[3] Evan A. Zimmerman, *Desert Ranching in Central Nevada*, 2 Rangelands 5, 185 (Oct. 1980), https://journals.uair.arizona.edu/index.php/rangelands/article/viewFile/9990/9602.

and wildlife in the Monitor Valley.[4] When given a choice, cattle, horses, and elk will prefer it in all seasons over other types of grasses and all types of forbs. Sheep, deer, and antelope also choose it over other grasses in spring, late fall and winter.[5]

My initial excitement over recognizing ricegrass in the Hage video was short-lived, though, as things quickly turned ominous once the narrator started to describe events in the Monitor Valley (as of 2018). According to him, this valley belongs to his family, and the federal government is trying to take it from them. The camera follows the lead cowboy, who is Wayne Hage Sr.'s son, Wayne N. Hage, and focuses on his back as his horse canters toward the grazing herd of cattle. In this shot, it is hard to miss the handgun that sits in a holster on his left hip as he reveals himself as the narrator and begins to shares his perspective that he might be "the last cowboy" in his family because the federal government is bent on destroying his family's livelihood and legacy. Interspersed with clips of Wayne Sr. standing in a meadow and still shots of various other locations on the ranch is an interview with Ramona Hage Morrison, Wayne N. Hage's sister and Wayne Sr.'s daughter. She describes her father's vision for the ranch as a model of western ranching, using the methods that ranchers have used for 150 years, and one that has been under constant threat. The seemingly placid Monitor Valley is, in her view, a battleground.

Although it is initially as easy to empathize with the Hages as it is with the Duttons of Yellowstone, their call to action has a very specific audience and omits a lot of detail. This battle they speak of has rules, after all, and they were rules that were designed by ranchers like them. European American ranchers, including the Hages' predecessors, were drawn to the West for its free land and water. As the nineteenth-century wave began to bypass the intermountain West, the federal government used strong incentives to urge westward immigrants to stop before they reached California and Oregon, and settle in more arid regions like Idaho, Nevada, and Utah. They did so by offering increasingly large parcels of land and abundant water through homestead acts and other disposal laws in effect at the time. Because of the aridity of the region, the government's thinking went, grazing livestock on these "desert lands" required a greater amount of land than it did in less arid regions, due to the relative scarcity of grasses and the ease with which cattle could graze them down to the roots. Thus, ranchers would need nearby public domain lands, which although typically less productive than the homesteaded lands, were useful for additional "range" if the lands within the homestead boundaries were depleted.[6]

4 Roemer & J.A. Schultes Barkworth, "Indian Ricegrass Plant Guide," p. 1, U.S. Department of Agriculture Natural Resources Conservation Service, https://plants.usda.gov/DocumentLibrary/plantguide/pdf/pg_achy.pdf.

5 Indian Ricegrass Plant Guide, p. 1.

6 Bryan Leonard & Shawn Regan, *Legal and Institutional Barriers to Establishing Non-Use Rights to Natural Resources*, 59 NAT. RESOURCES J. 135, 146 (2019).

As was the case for Ferry Carpenter and the founders of the Pine Creek Ranch, if homesteaders cultivated the requisite number of acres for the statutory period (which was as little as five years in some cases), the federal government would convey title to the homesteaded property in fee simple absolute.[7] During the height of the homesteading era, in the late nineteenth century, and continuing into the early part of the twentieth century, livestock grazing on federal lands was basically open, free, and unregulated.[8] The federal government tacitly acquiesced to ranchers' use of unclaimed federal lands, not through lack of diligence, but purposefully, because these trespassing ranchers and animals further established the footprint of the spreading American nation across the intermountain region, signaling to Spanish, Russian, and other foreign powers – including Tribal Nations – that the United States was growing, powerful, and there to stay.

Characterizing this land as "unclaimed land" or "open land," though, was not accurate because it was almost entirely Indigenous land prior to the waves of settler colonialism that the Mexican and later, US governments encouraged through their homesteading and agricultural laws and policies. Although they likely would not refer to their traditional agricultural practices using the terminology of the Hages, Indigenous Peoples throughout what is now the United States engaged in land and resource stewardship and agriculture through practices like prescribed fire, clearing fields, and selectively harvesting plants to increase their resiliency and productivity.[9] The deeper that initial European traders and explorers pushed into the continent, the more they discovered that the diversity of Tribes with different languages, cultures, and social norms belied the commonality of food sources in specific regions, due to intertribal collaboration in land and resource stewardship and a mutually understood "language" that allowed for communication of cultivation and other techniques, like the use of fire, from Tribe to Tribe.[10] Many Tribal ranchers and cultural stewards continue these traditions today.

The Doctrine of Discovery empowered the United States to remove Indigenous Peoples from their lands, but in recent years, the Doctrine itself has come under

[7] 43 U.S.C. §932 (1866) (repealed 1976); Bret C. Birdsong, *Road Rage and R.S. 2477: Judicial and Administrative Responsibility for Resolving Road Claims on Public Lands*, 56 Hastings L. J. 523, 526 (2005).

[8] Hoffmann, 24 J. Envtl. L. & Litig. at 248.

[9] Baldes, Jason. Native Memory Project, "Native Fire Management" (last accessed Oct. 16, 2024), https://nativememoryproject.org/voice/native-fire-management/.

[10] Sunmin Park, Nobuko Hongu, & James W. Daily, *Native American Foods: History, Culture, and Influence on Modern Diets*, 3 Journal of Ethn Foods 3, 171–77 (2016), ISSN 2352-6181, available at https://doi.org/10.1016/j.jef.2016.08.001. Many of these intertribal networks survive through the present day, such as the shared relationship between the Crow and Eastern Shoshone people involving a medicinal plant used by both Tribes that requires distinct fire cycles. The Eastern Shoshone call this plant "lightning root." Baldes, Jason. Native Memory Project, "Native Fire Management" (last accessed Oct. 16, 2024), https://nativememoryproject.org/voice/native-fire-management/.

increasing scrutiny, including from the Pope himself. Moreover, Tribal Nations that signed bilateral agreements to cede lands that became ranches like Pine Creek have argued for years that these treaties were signed under force of starvation or threat of military invasion, and the description of the lands subject to the ensuing treaty obligations was often flawed to the point of being impossible to defend against the waves of incoming settler colonizers, railroad companies, cattle companies, and miners.[11] These and other historical realities call into question the relationships of people to land depicted in the Hage video, which omits any reference to the Shoshone or other Tribes that once called this valley home.

Nearly a century of treaty making followed European contact, including after the Doctrine of Discovery was established in 1823. Throughout this era, Tribal Nations sold or traded their occupancy rights, but reserved certain rights in perpetuity for their people, including rights to use land and access resources like fish, bison, and other wildlife species hunted for food, as well as areas where plants were cultivated and harvested. Treaties and statutes promised the remaining territories (i.e., "reservations") for Tribal citizens' exclusive use, but these and other promises yielded when settler colonizer (or military) pressure did not relent. To solve these problems, Congress passed other laws and the Executive Branch pursued policies that effectuated child removal and family separation, the establishment or, and compulsory attendance at distant residential schools, and laws prohibiting Tribal members from speaking Indigenous languages, celebrating cultural events in ceremonies or otherwise, and practicing their religions. The purpose of these laws was to assimilate Tribal members into "mainstream" American society, but the power they conferred upon the executive branch and the agencies of the Department of Interior was more than assimilative.[12] The federal motto at this time was to "Kill the Indian: Save the Man," although the policies ultimately resulted in the deaths of untold numbers of Indigenous children and the permanent severing of ties to the reservation for countless others.[13] Equally devastating was the federal government's buffalo slaughter policies, which ultimately eliminated a primary food source for so many Indigenous Peoples of the plains and Rocky Mountain regions, while disrupting western grassland ecosystems in ways that are still revealing themselves, well into the 2020s.

[11] The Shoshone people have long maintained that much of Nevada is rightfully theirs, pursuant to an 1863 treaty signed at Box Elder, Utah, between Shoshone Tribal leaders and representatives of the federal government, which was ratified by Congress. Thus far, no court has been willing to validate these claims, including the United States Supreme Court. *Nw. Bands of Shoshone Indians v. United States*, 324 U.S. 335, 336 (1945).

[12] Walter R. Echo-Hawk, In the courts of the Conqueror: The 10 Worst Indian Law Cases Ever Decided, pp. 72, 73 (Fulcrum 2010).

[13] *Id.* at 73, 220 (noting that there is perhaps no more effective means of eliminating a culture, and diminishing its power, than taking its children).

Moreover, despite the generosity of the federal government to the non-Indigenous, settler colonizers at such a great cost to Indigenous Peoples and people of color more broadly, white western ranchers wanted more. And they got it. They got more land, more water, and permits and leases that allowed them more land and water still. The system that Ramona Hage Morrison claims as a basis for her family's rights to federal land and water is the same one that Ferry Carpenter helped to develop in the early 1900s. As discussed in the preceding chapters, the BLM and its predecessor agency, the Federal Grazing Service, promulgated regulations pursuant to the Taylor Act that have created an expectation on the part of ranchers like the Hages that they hold grazing privileges on public land as private property rights. Public lands ranches like the Carpenter Ranch and the Pine Creek Ranch, so prolific in the West, are distinguished primarily by one factor – they rely upon a mixture of private fee land and nearby public lands for additional pasturing and forage.[14] This concept started with the Spanish and Mexican ranchers discussed in Chapters 1 and 2, who used their governments' land to graze cattle, for hunting, and for growing crops.[15] Because the private land grants from regional governors and other authorities did not contain adequate pasture lands to sustain large ranching operations in the dry desert southwest, grantees used their fee property inside the varas as a base for their ranching operation and grazed their livestock on nearby unclaimed government land, the commons.[16] The ability to access the commons created a dependency on the nearby open public domain to satisfy the ranchers' need, and as the numbers of homesteaders grew, and the resources became scarce, homesteaders and other stock owners, including migrant sheep ranching operations, began to adopt a fear-based, scarcity mentality. Ranchers tried to exclude others from accessing what they saw as "their" public lands, by controlling water rights and monopolizing access to water sources, which allowed them to effectively control vast areas of land.[17] Yet, the pressure was unrelenting, as the wave of emigration from the east did not stop when the resources became scarce. By the early twentieth century, range wars became more frequent and intense, resulting in calls for congressional intervention.

As discussed in Chapter 5, these range wars were often fought between cattle ranchers and sheep operations. The cattle ranchers were often homesteaders like Ferry Carpenter, who settled on their homestead, lived there at least part of the year, and ran their cattle nearby. They were also usually white and ethnically northern or central European, as were the cowboys and ranch hands they hired. The sheep ranching operations often used vast areas of land, moving herds across state boundaries and over hundreds of miles in search of winter and summer pastures. With

14 Hoffmann, 24 J. Envtl. L. & Litig. at 245.
15 *Id.*
16 *Id.* at 248.
17 *Id.* at 249.

these operations came sheep herders, who were often Basque, Mexican, Mexican American, or Indigenous.[18] Chapter 4 explored how the introduction of foreign species of grasses began in earnest in the years surrounding the Dust Bowl era, which often had permanent consequences for entire ecosystems that continue to complicate climate and other management efforts, such as wildlife conservation and biodiversity. These invasive species have created an ecological and climate quagmire that regulators, ranchers, farmers, and conservationists will have to address as part of any climate mitigation or adaptation strategy for the future.

Laws like the Taylor Grazing Act, the Public Rangelands Improvement Act, and others were designed to organize grazing uses and stop the violence, while protecting the land being grazed from further damage. Yet, as discussed in Chapters 5 and 7, the laws and regulations simultaneously protected a defined class of federal lands ranches, through the base property and preference requirements, while foreclosing opportunities for other applicants. Although it is possible to buy base property and purchase the associated grazing preference, these costs can be prohibitive for many. The static regulatory definitions of base property and preference have made it nearly impossible for anyone lacking descendancy rights or significant financial resources to obtain grazing permits. Although permits have a limited duration of ten years, agency rules have always given priority to the renewal and issuance of new permits to existing permittees. The BLM has also historically required applicants to show more in the way of qualifications than the language of the Taylor Grazing Act and other applicable statutes required, which favors those in the established livestock industry. These requirements have served as a bar to new classes of applicants, which has kept the pool of grazing permittees overwhelmingly white since the days of the first permittees.

The environmental laws of the 1970s and 1980s brought tremendous positive changes to much of the nation, increasing protections for water quality, air quality, and incorporating science into federal agency approvals of highways, roads, dams, ski areas, mines, and development that could negatively impact the environment or human health."[19] They also ensured minimum protections for certain species of plants, insects, birds, and wildlife species on the brink of extinction. The growing popular support for environmentalism and conservation spurred these legal reforms and people celebrated them as progress.[20] In subsequent years, legal scholars have argued that some of these statutes should be used to anchor the national strategy

[18] Adam M. Sowards, *Why Sheep Started So Many Wars in the American West*, Zócalo Public Square (Oct. 5, 2017), available at www.zocalopublicsquare.org/2017/10/05/sheep-started-many-wars-american-west/ideas/essay/. In the New Mexico territory between 1870 and 1890, 619,000 sheep burgeoned to nearly five million in less than two decades.

[19] Robert L. Glicksman, *et al.*, Environmental Protection: Law and Policy, p. 2 (Wolters Kluwer 2019).

[20] Cary Coglianese, *Social Movements, Law, and Society: The Institutionalization of the Environmental Movement*, 150 U. Pa. L. Rev. 85, 88 (2001).

to combat climate change, and courts have begun to listen.[21] All of these interest groups would likely characterize these laws as the beginning of a protective layer of climate law and strategy.

Many farmers and ranchers had and still have a different perspective, though. The election of Ronald Reagan as President in 1980 gave a national platform to the Sagebrush Rebels, who were largely white, middle to upper class, owned land, and participated in grazing boards and cattlemen's associations, giving them a significant degree of local authority over land, water rights, and grazing rights. These ranchers valued private property, denied federal authority over public lands in the West, and they were often conservative Christians or members of the Church of Jesus Christ of Latter-Day Saints (also known as Mormons).[22] The Reagan Administration era was their launching off point, which ultimately spawned the likes of the Bundy militia and other white-Supremacist militant groups that sought to secure permanent ownership rights of federal lands for white ranchers throughout the West.[23] This social movement has significantly stymied the development of a comprehensive climate strategy in this region, as the Rebels view the environmental laws and their myriad regulations as government overreach in their worst form, especially as these laws negatively impact their farming and ranching operations.

Today, the grasslands of the West bear the scars of these centuries of colonization and dominion. Their soils are thin on nutrients and native grasses have been replaced by invasive species. They are heavily impacted by urban growth, suburban, and exurban development, and are highly vulnerable to fires and drought. They are subject to a complex patchwork of laws and regulations that vary depending, in many cases, on the race of their nineteenth-century owners, and yet these laws and regulations continue to proscribe these lands' current use and management. So, while it has become clear to ecologists and climate scientists that grasslands will be a critical component of a US strategy to combat climate change, the existing laws and regulations may hinder or slow those efforts significantly unless some critical reform is achieved.

That the West has served as a bastion for a small cadre of real-life John Duttons is a fundamental regional truth. Yet, even in Yellowstone, the hegemony came to an end, with the death of Kevin Costner's character kicking off the storyline of season 5's second part. In 2024, there are rumors that the ranch could be sold. Similar rumors dog the Hages. If their public claims are to be believed, they will lose their ranch because they cannot continue ranching without access to their hundreds

[21] *See* Massachusetts v. E.P.A., 549 U.S. 497, 528 (2007) (holding that the Clean Air Act authorized EPA to regulate greenhouse gas emissions from new motor vehicles).

[22] Ian Bartrum, *Searching for Cliven Bundy: The Constitution and Public Lands*, 2 Nev. L. J. Forum 67 (2018).

[23] Carl Segerstrom, *The Washington, D.C. Siege Has Western Roots and Consequences*, High Country News (Jan. 8, 2021).

of thousands of acres of public grazing allotments. This might also be the fate of the system of laws, incentives, and other policies that their predecessors used to secure power in this region, especially as national conversations about land use, conservation, and climate change intensify. Any strategy for building a climate-resilient West will incorporate these grassland ecosystems, rendering them impossible to ignore in the national conversations about climate resiliency, adaptation, and mitigation.

Ideally, the process of incorporating these lands into a comprehensive climate strategy will avoid perpetuating the racism and other problematic biases and prejudices of the past. According to Professor Jessica Shoemaker, through homesteading and other disposal era statutes, "America constructed a *legal* system that allocated land to its white citizens, to the exclusion of people of color. These choices radically transformed the American landscape and dispersed nearly exclusive white agricultural landownership."[24] They also created expectations in the privileged classes (and races) that permeate western agriculture and land management today. As Shoemaker reflects, "[t]his history of racism … might be confined to the past if everyone had equal opportunity to acquire land today – if labor and hard work were rewarded fairly and parallel opportunities for land access distributed equally."[25] But, as the preceding chapters have shown, they are not. Rather than repeating these tragic mistakes of the "lords of yesterday," the goal for the West in the future should be a resource-allocation system free from those barriers and structures.[26]

Chapter 10 includes several proposals for legal reforms that would begin to set the region on this path. The time seems to be right in the early decades of the twenty-first century, as social justice, racial justice, and climate justice are coming for the modern West. Indigenous Nations are asserting their sovereign powers to a degree not seen since the 1930s, and they have a national audience for their claims to ancestral lands, justice for their missing and murdered, for their stolen children, and a unifying voice expressing demands for Tribal sovereignty, food sovereignty, and for a national reckoning with federal policies of colonization and assimilation. They are in some ways easing into this new future, through shared environmental governance structures like comanagement of protected national public lands and negotiated exercises of treaty hunting and fishing rights. But a broader reckoning is coming for the West.

When that reckoning begins, it will be necessary to peel back the layers of law and policy, perhaps even to the beginning, when the United States treated with Tribes and used a nation-to-nation framework to navigate issues of land tenure, water

24 Jessica A. Shoemaker, *Fee Simple Failures: Rural Landscapes and Race*, 119 MICH. L. REV. 1695, 1721 (2021).

25 *Id.*

26 *Id.* at 1722.

rights, access to game, fish, and plants, and other necessities of existing as neighboring nations occupying one land base. The justification to look so far back, into the oldest volumes of the United States Code, is to ensure that any treaty promises that were made can begin to be understood and incorporated into the new framework. Moreover, as the preceding chapters have shown, certain laws and policies played a central role in consolidating and in some cases, permanently cementing the framework of disparate access to "grass." The power and influence of this group must be addressed, but carefully and inclusively, to avoid inflaming the debate with rhetoric like that which led to the heated confrontations at Bunkerville and Malheur.

Also, not every rancher is a Sagebrush Rebel, and there are no doubt many ranchers less famous than Cliven Bundy who attempt to be ecological stewards of the land they till and cultivate. The 26,000 or more permittees holding grazing privileges on the federal lands will remain in many ways indispensable to any ecological change that a policy maker or electorate might seek to effectuate because their participation will likely be required, at least to some degree, to accomplish the reforms discussed in Chapter 10. And as mentioned in Chapter 10, either resource scarcity or climate change, could be the key that unlocks the door to the future.

The reckoning coming for the West also will require a better understanding of grasslands and how they are influenced by agricultural activity. Grazing in arid regions like that of the Colorado Plateau, the Great Basin, and the southwest is often dramatically affected by annual rainfall, soil health, and fire. Native grasses have a complex relationship with fire, though, needing it to some degree, but not too frequently, and at an intensity that doesn't eliminate their ability to propagate.[27] The alteration of the precontact relationship between Indigenous Nations and their fire stewardship practices, among other causes discussed in earlier chapters, has created circumstances that give rise to much more powerful and widespread fires. When combined with the introduction of fire-loving invasive species like cheatgrass, this has in recent years, caused giant, mega-fires that pose serious threats to federal, state, and Tribal land managers alike. Fire has been the disrupter to end all disrupters.

The Hages' video about their ranching way of life in the Monitor Valley contains a long list of grievances – that the federal government has taken their land, their water, their grass, and their access. The Hages seem most irritated by the fact that the federal government deigns to regulate them at all, nevermind the fact that their title might be subject to Indigenous treaty claims and that there could ostensibly be other purposes for which the American public values this land. As I watched this video, a quote from Booker T. Washington came to mind, and it struck me as a fitting bookend to the Hages' storyline in the video: "It is at the bottom of life we must begin, and not at the top. Nor should we permit our grievances to overshadow

[27] Vachel A. Carter, Andrea Brunelle, & Mitchell J. Power *et al.*, *Legacies of Indigenous Land Use Shaped Past Wildfire Regimes in the Basin-Plateau Region, USA*, 2 Commun. Earth Environ. 72 (2021). https://doi.org/10.1038/s43247-021-00137-3.

our opportunities." Speaking to the former slaves gathered at the Atlanta Cotton States and International Exposition in 1895, but addressing a broader audience, he emphasized that:

> There is no escape through law of man or God from the inevitable
> The laws of changeless justice bind
> Oppressor with oppressed;
> And close as sin and suffering joined
> We march to fate abreast.

Index